IS COMPLETE

BOROUGH OF POOLE

500062189 V

HEAD OVER HEELS IN THE DALES

'Could you tell me how to spell "sex", please?' The speaker was a flaxen-haired, angelic-faced girl of about six with wide innocent eyes. So opens Gervase Phinn's new book about his years as a school inspector, set against a background of the peerless Yorkshire Dales. He finds himself here facing one of those awkward situations—when a child's innocent remark floors him. The team of inspectors, working in Fettlesham, remains the same although news of an early retirement makes Gervase Phinn, Inspector for English and Drama, seriously consider applying for the senior post. However, his fiancée, Christine Bentley of Winnery Nook School, is less keen: 'I want to see my husband other than at weekends,' she says. In the schools themselves, Gervase faces every challenge with humour that is rarely far from the surface. As another school year passes, with the changing seasons in the Dales never failing to move him, Gervase and Christine Phinn settle down to blissful married life.

HEAD OVER HEELS IN THE DALES

Gervase Phinn

BOROUGH OF POOLE

- - MAR 2002

LIBRARIES

CHIVERS PRESS
BATH

First published 2001
by
Michael Joseph
This Large Print edition published by
Chivers Press
by arrangement with
Penguin Books Ltd
2002

ISBN 0 7540 1736 2

Copyright © Gervase Phinn, 2002

The moral right of the author has been asserted

All rights reserved.

British Library Cataloguing in Publication Data available

Printed and bound in Great Britain by
BOOKCRAFT, Midsomer Norton, Somerset

For Jenny Dereham
my ever-patient editor, and dear friend

Acknowledgement

The poem 'School Visitor' (*opposite*) is taken from *The Day Our Teacher Went Batty*, published by Puffin Books (2002).

School Visitor

Good morning, Mr Manning,
Do please take a chair.
A cup of tea is on its way,
Are you comfortable there?
I must say that your letter
Caught me unprepared.
The children are so nervous,
And the staff—quite frankly—scared.
Now I think you'll find the pupils here
Really try their best.
The reading's good, the writing's neat
Feel free to give a test.
I know this is a little school
But we do strive for perfection.
I must say that we've never had
A thorough school inspection.
Oh, you're not the school inspector?
And Manning's not your name?
You came about the toilets
 And the blocked-up kitchen drain?

CHAPTER ONE

'Could you tell me how to spell "sex", please?' The speaker was a flaxen-haired, angelic-faced girl of about six with wide innocent eyes and a complexion a model would die for.

'I . . . b . . . b . . . b . . . beg your pardon?' I stuttered.

I was sitting in the corner of the infant classroom of Staplemoor County Primary School on a bright September morning, the second week into the new school term, there to observe the first lesson of the day. The children had just settled down to write their stories when the little angel approached me, paper in hand, pencil poised.

'"Sex." Could you spell "sex" for me, please?' she repeated, smiling widely.

I had been a County Inspector of Schools in Yorkshire now for a little over two years and during that time I thought I had become accustomed to the precocious young children I had met. I had been delighted by their humour, intrigued by their responses to my questions and amused by their sharp observations on life. But on a few rare occasions, like this one, I had been completely lost for words. My colleague and immediate superior, Dr Harold Yeats, had warned me early on in my career about such potentially hazardous situations. He had told me, that when faced with an inquisitive child who asks a tricky question or raises an embarrassing topic, to smile widely, nod sagely and be as evasive as possible.

'It's like fishing for trout, Gervase,' he had once

1

confided in me. 'You need to know when to let out the line and when to reel it in. Give it plenty of space, let it tire itself out and then it will stop thrashing. Don't be too quick to explain things to young children—you could get yourself into hot water. Just listen and take your time.'

I took Harold's advice. 'Why do you want me to spell *that* word for you?' I whispered.

'I need it for my story,' replied the child.

'What is your story about?' I asked gingerly.

'I just want you to spell "sex".'

'Yes, but could you tell me a little about your story?'

'Why?'

This was getting harder. 'Well, I would like you to.'

The child shook her head and breathed out heavily. She answered me in a voice which had an exasperated edge to it. 'If you must know, it's about a little black beetle who lives in a big, big garden and is sad and lonely and nobody loves him. All the other little creatures have friends but he is all by himself. He just sits there all day long on the compost heap feeling really, really sad and wishing he had someone to play with. Then, one day, a lady beetle climbs onto the compost heap—'

'A lady beetle?' I said.

'That's right, a lady beetle.'

I had a glimmering of what was coming next. 'I see,' I sighed, frantically thinking of the best way to get out of what was likely to become a very uncomfortable situation.

'And then,' continued the child brightly, 'she sees the lonely little beetle and asks him who he is. He tells her that he is just a sad and boring little bug

2

and he's ugly as well and nobody loves him. She tells him he's a beautiful beetle, the beautifulest beetle she has ever seen in the whole wide world and she asks him if she can stay with him for ever and ever. They love each other and then they have lots of little baby beetles.'

'I thought they might do,' I said under my breath.

'But all I want is "sex"!' she said, rather too loudly for comfort.

'Just keep your voice down a little,' I told her. 'What about "cuddle up" or "snuggle"? Those might be better words to use.'

'I don't want "cuddle up" or "snuggle",' she replied tartly, clearly irritated by the delay. 'I want "sex".' Her voice was now loud enough to attract the attention of the headteacher who swiftly appeared on the scene.

'My goodness, Mr Phinn,' she said, 'you and Melissa seem to be having a very interesting conversation.'

'It's about "sex", miss,' said the little girl.

Before I could explain, the child, giving another great heaving sigh, announced, 'He won't spell "sex" for me, Mrs McCardle. I've asked him but he won't spell it. I don't think Mr Phinn's too good at spelling.' The teacher arched an eyebrow. 'You see,' continued Melissa, holding up her paper for Mrs McCardle to see, 'I can spell the first bit but it's the "sex" bit I can't do.'

'Tell Mr Phinn what the full word is, Melissa,' the teacher told her, a knowing twinkle in her eye.

' "Insects",' announced the child. 'I want to start my story: "Beetles are insects." I can do the "in" but not the "sects".'

3

I think it is fair to say that my inspection of Staplemoor Primary School had not got off to a very auspicious start.

'Perhaps you would like to visit the juniors for a short while, Mr Phinn,' suggested Mrs McCardle, 'and then join us again in the infants after morning break. Would that suit?'

'That would suit very well,' I replied, retreating gratefully to the adjoining classroom.

*   *   *

The junior teacher, Mr Spencer-Hall, was a lean, weary-looking individual of indeterminate age with a pained expression, fluffy outcrops of ginger hair and large spectacles which had the habit of slipping down his nose as he talked.

'I've always had a secret dread of school inspectors,' he informed me morosely, pushing up his glasses and producing an expression a child might pull when faced with a plate of cold cabbage. 'I've only met two school inspectors in my whole career and they put the very fear of God in me, they really did. I had sleepless nights for weeks after their visits and I'm sure they brought on my asthma.'

'Well, I hope my visit is going to be less distressing, Mr Spencer-Hall,' I told him cheerily.

'What exactly are you going to be doing, Mr Phinn?' he asked with an even more woeful look on his face.

'Well, I thought I might observe a bit of your teaching,' I replied, 'and then—'

'Oh dear,' he moaned, 'you mean *watch* me?' There was a stiffening of the shoulders then a

4

sharp intake of breath. 'I don't like the sound of that. I don't like being watched, I really don't. I'm never at my best when I'm being observed.'

'Then I would like to hear the children read,' I continued, deciding to ignore these last comments, 'look at their written work, test their spellings and talk to them a little.'

'It all sounds terribly daunting to me,' he groaned, biting his bottom lip, 'but I suppose you have a job to do and I'll just have to grin and bear it.' He smiled like an undertaker. 'Won't I?'

'I'm afraid you will, Mr Spencer-Hall,' I said. 'That *is* my job, watching teachers teach.'

'And I suppose there will be a report?'

'Yes, there will,' I replied, 'which, of course, I would be happy to discuss with you.'

'Oh dear,' he moaned again. 'I don't like the sound of that either.'

'The point behind my observing your lesson, Mr Spencer-Hall, is to give you an objective view of your teaching, help you improve and also offer some advice and support. I think you will find it quite painless.'

'Well, Mr Phinn,' he said sadly, 'those two school inspectors who visited me before, the ones who put the fear of God in me and kept me awake at night and brought on my asthma, had the very opposite effect. It was about as painless as having a boil lanced. They made me ill. One had the manner of a police-cell interrogator and the other looked as if he'd been dug up. Seeing them scribbling away in their little black books put me off my stroke and no mistake. I just went to pieces.'

'Well, I hope you will not find me quite as frightening,' I told him. 'Just imagine that I am not there, Mr Spencer-Hall.'

'Easier said than done,' he groaned.

I prepared myself for what I imagined would be an endlessly dull lesson. As it turned out, Mr Spencer-Hall's teaching was not that bad. As soon as he faced the children he became more confident and animated. The children listened attentively as he explained how they might make their writing more vibrant by strengthening their verbs. The idea was that they should produce alternatives to a chosen word.

'What about "looked"?' the teacher asked.

Back came 'glanced', 'peered', 'watched', 'glimpsed', 'gaped', 'eyed', 'peeped', 'stared' and many others.

'And what about "walked"?' he asked next.

Again there was a lively response: 'limped', 'staggered', 'trotted', 'swayed', 'reeled', 'tottered' and a host more.

The words were listed neatly on the blackboard in a careful cursive script and then the children were set the task of including some of them in a piece of writing.

Mr Spencer-Hall was not the most dynamic and enthusiastic teacher in the world but the lesson was well planned and the children were keen. When the teacher glanced nervously in my direction, I gave him a reassuring smile and made sure I was not 'scribbling away in my little black book'. He sighed, put on a martyred expression, slid his spectacles up his nose and continued.

The first child I heard read that morning was William, a moon-faced boy of about ten or eleven, with apple-red cheeks, a thatch of black hair and a ready smile. He presented himself to me armed with an extremely thick and ancient-looking reading book, a folder of his written work and a bizarre construction made of cardboard, matchboxes, lavatory rolls, lollipop sticks and tissue paper. The cardboard creation resembled the sort of building which might have survived a nuclear holocaust.

'Shall we mek a start, then?' he asked me bluntly, shuffling onto the chair next to me and rubbing his hands together like someone about to embark on an adventure. 'What's tha want to talk to me abaat fust, then, Mester Phinn, mi readin', mi writing or mi design technology?'

'You're a bright and confident lad and no mistake,' I told him.

'Aye, well, mi granddad says not to be backwards in comin' for'ards. "Allus speak tha mind. Say what thas got to say and then shurrup." That's what he says.'

'Very true. Shall we start with that incredible construction of yours, then, William? It certainly is unusual. Is it a factory of some sort?'

'Nay, nay, Mester Phinn, it's an oil refinery. I like doin' models. I'll show you mi abattoir later on, if tha likes. It's got caging pens, holding area, slaughter chamber—'

'Yes, I'd like that,' I replied, trying to sound enthusiastic.

William then explained to me, in some detail, the workings of an oil refinery, asking me finally if I had understood.

When we got to the reading, the boy shuffled again on his chair and opened the heavy tome, sliding his second finger along the top of the page and running it behind like a seasoned reader.

7

'Who taught you to turn pages like that, William?' I asked.

'Granddad. He's a gret reader is mi granddad. Can't get enough books. When we goes to t'library, he gets reight cross when he oppens a book and sees all them grubby thumb marks on t'bottom o' pages. He reckons you 'ave to 'ave respect for books. That's how yer turn the pages of a book, tha knaas, from t'top.'

'Yes, that's right,' I agreed.

' 'Old a book in your 'and and you're a pilgrim at t'gates of a new city.'

I was stunned into silence. 'What was that you said?'

'Hebrew proverb,' said the boy, scratching the thick thatch of black hair. 'Learnt it off mi granddad. He's a gret one for proverbs and psalms, is mi granddad. He's a preacher, tha knaas.'

'A teacher?'

'Nay, a preacher.'

'Really?'

'Methodist. He reads his bible every neet. He showed me how to turn t'pages wi'out damaging t'book. He reckons that John Wesley learnt to read upside down, tha knaas. 'As thy 'eard o' John Wesley?'

'I have indeed,' I told him.

'Amazin' man was John Wesley. He was one o' nineteen children, tha knaas.'

'Really, I didn't know that.'

'They say he travelled near on a quarter of a million miles on his 'orse bringing t'word of God to folks. Spent a lot o'time in Yorkshire did John Wesley.'

'Amazing.'

'He used to listen to his father reading t'bible to 'im every neet as a little 'un and he used to follow t'words which were upside down to 'im, o' course. My granddad reads bible to me. Not upside down, though. I know all t'stories: Samson, Daniel in t'lions' den, Moses, Noah, Jacob, Joseph. There's some lively stuff in t'bible.'

'And which is your favourite bible story?' I asked.

'Waay, it 'ud 'ave to be David and Goliath.'

'Why is that?'

'Well, it's a cracking good tale, i'n't it? Old Goliath comes ovver dale, huffin' and puffin' and shoutin' and screamin' and wavin' his reight big sword abaat like there's no tomorra and tellin' t'Israelites to send out their champion. Out comes little David, wi' nowt but a sling shot in 'is 'and. "Waaaaay!" rooars old Goliath. "Tha must be jokin'. Is this t'best thy lot can do? Little squirt like thee! I could tread on thee and squash thee. I could spit on thee and drowan thee. I could breath on thee and blow thee into t'next week. Send out a proper champion not a little scrap like thee. I'm not feightin' thee." Anyroad, David says to 'im, "I'm thee man," and he reaches into t'beck and pulls out a pebble t'size of a pullet egg and pops it in 'is sling shot and lets fly. By the 'eck, it di'n't 'arf shift and it 'its old Goliath smack between 'is eyes.'

'That must have really hurt him,' I ventured.

''Urt him? 'Urt 'im?' the boy cried. 'It ruddy well killed 'im!'

I looked down and tried to suppress my laughter. 'Well, what about this book of yours, then, William? Tell me a little bit about it and then perhaps you would like to read me a page.'

'I can do that wi'out any trouble at all, Mester

9

Phinn,' he told me confidently. 'Now then, this book is abaat exploration in t'Arctic.'

'It's a very old book,' I observed, fingering the shabby cover and staring at the cramped print and yellowing pages. It had a rather unpleasant, musty smell to it.

'Aye, I got it from a charity shop. Dun't really matter what it looks like, though, does it? It's what's inside what counts, my granddad says. Same wi' people, he says. "Many a good tune played on an owd fiddle." He says that an' all.'

'Very true,' I agreed. 'Off you go, then, William. Read me a couple of paragraphs.'

The boy took a deep breath, cleared his throat noisily and began, his body hunched and his face close to the page, ' "The gale raged about the tent. Captain Scott decided that they must continue with the march despite the appalling weather. To stay there would have meant certain death in the icy wasteland. Facing chasms and crevasses, thick-crusted snow and massive mountains of ice, the explorers plodded on. Their cracked lips were broken and raw, their fingers numb with cold and their feet frozen beyond feeling. Slipping and falling, sliding and stumbling, plunging blindly into yawning ravines and escaping only by a miracle, Captain Scott and his party marched onwards." ' The boy paused and thought for a moment before commenting, 'He's a gret one for t'verbs, this writer, i'n't he?'

'He is,' I agreed, chuckling.

'Not so 'ot on t'adjectives, though.'

'No,' I agreed, thinking that Mr Spencer-Hall's lesson had had some impact.

'He died, tha knaas.'

'Who did?' I asked.

'Captain Scott. He were found frozen to deeath.'

'Oh, yes, I know. It was a very sad end.'

'Aye, he died all right.' The boy thought for a moment. 'It gets reight cowld up where I lives but not as cowld as that. Shall I go on?'

'No, that's fine, William,' I said and then added, 'It's a marvellous story, isn't it? A story of great courage and determination.'

'It is that,' agreed the boy. 'It is that.'

'And you're a grand reader, William.'

'Aye, I'm not too bad, even if I says so mi'self.'

The boy's folder was impressive. There were stories and vivid descriptions, little anecdotes and lively accounts. It was clear that Mr Spencer-Hall had covered a good deal of ground with his pupils and that he had taught them well.

One poem in William's folder appealed to me in particular. 'I guess this is about this remarkable granddad of yours, William,' I commented.

'It is that,' said the boy. 'And he were reight chuffed wi'it an' all. It's called *T' Dalesman*.'

'I'm sure he was very proud. Would you read it for me?'

William shuffled in his chair, coughed and read his poem loudly and clearly.

> Old man, sitting on the stile,
> Hands like roots and haystack hair,
> Smoky beard and sunshine smile,
> He doesn't have a single care.
>
> Old man, staring at the bield,
> Falcon-nosed and raven's eye,

Thin as the scarecrow in his field,
He stands and sees the world go by.

'What's a "bield", William?' I asked.

'Tha not from around here, then?'

'No, I'm not.'

'An "off-comed-un", are you?'

Since starting work in rural Yorkshire, I had been called this more times than I can remember—someone from out of the dale, a foreigner. 'I am indeed an "off-comed-un",' I admitted.

'Sometimes in a field tha'll see a wall,' the boy explained. 'It gus noweer, it dunt divide owt, it just stands theer, just a bit o' drystone wall. People passing—"off-comed-uns", visitors and the like—they often wonder what the heck it is.' He scratched the thatch of thick hair.

'Well, what is it, William?' I asked.

'I'm just abaat to tell thee, Mester Phinn. That bit 'o wall is a "bield". It's for t'sheep to get behind for a bit o'shelter when t'wind lashes at 'em and rain soaks 'em through. It's a sort of refuge.'

'I see. Well, that's something I've learnt this morning.'

'Mi granddad says you nivver stop learnin'.'

I tested William on his spellings, punctuation, knowledge of vocabulary and grammar and was well satisfied.

'It's been a real pleasure talking to you,' I told him, closing the folder of work.

'Likewise, Mester Phinn,' he replied. Then, getting to his feet, he patted me on the back as a grandfather might do to his grandson. 'Tek care,' he said, 'and if tha wants to see mi abattoir, it's in t'corner.' Then he departed with his book, folder and oil refinery, whistling merrily as he went.

Most of the questions school inspectors ask in the course of their work are pseudo questions. We know the answers; they are not genuine in the sense that we are asking something which, for us, is obvious. When I ask a child to spell a word, I already know the spelling. When I ask if he knows what a noun is, I am fully aware of what it is and am just testing him. But there have been many occasions on my travels around the schools in the Dales where the questions I have asked are genuine, when I have no idea of the answer. After William had returned whistling to his seat, I added yet another word—'bield'—to my Yorkshire vocabulary and wrote it down in my little black book alongside 'arran' (spider), 'barfin' (horse collar), 'biddy' (louse), 'chippy' (starling), 'fuzzock' (donkey) and other wonderfully rich and descriptive dialect words.

The next pupil was something of a contrast. He was a shy, mousy little boy who fidgeted in his chair but managed to keep his hands clasped tightly in front of him as if bracing himself for some unseen and impending horror. He had deep-set brown eyes with thick lashes and kept glancing nervously in my direction. I could see that he found me rather intimidating despite my efforts to put him at his ease. He answered my questions in monosyllables, read quickly and in a trembling voice and was very pleased when I curtailed our interview. He scuttled away and buried his head behind a big book.

The third child, a large healthy-looking girl sporting straw-coloured hair gathered up in enormous bushy bunches, deposited her reading book and folder of written work in front of me, plopped onto the chair and stared up with a wearisome expression on her round face. It was clear that this pupil, unlike William, was not overly enthusiastic about showing me her work but, unlike the nervous little boy, she was by no means daunted by the presence of the stranger in the dark suit.

I smiled. 'And what is your name?'

'Janice.'

'Well, Janice, I'm Mr Phinn and I am here to see how well you are getting on in school.' She nodded. 'And how do you think you are getting on?'

'All reight,' she replied, somewhat sullenly.

'Working hard?'

'Yeah.'

'And keeping up with the work?'

'Yeah.'

'And what do you enjoy best about school?'

'Goin' 'ome,' she told me bluntly.

'Well, would you like to read to me?'

'I'm not dead keen, but I will if I 'ave to.'

'Let's have a look at your book.' The girl flicked open a thin green volume entitled, *An Anthology of Animal Verse*. 'Ah, a poetry book. Do you like poetry then, Janice?'

'Not really,' replied the girl before adding, 'It's just that poems are shorter than stories and easier to read.'

The poem, called *Nature's Treasure* by Philomena Phillpots, described in the preface as 'The Dales Poetess', was delivered slowly and loudly, the reader stabbing the words with a large finger like someone tapping out an urgent Morse code message.

14

Oh, what lovely little lambs
Prancing in the spring!
Hear their happy bleating,
Oh what joy they bring!

I groaned inwardly and had to sit through six more verses, all as trite as the first.

'Is that it, then?' asked Janice, snapping the book shut and looking up at me. She was clearly keen to get away. I suggested that she might like to tell me a little about what she had just read.

She considered the prospect for a moment before replying. 'I 'ave enough trouble wi' readin' it, ne'er mind havin' to tell you abaat it as well.'

'Do you like reading then, Janice?' I asked cheerfully.

'No.'

I gave it up as a bad job. 'Well, shall we look at your written work?'

'Can if tha wants.'

Janice's written work consisted largely of spelling exercises, short pedestrian passages of prose, a few poor-quality rhyming poems and numerous descriptions, rather more lively and descriptive, of calving, lambing, sheep-shearing and other farming matters.

'You keep cows on your farm then, do you, Janice?'

'Yeah.'

'And pigs?'

'Yeah.'

'And what about sheep?'

'What about 'em?'

'Do you have any?'

'Yeah.'

This was hard work but I persevered. 'And do you help with the lambing?' I asked.

'Yeah.'

'It must be wonderful each year to see those little woolly creatures, like the ones in the poem, all wet and steaming in the morning air, with their soft fleeces, black eyes like shiny beads and their tails flicking and twitching.'

'It's all reight,' she said, stifling a yawn.

'And what do you like best about lambing?'

She considered me again with the doleful eyes before telling me without batting an eyelid, 'Best part's when me and mi brother slide on t'afterbirth in t'yard.'

'Really?' I said, and thought of Philomena Phillpots' truly awful little verse about 'lovely little lambs prancing in the spring'. It was a world away.

*　　　*　　　*

At morning playtime I joined Mrs McCardle in her room.

'Your face was a picture with little Melissa and no mistake,' the headteacher told me, shaking her head and smiling. 'You looked like a little boy who had just had his ice cream snatched from his hands—completely stunned. I must say I didn't realise what word she wanted until I saw the beginning of her story in her book. It happens so often, doesn't it? I recall once when a child asked me to spell "virgin" and I did exactly the same as you. "Why do you want that particular word, James?" I enquired. "I need it for my story, miss," he announced. "But I asked you to re-tell the parable of The Good Samaritan and I don't recall

16

there being a virgin in that story," I replied. "But you asked us to do our own 'virgin' of it, miss," he responded. He meant "version", of course.' Mrs McCardle shuffled some papers on her desk. 'Anyway, how did you find Mr Spencer-Hall and his class?'

'Well, the junior children seem to be doing well,' I replied, 'although there is a range of ability. There are some very lively and able children and others who clearly need a great deal of support. However, standards are generally pretty good. I'll be sending a full report next week and will call in again when you have had a chance to read my recommendations.'

'I'm pleased to hear that,' said the headteacher. 'Mr Spencer-Hall's been like a cat on a hot tin roof since he heard you were coming, whittling and worrying and moaning and groaning. He's a bit long in the tooth is Mr Spencer-Hall and has been here many years but he works hard, prepares his lessons well and the children produce some very praiseworthy work. Sometimes his Prophet of Doom manner is a bit tiresome but his heart's in the right place.'

'William's an interesting boy,' I said.

'Oh, William Turnbull! He's a character and no mistake. Did you manage to get a word in? He's got what my mother used to call "verbal diarrhoea". He never stops talking.'

I don't know about William having verbal diarrhoea, I thought, but Mrs McCardle could certainly give him a run for his money when it came to talking.

'You know, Mrs McCardle,' I told her, 'William is an accomplished poet and I would love a copy of

17

his 'Dalesman' poem if I may.'

'Of course, Mr Phinn, I'm sure he'd be delighted to let you have a copy.'

*　　　*　　　*

In the infant classroom, to which I returned later that morning, the children were busily engaged writing their stories about insects.

'Do feel free to wander and have a chat with the children,' said Mrs McCardle.

One child, tongue stuck out in concentration, was colouring in a grey spidery-legged creature.

'Daddy-longlegs?' I remarked.

'Crane fly,' she corrected, pertly.

'Ah yes. Would you like to tell me a little about your project?'

'We've been looking at all sorts of insects,' said the child, placing her pencil carefully on the desk. She was a precocious little thing with shiny blonde hair and bright brown eyes. 'Mrs McCardle brought some maggots in for us to watch them change into flies.' Her voice took on a conspiratorial whisper. 'And some escaped. They wriggled out of the tank and we had flies everywhere. Mrs Todd—she's our cleaner—was not very pleased. Toby brought in a wasps' nest that he found in his garden. What else? Oh, we have a wormery where you can see the worms making tunnels, and a tank where we have beetles and bugs.' She thought for a moment before asking, 'Is that called a buggery?'

Here we go again, I thought, and moved on swiftly.

I came again upon Melissa who was putting the finishing touches to her story about the lonely beetle and his amorous adventures on the compost heap. I asked her how she was getting on with her story.

'It's going very well, thank you,' she told me.

'I would love to see it when it's finished,' I told her.

'OK.'

Next to her was an awkward-looking boy with spectacles and big ears. He was sitting in thoughtful silence, his elbows on the desk, his hands propping his chin. 'I'm just thinking for a minute,' he told me seriously. 'My story's about a bee who's lost his buzz and can't find his way back to the hive but I don't know how to spell "nectar".'

'Well don't bother asking Mr Phinn,' chipped in Melissa, 'he's not very good at spelling, are you, Mr Phinn?'

CHAPTER TWO

That visit to Staplemoor County Primary School was the first of the new term but, as every school inspector—and indeed every teacher—knows, a vast amount of work has to be done between the end of the summer term and the beginning of the next when the new school year begins. Soon after the schools had broken up for summer, I had taken a few days off to visit my parents in Rotherham since there was some important news to tell them. Now back, I faced a pyramid of paper on my desk which had to be dealt with before I could escape for some holiday. However, as I sat there staring at the daunting pile, I thought about the school year we had just finished.

It had been a really interesting year. I had arranged courses and conferences for teachers, directed workshops, carried out various surveys, attended appointment panels, advised school governors and hosted important visitors from the Ministry of Education and Science—all this in addition to inspecting schools.

Yes, I thought to myself as I stared at the untouched mountain of paper, it had been a good year, but I reckoned it would be dull indeed compared to the year which lay ahead of me. That promised to be the most exciting one in my life so far, for, at the end of the previous term, I had asked the woman I loved to marry me and—bingo!—she had said yes.

On this July morning, I had arrived early at the inspectors' office, in buoyant mood despite the dismal weather. It was a dark, rain-soaked landscape that rolled past the car window as I drove the short distance from my flat above the Rumbling Tum Café in Fettlesham High Street to County Hall. The room where I worked, and which I shared with my inspector colleagues, was cramped and cluttered. There were four heavy oak desks with brass-handled drawers, four ancient ladder-back swivel chairs, four grey metal filing cabinets and a wall of dark bookcases crammed with books, digests, journals, folders and files. A couple of unhealthy-looking spider plants struggled for life on the shelf by the window.

Just as I was about to tackle the pile of paper, there was a clattering on the stairs leading up to the office. This signalled the imminent arrival of Julie, the inspectors' secretary, in those ridiculously high-heeled shoes she was fond of wearing. Julie, with her bubbly blonde hair, bright open smile and constant chatter, brightened up the dullest of days. She was ever-cheerful, wonderfully efficient and her ready wit combined with typical Yorkshire bluntness helped her immeasurably to keep the school inspectors in order. I suspect we were not the easiest of people to work for.

Besides myself, in charge of English and drama, there was Sidney Clamp, the immensely creative but entirely unpredictable and sometimes outrageous inspector in charge of creative and visual arts; David Pritchard, the lively little Welshman responsible for mathematics, PE and games, who fired words at all and sundry like a machine gun, and Dr Geraldine Mullarkey, the newest and quietest member of our team and who was in charge of science and technology. Down the corridor was our team leader, Dr Harold Yeats, the Senior Inspector, one of the gentlest and kindest of people it had been my pleasure to know, and next to his room was the secretary's small office which we all referred to as 'the broom cupboard'.

Julie now bustled in loaded down as usual with various bags. She was soaking wet and windswept. 'So what happened to summer then?' she asked as she dropped the dripping bags on the first empty desk. 'It's teeming it down out there. It's supposed to be bright and sunny at this time of year. July? It's more like the monsoon season.' She shook herself like a dog emerging from the sea. 'Why is it that the only time I forget my blessed umbrella, the heavens open? And why is it that you're left standing for half an hour at the bus stop and then three buses come at once? And why is it there's no

21

bus shelter on Sandringham Road? And why is it that madmen in cars wait until you cross the road before they drive through the puddles? I must look like something the cat's brought in.' She stood staring at me, puffing and spluttering and dripping.

'Good morning, Julie,' I said, getting up to help her off with her saturated jacket. 'Let's get these wet things off.'

'Thanks,' she said, pulling off her jacket. 'I feel as if I've been dragged backwards through a car wash. My hair must look a sight.' She pulled a strand of wet hair in front of her face to inspect it. 'What are you in so early for? It's only just after nine. Schools have broken up, you know. You don't need to get in here at the crack of dawn. Mr Clamp and Mr Pritchard won't be in till ten.'

'I intended to a make start on all this paperwork,' I said, gesturing to the mountain before me, 'but haven't got very far. Look, you go and dry off and I'll make some coffee.' I took her wet jacket and draped it over a chair to dry.

'Ta, I will.' She picked up her jacket and headed for the door but stopped suddenly, turned and gave me a knowing smile. 'Oh, what about *you*, then?'

'Me?' I asked. 'What about me?'

'Bit of a dark horse, aren't you? I hear wedding bells are in the air.'

'Oh, that. Yes, Christine and I are getting married.'

I had first met Miss Christine Bentley, headteacher of Winnery Nook Nursery and Infants School, when, as a newly-appointed County Inspector, I had visited her school some two years before. As I had tried to comfort a very distressed little girl at the school entrance, this vision had

22

appeared before me and had given me such a smile that my legs went weak. Christine had the deepest blue eyes, the softest mass of golden hair and the smoothest complexion I had ever seen. She was stunning. I had been completely bowled over, it had been love at first sight, but I had found it difficult to put my feelings into words. However, the more I had got to know her, the deeper that love became. I just could not get her out of my mind. I would be attending an important conference but sit thinking about her. I would be in a meeting and my thoughts would wander to a picture of her surrounded by a group of wide-eyed infants. I would be perched at the back of a classroom and would visualise her smiling that easy smile and gazing at me with those clear blue eyes. I would lie in bed at night with a longing so powerful it felt like an illness. I was like a love-sick schoolboy. Finally, I had had the courage to ask her out. We began to spend more time together. Now she was to be my wife and we had a lifetime together ahead of us.

'Congratulations,' Julie said, interrupting my thoughts. 'It was about time you asked her.'

'How did you know?'

'You really don't imagine that news like that stays a secret for long at County Hall, do you? The jungle telegraph was going the day after you proposed.'

'I don't see how anybody possibly could have known,' I said, puzzled.

'Haven't you forgotten about the Queen of the Jungle?' Julie's upper lip arched like a mad dog and there was a wild gleam in her eye. 'That dreadful woman was on the tom-toms in no time.

She spread it round County Hall like somebody fanning a forest fire. It's a wonder she didn't send out one of her mile-long memos letting everyone know, or announce it over a loudspeaker in the staff canteen.'

'Ah,' I sighed, 'I'd forgotten about Mrs Savage.'

'I wish I could,' remarked Julie wistfully.

Mrs Brenda Savage, Personal Assistant to Dr Gore, the Chief Education Officer, was not a well-liked woman. She was humourless, patronising and liked her red-nailed fingers in every pie around. She was also excessively nosy and very fond of her own voice and all of us had been on the receiving end of her sharp tongue at one time or another.

'Anyway,' asked Julie, gathering up the wet bags off the desk-top, 'how did the Black Widow find out?'

I explained to Julie that I had proposed to Christine on the last day of term in what I thought would be a secluded restaurant, Le Bon Appetit, in the little Dales village of Ribsdyke. By sheer coincidence, Dr Gore and Mrs Savage had been having dinner there as well that evening and had witnessed my hysterically happy outburst when Christine had said, 'I will.'

With a thud, Julie dropped the bags and her jacket back onto the desk, put her hands on her hips and said sharply, 'Well, what was *she* doing having dinner with Dr Gore?'

'You'll have to ask her that,' I teased.

'Ask *her*? Ask *her*?' Julie repeated, screwing up her face. 'I'd as soon play "Postman's Knock" with a sex-starved crocodile. I never speak to that woman unless I have to. She treats me as if I was something discovered on the sole of her shoe. She's

24

only a jumped-up office clerk. Anybody would think she was secretary of the United Nations the way she carries on. Lady High and Mighty. She forgets that some people remember her before she had that face job and when her voice didn't sound like the Queen being garrotted and when that hair of hers was natural and wasn't out of a bottle. As my mother says, "You can never escape your roots."'

'Well, who knows, she might very well be the future Mrs Gore,' I said mischievously. 'They certainly seemed to be getting on very well. Quite intimate, actually.'

'No!' gasped Julie. 'You don't think she's getting her hooks into Dr Gore, do you? She's been through three husbands. Do you think she's trying to make him husband number four? That would be awful. She's bad enough now but if she married the CEO she'd be unbearable. She'd be lording it—'

Julie's monologue was interrupted by the shrill ringing of the telephone on my desk. I picked it up.

'Hello, Gervase Phinn here.' It was the woman herself—the formidable Mrs Savage.

'Good morning, Mr Phinn, Brenda Savage here,' she said with slow deliberation. I waited but there was no polite, 'How are you?' or 'Congratulations on your forthcoming marriage.' She was her predictably coldly formal self. 'Are you still there?'

'Good morning, Mrs Savage,' I replied cheerfully, grinning in Julie's direction. I resisted the temptation to say 'Speak of the devil . . .' but asked instead, 'What can I do for you?'

Julie took a blustering breath and left the office. '*I'll* make the coffee,' she said on the way out, 'and I'll put plenty of brandy in it.'

25

'Mr Phinn,' continued Mrs Savage slowly, 'I don't appear to have the inspectors' programmes for next week.'

'Really,' I said.

'I have mentioned to you all, on numerous occasions, how very important it is to have details of the inspectors' proposed timetables in case Dr Gore or one of the councillors needs to make urgent contact.' I attempted a reply, intending to inform her that since schools were on holiday we would all be in the office and that filling in the forms would be a waste of time and effort, but she carried on regardless. 'I have rung Dr Yeats's number several times now but there is no response. Could you inform him, when he does arrive, that it is imperative that I have the programmes on my desk by the end of the day? I really do not have the time to be constantly reminding you inspectors about these and other matters. Now, I have work to attend to,' she said, as if I were deliberately detaining her and without waiting for a reply she ended the call.

'Insufferable woman,' I muttered to myself.

'What did Lady Macbeth want then?' Julie asked when she returned with two mugs of coffee which she set down on the desk in front of me. She wore no shoes and her hair, which had dried out a little, looked wild and wiry.

'The inspectors' programmes.'

'Well, she can wait,' Julie said bluntly, straightening her crumpled skirt.

'I'll take them across later,' I told her. I patted the pile of paper on my desk. 'I need to start on this little lot first.'

'Dr Yeats hasn't given me the programmes yet,

so you can't. Anyway, why should you be at her beck and call? She's got legs. Wouldn't do her any harm to get off her fat backside and leave that fancy office of hers and come and get them. She's got precious little else to do all day except sharpen her nails.'

'I must say, I thought Harold would be in by now,' I said.

'He usually is,' replied Julie, cupping her hands around the mug. 'He spends most of the school holidays at his desk but he hasn't been around for a couple of days. I hope he's all right. I found him in his office one day last week, just staring into space. I had to cough to get his attention. I even found a couple of mistakes in his last report, not up to his usual meticulous standard.'

'Do you think he's ill?' I asked.

'Well, he said not,' replied Julie, 'when I asked him last week. But if you ask me, something's bothering him.'

'We have our inspectors' meeting later today,' I told her, 'so I'll find a minute to have a quiet word with him then.'

'Might be an idea,' agreed Julie, heading for the door. 'I was thinking it could be the male menopause. I was reading about it in a magazine this weekend. Most men go through it. My dad did when he was about Dr Yeats's age. It's when men start to go bald, get a paunch, see time ticking away and try to prove that they aren't "over the hill". They start looking at bimbos, take up jogging, dress in clothes that are far too young for them and come out with the oddest things. Do you know, my Dad came into the kitchen one morning and said—'

'I'll have a word with Dr Yeats, Julie,' I said, 'but

27

now I really must get on.'

'Yeah, have a word with him,' she said thoughtfully. Then her face changed and she snapped, 'Oh, and if the Wicked Witch of the West phones again, tell her to go chew a brick.'

* * *

As the clock on Fettlesham's County Hall tower struck ten, Sidney and David arrived at the office. I could hear them squabbling like quarrelsome little schoolboys all the way up the stairs. The door burst open and Sidney made his usual dramatic entrance, followed closely by David, clutching a wet umbrella. I might have been invisible for all the notice they took of me.

'You're like a Welsh terrier, David,' Sidney was saying, waving his large hands expansively in the air as if discouraging an irritating fly. 'You *will* persist in your pedestrian views like a snappy little dog worrying a rabbit. You just won't let it lie. You would argue with a signpost given half a chance.'

David hooked his umbrella on a shelf, tucked his briefcase away, sat down, placed his hands on the high wooden arm rests and took a slow, deep breath. 'The trouble is, Sidney,' he said in a deliberately measured voice, 'you never like anyone to disagree with you, to have an alternative version of things, another point of view. You are blinkered, entirely unable to accept that just for once you may indeed not be the fount of all knowledge.'

'Everyone has a right to my opinion,' said Sidney.

'As my Welsh grandmother used to say—'

'Oh, save me from the Celtic words of wisdom,'

28

interrupted Sidney. 'This Welsh grandmother of yours sounds a pain in the neck, endlessly giving everyone the benefit of her homely advice. I would have consigned her to an old folks' home years ago.'

'As my dear and very much loved Welsh grandmother used to say,' said David, undeterred by the interruption, ' "Just because someone talks with conviction and enthusiasm doesn't mean they know what they're talking about. Fancy words butter no parsnips." '

'Good morning, David. Good morning, Sidney. Now, what's all this about?' I asked. 'I could hear you arguing from the bottom of the stairs. As soon as one of you stops for a breath, the other begins again.'

'We are not arguing, Gervase, we are having a professional disagreement,' explained Sidney, acknowledging my presence for the first time. 'David is saying that I don't know what I'm talking about when it comes to art, which is, as you know, my specialist subject.'

'I am merely saying,' said David, 'that I am entitled to have a view.'

'Well, let's ask Gervase,' said Sidney, rattling the change in his pocket and staring out of the window.

'Don't bring me into it, Sidney,' I said, shaking my head. 'I always seem to end up in the middle, pleasing neither of you.'

'Listen, Gervase, would you accept that I know more about art than David?'

'Well, I suppose so but—' I began.

'Which, of course, is not really unsurprising since I am the inspector responsible for creative and visual arts, with a degree in fine art and a master's degree in art. So, David, do you at least recognise that I know more about art than you?'

David lifted both his hands to his face, took off his spectacles and folded them on the desk in front of him and breathed loudly through his nose. 'Yes, but the point is—'

'Do stop making that infernal blowing noise, David,' interrupted Sidney yet again, 'you sound like an asthmatic whale. Now, as you agree that I know more about art than you do . . .' at which point I switched off. I knew these two: once they got into an argument it was like a bone between two dogs.

A few moments later, they paused in their verbal battle when Julie arrived at the door.

'Morning,' she said.

'Good morning, Julie,' said David.

'Good God, Julie!' exclaimed Sidney rising from his chair. 'Whatever have you done to your hair? It looks as if you've had your head in a spin drier.'

'What a flatterer you are, Sidney,' I said.

Julie ignored Sidney's remark. 'Do you want coffee?' she asked.

'That would be splendid,' said David. 'Then if Mr Clamp will leave me alone, I shall make a start on my in-tray.'

'The thing is, David,' Sidney interrupted, 'I do not profess to possess a deep-seated knowledge about mathematics, therefore I keep my own counsel. I am somewhat tentative about making pronouncements about things of which I know little. You, on the other hand—'

As he was about to hold forth yet again, Julie turned to me and said, 'Aren't you going to tell them the news?'

'Well, I would have,' I replied, 'if I had been able to get a word in.'

'Don't give me any bad news,' said Sidney, sitting back down. 'It's the school holidays and I don't want bad news, extra work, contentious issues, problems or difficulties. I have had enough of those this year. I intend clearing my desk in the next few days and then spending two glorious weeks in Italy. Well, what is this news that is so important?'

'I'm getting married,' I said. 'Christine has said she will marry me.'

'Dear boy!' exclaimed Sidney, jumping from his chair and thumping me vigorously on the back. 'Why ever didn't you say, letting us ramble on? What wonderful news! Well done! At last, you are to make delectable Miss Christine Bentley of Winnery Nook, the Aphrodite of the education world, the Venus of Fettlesham, an honest woman.'

'You haven't *got* to get married, have you?' Julie enquired of me from the door. 'I mean she's not—'

'No, of course she isn't,' I laughed.

'Congratulations, Gervase,' said David, reaching over to shake my hand. 'You are made for each other.'

'Thank you, David.'

'And when is the big day?'

'We're thinking of next April,' I replied.

'Not hanging about, are you?' observed Julie.

'Of course, you're quite right not to wait,' Sidney remarked, leaning back expansively in his chair and placing his hands behind his head. 'I mean, neither of you are getting any younger.'

'We're not quite in our dotage,' I replied.

'No and neither of you are spring chickens, either. I mean, if you're thinking of starting a

31

family you need to get cracking.'

'Now he's a self-styled marriage counsellor,' snorted David. 'An expert on marital affairs. If I were you, Gervase, I would take his comments, like the ones about modern art, with a great pinch of salt.'

'You see,' spluttered Sidney, 'just like a snappy little Welsh terrier. He will not let it lie.'

'Hush a moment,' commanded David, raising a hand. 'If I am not mistaken, those fairy footsteps on the stairs tell us our esteemed leader is on his way up.'

Harold Yeats, Senior County Inspector, was a bear of a man, well over six feet tall and with a great jutting bulldog jaw. He looked the last person in the world to be a school inspector. With his broad shoulders, arched chest and hands like spades, he looked more like an underworld enforcer or a night club bouncer. But Harold was a gentle giant, warm-hearted, generous and courteous to all. He also had an encyclopaedic knowledge and an amazing memory.

'Harold!' boomed Sidney as he caught sight of him at the door. 'Gervase is to tie the knot.'

Harold squeezed past Julie and entered the office. He smiled warmly, revealing a set of tombstone teeth, and shook my hand. 'Yes, yes, I heard from Dr Gore this morning. Congratulations, Gervase. She's a lovely young woman, Miss Bentley. You are a very lucky man.'

'I know,' I said.

'Dr Yeats,' said Julie, 'may I ask where you've been? I was expecting you a lot earlier.'

'With Dr Gore, Julie,' he replied. 'Didn't I tell you?'

32

'No, and if you've seen Dr Gore, did Brenda the barracuda find you?'

'The *what*?' asked Harold, his brow furrowing.

'Mrs Savage. She wants the inspectors' programmes for next week.'

'Ah, yes, I did see her when I was leaving Dr Gore's office and she mentioned something of the sort. But that can wait. Now, look everyone, would you all sit down for a moment, there's something very important I have to say. I did think of waiting to tell you at a full team meeting but, as you know, Geraldine is on the Association of Science in Education Conference in York this week so won't be able to join us.'

'I was wondering where our pale Irish beauty was,' remarked Sidney. 'She's not the most forthcoming of people. I had no idea she was on a course this week.'

'Well, she is,' said Harold. 'Anyhow, if you would all give me your attention and you, too, Julie, if you would stay for a moment, please. If I delay telling you all, the news is sure to leak out and I do want you to be the first to know.'

'Leak out!' repeated Julie, sneering. 'If Mrs Savage gets to hear of it, whatever it is, there'll be a tidal wave, never mind a leak, going through County Hall.'

'Ah yes,' said Harold. 'Well, I expect Mrs Savage will get to know sometime today.'

'If it's bad news, Harold,' said Sidney, 'I don't want to know. It's the start of the school holidays and I need a rest. I do not want depressing news, extra work, contentious issues, problems, difficulties or complaints.'

Harold gave a weak smile. 'Well, Sidney, I don't

33

know whether it's good or bad news to be honest.' He paused and touched his brow with his long fingers. 'I'm going to retire.'

'*Retire?*' we all shouted in unison.

'That's right, I've decided to finish but not immediately. I'll be around for some time yet. Dr Gore has asked me to see out the next academic year which is only fair. That gives him the chance of advertising my job, shortlisting and interviewing in good time for my replacement to start next September. That's why I was with Dr Gore this morning.'

'Whatever has brought this on?' exclaimed David.

'I've been thinking about it for some time,' said Harold.

'But why, Harold?' I asked. 'Are you all right, physically, I mean?'

'Oh yes, I'm fine, there's nothing wrong with me—apart from feeling things are getting a bit too much. All the travelling and the late evenings have taken their toll this past year. I've been reviewing things a little lately, my future, what I want to do with the rest of my life and, to be frank, I'm ready to finish.'

Julie arched an eyebrow and gave me a knowing look.

'You can't finish, Harold!' snapped Sidney. 'It's out of the question.'

'Yes, I can, Sidney,' said Harold softly. 'I've had enough. Last term was particularly difficult. That school closure was such a time-consuming and wearisome business, then the increased number of inspections and the additional demands from the Ministry. I'm tired, Sidney, I'm very tired. All those

34

conferences away from home, weekend courses, difficult meetings, lengthy reports, inspections and late nights attending this, that and the other. I don't have to tell you what it's like. I'm ready to pass the baton to a younger person with more stamina than I have at the moment. I suppose it came home to me a couple of weekends ago. Janet and I went for a day to Scarborough to blow away a few cobwebs. We were walking along the North Shore and we came upon a man in a sort of booth with a big sign in the front saying that if he was unable to guess your age within a year you would win a prize. Well, I won a prize. I'm fifty-nine next birthday and he guessed my age at sixty-four.'

'Oh, Harold, that's nothing,' said Sidney. 'I mean, look at David. He looks considerably older than you and he's still managing to carry on.'

'Thank you, Sidney,' sighed David.

'When we were inspecting that little school at Barton Moor together last term one little boy, you must remember, David, asked if you were Dean's great-granddad, there to talk about your experiences in the trenches. Do you recall?'

'I had forgotten, but am most grateful to you for reminding me,' David told him.

'So you see Harold,' continued Sidney, 'you're only as old as you feel.'

'The problem is, Sidney,' said Harold, giving another weak smile, 'I sometimes feel about eighty.'

'We all feel tired at the end of a busy term, Harold,' I said. 'You'll feel a whole lot better after a holiday and a good rest.'

'Exactly,' agreed Sidney. 'Now, put further thoughts of retiring from your mind.'

'I'm afraid I can't do that, Sidney,' said Harold. 'I'm ready to finish and I have made up my mind. Which is exactly what I have told Dr Gore. As I said, I wanted to give him time to find the best replacement, so you won't get rid of me just yet.'

'But when do you intend to finish?' asked Julie who, until now, had been stunned into silence.

'As I said, I hope to see out the academic year. Probably July, perhaps a little earlier. I shall take things a bit easier and cut out some of the late meetings.'

'Good God, Harold, you're serious,' whispered Sidney.

'Well, I'm devastated, Harold,' said David. 'I don't mind saying so. I'm completely lost for words.'

'Hasn't that proverbial old Welsh grandmother of yours got an apt little saying for the occasion?' asked Sidney, shaking his head.

'I suppose she'd say what she said about Lloyd George,' said David sadly. ' "We will never see his like again." '

'That's most kind of you, David,' said Harold, 'but life does go on. None of us is indispensable.'

'This is a shock, Harold,' I said. 'It really is.'

'It's quite dreadful news, Harold, dreadful,' continued Sidney. 'I feel physically sick. I just cannot take it in. I mean, I'll probably hate your replacement.'

'Beggar the thought,' said David. 'You not get on with people? The very idea.'

'I suppose the person taking over could be an internal promotion, someone on the team already,' said Sidney. 'Please don't think I am considering applying myself, I am far too long in the tooth.

Geraldine has just started so she's out of the running and David is definitely past it.'

'Thank you,' chipped in his colleague. 'Remind me to check when my stair lift is being installed.'

'You know what I mean, David,' Sidney told him. 'No, I was thinking of Gervase. What about Gervase taking over? He could do it.'

'Now hold on, Sidney,' I said hurriedly.

'That is really not for me to say, Sidney,' said Harold. 'The post will be advertised and Gervase's application, should he wish to apply, will be considered along with the rest.'

'But you could put a good word in with the powers that be, Harold,' persisted Sidney.

'You over-estimate my influence, Sidney,' replied Harold.

'Now, the suggestion of Gervase having a go for the job,' said David thoughtfully, 'is not at all a bad idea, something on which we could certainly agree, Sidney. "Better the devil you know", as my Welsh grandmother was wont to remark.'

'Do I get a say in all this?' I asked. Before anyone could answer, the telephone on my desk rang and I snatched it up. 'Yes, Mrs Savage, Dr Yeats is here. I'll pass you over to him.'

*   *   *

For the remainder of the day I attempted to knuckle down to some serious work in the hope of clearing my desk of as much paper as possible, but my thoughts kept wandering. I had started the day thinking about the past year and now I could not get the year ahead out of my mind. There would be the wedding, of course, married life, buying a

37

house and now there was something else—Harold's shock announcement. 'What about Gervase taking over?' Sidney had said. I would have to think long and hard about that one.

CHAPTER THREE

Connie, the caretaker of the Staff Development Centre, was a good-hearted, down-to-earth Yorkshire woman with an acerbic wit and wonderful command of the most inventive malapropisms and *non sequiturs*. She had no conception of rank, status or position and treated everyone exactly the same— with a bluntness bordering on the rude. If the Pope himself were to pay a visit to the Staff Development Centre and make use of the washroom facilities, Connie would no doubt have detained His Holiness as he departed, with the words: 'I hope you've left them Gents as you found them!' Were the Queen to grace the portals of the SDC, Connie would have no compunction in telling Her Majesty to wipe her feet before entering and to return her cup to the serving hatch after use. Should the Prime Minister enter the building, Connie would have not the slightest hesitation in asking the right honourable gentleman, as she asked all visitors, if he had parked his car well away from the front doors because blocking her entrance was a health and safety hazard. It was unthinkable that she was at the end of any chain of command, that she could be directed to carry out instructions or, perish the thought, be given such a thing as an order. It was Connie who was at the controls when people were on her territory.

Connie could be quite unnerving. Teachers attending courses at the Centre would be listening to a speaker and, glancing up, would see Connie's round, florid face grimacing at the door. During the coffee-break they would find an ample woman with a bright copper-coloured perm and dressed in a brilliant pink nylon overall hovering in the background, usually surveying them with a malevolent expression. At lunchtime they would be eating their sandwiches nervously, making certain not a crumb fell on the spotless carpet, sensing that small sharp eyes, like those of a blackbird searching for a worm, were watching from behind the serving hatch. And when, at the end of the day, the equipment had been put neatly away, the chairs carefully stacked, the rooms left in an orderly fashion, litter placed in the appropriate receptacles and all crockery returned to the kitchen, Connie would stride around her empire, feather duster held like a field-marshal's baton, her nylon overall crackling, to make sure that everything was left as it had been found earlier that day. And woe betide anyone who flouted these unwritten rules.

The Staff Development Centre, where all the courses and conferences for teachers and most of the staff interviews took place, was a tribute to Connie's hard work and dedication. She scrubbed and scoured, polished and dusted, mopped and wiped with a vengeance. The building, inside and out, was always immaculately clean and tidy, not a speck of dusk or a scuff mark was to be seen anywhere and it always smelt of lavender furniture polish and carbolic soap. The toilets were her pride and joy. The porcelain sparkled, the brass pipes shone, the tiles shimmered, the floors gleamed. The Staff Development Centre was Connie's palace. If any one of us was ever inclined to suggest to her that she should show a little more deference and respect, that person would desist, knowing that deep down this woman had a heart of gold and that no one could do the job better than she. Everyone who knew her was prepared to tolerate her abrupt manner and sharp tongue for those very reasons. Everyone, that is, except Sidney. Sidney—noisy, unpredictable, untidy, madly creative—was someone guaranteed to ruffle the feathers of her duster and wind Connie up to distraction.

I arrived at the SDC one dull Friday afternoon in the third week of the new term to prepare for an English course I was to direct the following Monday. In the entrance hall stood Connie, in fierce discussion with the man himself. She was dressed, as usual, in her pink nylon overall and was clutching her feather duster magisterially.

'Look here, Connie,' Sidney was trying to explain to her, 'you have to accept a bit of a mess. For goodness sake, it was an *art* course. Art is not like mathematics, you know, it's not orderly, it's not methodical, it's not tidy. We artists use messy materials like paints, charcoals, crayons, clay, cardboard, glue, pencils, paper.' He waved his hands about theatrically as if conducting some invisible orchestra. 'People have to express themselves in art, be creative, imaginative and they are therefore often untidy. It's par for the course.'

Connie pulled one of her many expressions of distaste, the face of someone suffering from acute indigestion. 'Well, it's not part of *my* course, Mr Clamp,' she retorted, 'and I don't want these artists, as you call them, expressing themselves like that in *my* Centre. They can clear up after themselves. They do have hands, I take it, if they are doing all these creative carryings-on. Then they can use those hands to clear up and they don't need to leave a trail of debris and destruction behind like what they have this afternoon.'

'Hardly a trail of debris and destruction,' sighed Sidney.

'Oh, yes, they did, Mr Clamp, and I can't be doing with it. Even my little grandson wouldn't leave a mess like that.'

Sidney continued to wave his hands elaborately before him. 'Einstein said that genius is seldom tidy.'

'I don't care what Einstein or any of your other artificated friends have to say. I am not cleaning up that mess and that's that. It's all very well for you and this Einstein to leave the room as if a bomb has hit it, I'm the one left to pick up the pieces. I'm telling you, I don't intend picking up those pieces that you've left today. I mean, it's just not fair to expect me to do it, Mr Clamp.'

'First of all, Connie,' said Sidney, 'Einstein is dead.'

'Well, I'm very sorry to hear it, I'm sure, but that's no excuse for the mess that was left in that room. It was spotless when you went in this morning, you could have eaten your dinner off of that floor, and look at it now. Anyway,' she said, flourishing her feather duster along a window ledge, 'it's my bingo night and I'm not missing the first house just because I have to stop here to clear up.'

'Good afternoon,' I said in a loud and cheerful

41

voice, determined to get their attention since until then neither seemed to have noticed me.

'Hello, Gervase,' moaned Sidney.

'Good afternoon,' said Connie through tight little lips. 'Anyhow, I've said what I had to say, Mr Clamp, and I insist that you will see to it that that room is left as you found it before you go. I could let this Centre go to rack and ruin but I keep it nice and tidy.'

'I know you do, Connie,' began Sidney.

'It's no skin off my feet if it was just left but you'd be soon complaining if you found the room like that at the start of *your* course.'

'Very well, Connie,' Sidney told her, bowing with a flourish. 'I give in. I surrender. I yield. I shall remain behind and return the art room to its pristine splendour and perhaps my kind and obliging colleague here will lend a helpful hand.'

'Oh, no!' I spluttered. 'I'm sorry, Sidney, but I have a course to prepare and then I'm meeting Christine at Mama's Pizza Parlour. You're on your own.'

'What happened to friendship and camaraderie?' asked Sidney to no one in particular. 'Whither went The Good Samaritan?'

'He probably didn't have a date and it wasn't his bingo night,' I replied flippantly.

'Very droll,' said Sidney.

'Well, just so long as it gets done,' came Connie's final riposte before she marched off down the corridor, flicking the feather duster at invisible dust and crackling as she went.

'That woman,' said Sidney through clamped teeth, 'will drive me to drink.'

'Speaking of drink,' I said, 'I'll see if I can get

42

Connie to rustle you up a cup of tea before you start the blitz of the art room. You might be there some time.'

'She'll probably put toilet bleach in it if she knows it's for me, and considering the mood I'm in at the moment, I would probably drink it. But, come on, Gervase,' he pleaded, 'lend a hand, there's a good fellow.'

'I'm sorry, Sidney, but I can't. I just don't have the time.'

'That dragon in pink will be watching my every move.'

'Don't judge her too harshly,' I said. 'Her heart's in the right place.'

'The right place for Connie's heart, dear boy,' replied Sidney, summoning up a faint smile, 'is on the end of a stake.' With that he departed for the art room to tidy up.

Having checked the equipment in the English room, set out the chairs, displayed a range of books and materials and put a programme on each table, I headed for the kitchen. By this time Sidney, who had made a half-hearted attempt to clear up the mess in the art room, had crept away. Connie was vigorously wiping the Formica top of the serving hatch.

'Right, that's sorted,' I told her.

'I hope the art room is,' she snapped. 'That Mr Clamp will drive me to drink. I don't know how you can share an office with him. I've never met anyone so untidy. And that Mr Pritchard is not a whole lot better, forever leaving his equipment all over the place. Anyway, have you got everything you need for Monday?' she asked.

'Yes, all ready and prepared.'

43

'I put another bulb in the overhead projector, just to be on the safe side.'

'Thank you, Connie.'

'And I put some extra paper on the flip chart.'

'That's very good of you.'

'And I've put out some more felt tip markers. I know how you like to write.'

'Thank you, Connie.'

'Do you want a cup of tea?'

I glanced at my watch. I was not intending to go home before meeting Christine so had a bit of time to kill. 'Yes, thanks.'

As Connie clanked and clattered in the cupboard behind the hatch, I had visions of her and Sidney, having driven each other to drink, ending up in the same drying-out clinic. Not a happy thought, and I pushed it from my wicked mind.

'So, was your summer holiday better than last year?' I asked her. Connie had had a disastrous time in Ireland the previous summer.

'We didn't go nowhere this year,' she said, prising the top off a large tin of biscuits, 'except for a couple of weekends in the caravan at Filey, and then it rained all the time.' She adopted another expression from her extensive repertoire. 'My father went into hospital and I was traipsing back and forth for most of the time.'

'I'm sorry to hear that, Connie,' I said. 'Is it serious?'

'He had a stroke. He was at the Legion playing dominoes when it happened. Next thing he was in casualty and he's been in ever since. He's getting on, you know. Ninety-two next birthday and he still lives on his own. He's very independent is Dad, and been fit as a butcher's dog until now. Never had so

44

much as a cold in his life before this happened, and he was down the pit for nearly forty years. He smokes like a chimney, eats a full fried breakfast every morning, black pudding included, and he likes a drink. The doctor said it had caught up with him. I said to the doctor, "Well, whatever it is that's caught up with him, it's took its time." "Well, you have to expect these things at his time of life," says he. "He's a good age." "Yes, well, that's as may be," I told him, "but I want my father looking after. I don't want any of this euthenoria business you read about. If he goes into one of them comas," I told him, "don't you dare turn him off. He fought for his king and country. He deserves top treatment, the RIP sort." That's what I told him.'

'So he's still in hospital, you say?' I asked, attempting to suppress a smile.

'Yes, still there. Mind you, he's a lot better than he was when he went in. He was sitting up and entertaining the nurses when I last saw him.'

'Well, that's good news,' I said. 'Perhaps you'll be able to get a holiday later this month.'

'No, I don't like leaving this place in term time, what with all the courses and conferences and interviews on. More trouble than it's worth. Can you imagine what mess I'd find in the art room if I left it for a couple of weeks?'

I swiftly steered her away from a continuation of the saga of Sidney and the art room. 'Well, I hope it won't be too long before your father's home.'

'Oh yes, well, we'll just have to hope and pray. He was wanting to go to the Cenotaph in London again this year with his British Legion pals. He's a Dunkirk veteran as well, you know. He always looks forward to his trip to London. All dressed up in his blazer and flannel trousers with creases like knife edges, wearing his medals, but I shouldn't think he'll make it this year. I'm so proud of him when I see them marching past the Cenotaph. They want to get some of these young hooligans in the army. They have no appreciation or gratitude for what the older generation did for them.' Connie began pouring the tea.

'Well, I hope he'll be home soon,' I said, accepting the proffered mug. I decided it was time to change the subject. 'I'm getting married, you know.'

'You're not, are you?' she gasped, pausing in her pouring. 'Is it that nice young woman with the blonde hair, Miss Bentley?'

'Well, it's not likely to be anyone else, Connie, is it?' I laughed. 'I'm not exactly your Casanova.'

'Well, you never know,' she said, starting to pour her tea again. 'You seem to be very pally with that little nun. That Sister Brenda.'

'Sister Brendan.'

'That's her. You seem to hit it off with her and no mistake. She's forever on your courses.'

'Nuns are celibate, Connie,' I told her.

'They're celi-what?'

'They're not allowed to get married.'

'Yes, well, as I've said to you before, I had no idea she was a nun when I first met her. I was talking to her as if she was a normal person. There was no long black skirt or headgear. I didn't know she was a nun. She looked like an air hostess in that dark blue suit and with her hair all buffeted up. If they can drive cars and dress like that, I reckon it won't be long before they're getting married. Anyway, I hope you and Miss Bentley will be very

46

happy.'

'Thanks, Connie.'

'You've not known her that long, have you? In my day, we used to walk out together for a few years before we decided to get married. I think the reason for all the divorces these days is that people rush into it.'

'I've been going out with Christine for nearly two years.'

'That doesn't mean a thing. No, gone are the days of long courtships and chaperones and getting engaged and asking fathers for their daughter's hand. These days, most people don't seem to bother with marriage. They "live over the brush", as my mother would say. They don't have husbands and wives nowadays, they have partners. I ask you! That's what you have on the dance floor, a partner. You wonder what the world's coming to, don't you? Take my cousin's girl. She's at West Challerton High, supposed to be doing her exams this year. She changes her boyfriends as often as she changes her knickers. I said to my cousin, "It'll end in grief, you mark my words."' Connie took a gulp of tea and grimaced. 'Anyway, I hope you'll have a very happy life together.'

'Thank you, Connie.'

'Ted and me have been married for thirty-five years, you know, and hardly a cross word has passed between us.' I had met Ted on a few occasions. He was a small, quiet man with a permanently worried expression. I guessed that Connie's long-suffering husband had thrown in the towel years ago.

Connie topped up her mug and then picked a biscuit out of the tin. 'I'm glad you've called in

47

today because I wanted to have a quiet word with you.'

Oh no, I thought, what now? 'Did I leave the room in—' I began.

'No, no, nothing like that. You're quite tidy compared to the others.' Damned with faint praise, I thought. 'It's Miss Pilkington I wanted to have a word with you about.'

Miss Pilkington was the headteacher of Willingforth Primary, the school which Connie's grandchildren, Damien and Lucy, attended. I had never heard Connie describe anyone in such glowing terms as she had done this headteacher. 'She's excellent, Miss Pilkington,' Connie had confided to me one day, as she had washed the dishes at the end of a training course. 'A woman after my own heart. She doesn't stand no nonsense, I can tell you, not like some of these airy-fairy, wishy-washy teachers you hear about.' Connie had gone on for a good ten minutes telling me how happy her grandchildren were at Willingforth, how much they were learning and what a beautifully clean school it was. When I had finally got around to visiting the school I had found that Connie's assessment was spot on.

'So what about Miss Pilkington?' I asked now.

'She's having a bit of trouble at the moment. I mean, I don't suppose it's for me to say really. As you well know, I'm not one for gossip, but I do think one of you inspectors ought to call in—and not Mr Clamp, he'd only make it worse.'

'Well, it's funny that you should mention Willingforth,' I said. 'I've had a request from Miss Pilkington to go and see her next week.'

'Ah well, that's it then. I'll say no more.' She took

48

a gulp of tea. 'But if they don't remove him, there'll be fireworks.'

'Remove him?' I repeated, intrigued.

'As I said, I'm not a hot gossiper but I shall say my piece and then say no more. My Lucy came home at the beginning of this term with tales that would make your hair curl.' She produced a new and wonderfully gruesome expression from her repertoire of faces. 'There's this new boy. Terry they call him. Terry the Terror. Terry, the storm in a T-shirt. He's come from a really bad home, I heard, being fostered by a doctor in the village. And he's a right little handful. "Put the paste on the table, Terry," says Miss Pilkington to him and he does just that. He pastes all the table-top as if he's painting a picture. "I can see your coat on the floor, Terry," says Miss Pilkington to him. "Yes, so can I," he says, walking past. Cheeky little devil. He's rude, badly behaved and my Lucy says he spits and swears. He wants a good smack, that's what he wants. Course you're not allowed to lay a finger on them these days, are you? I tell you, it never did me any harm. Miss Pilkington's at the end of her tether with this lad, so my daughter tells me.' Connie took another gulp of tea. 'And there's moves afoot.'

'Moves?'

'To have him sent to another school.'

'Well, I'm going to be there next week, Connie,' I told her. 'Thanks for the tea. I'll see you on Monday. Oh, and I hope your father improves.'

*   *   *

Half an hour later, I was sitting at a corner table in Mama's Pizza Parlour, waiting for Christine.

49

Mama's was a small family restaurant, rather dark but very atmospheric and tucked away down a narrow alleyway just off Fettlesham High Street. We had arranged to meet there early before going on to see an amateur production of *Antony and Cleopatra*, performed by the Netherfoot Thespians. One of Christine's friends was taking part. I was intrigued to find out how a group of motley amateurs would stage such an epic Shakespearean drama.

As the clock struck six Christine arrived. She made heads turn as she walked towards me.

'Excuse me, young man,' she said, 'may I join you?'

'Of course,' I replied, 'but I must warn you, I find you a devilishly attractive woman and I might just leap over the table and have my wicked way with you.'

'Sssh,' she said, laughing, 'people will hear. Have you been waiting long for me?'

'All my life,' I sighed. 'I've been desperately hoping against hope that one day I would meet the woman of my dreams. Let me swim in those limpid pools which are your eyes, hold your lithe body in my arms and smother hot kisses on those yielding lips.'

'Will you be serious! If you won't be sensible I shall pour this jug of water over you. That should cool your burning ardour.'

How lovely she was, I thought to myself as I looked at my wife-to-be across the table. What a lucky man I am.

'So how's Harold?' Christine asked, glancing down the menu.

I had told her of Harold's intention to retire at

the end of the school year and had raised with her the possibility of my applying for his job. She had been less than enthusiastic, suggesting I would have enough on my plate with what was already a relatively new job, a new wife and a new house, without taking on additional responsibilities at work.

'Of course, I'll back you if you really want to go for it,' she had told me, half-heartedly, 'but don't you think it's a bit soon for you to start applying for a senior position like that? Think of all the extra work. I would like to see my husband other than just at the weekend.'

'You sound as if I've already got it,' I had said, rather disappointed by her response.

'Well, you must be in with a chance,' she had replied. I had certainly been thinking about it a great deal since Harold had made the shock announcement a couple of months before, and it was clear that it had also been on Christine's mind as well, although we hadn't spoken much about it.

'So, how's Harold?' she asked now.

'Oh, he's fine. I told him at the beginning of the school holidays, when he looked worn out, that the summer break would recharge his batteries. He certainly seems back to his old self: getting in early, working late, attending all those meetings. Personally, I think he needed a good holiday.'

'Perhaps he'll change his mind.'

'About what?'

'About retiring.'

'No, I don't think so. He's pretty determined.'

'And are you?' asked Christine. She looked up from the menu.

'Am I what?' I asked.

51

'Determined—to apply for this job?'

I opened my mouth to answer but the waiter arrived at the table with a bottle of champagne in a silver bucket.

'For you, madam, and you, sir,' he said.

'Oh, how lovely!' cried Christine. 'What a nice thought.' She leaned over the table and squeezed my hand.

'I didn't order any champagne,' I said.

'A gentleman called in earlier,' the waiter informed me. 'It is with his compliments.' He plucked a card from his waistcoat pocket and placed it on the table before me.

'Congratulations,' it said in a large unmistakable script, 'on capturing the most beautiful woman in Yorkshire. I am sure you will both be idyllically happy. Give Christine a kiss for me. SC.'

'Sidney,' I said, shaking my head and smiling. I passed Christine the card.

'How sweet of him.'

After the waiter had opened the champagne, and had poured us both a glass, I toasted my future wife. 'To us, my darling, and to what lies ahead of us.'

Her blue eyes shone. 'To us.' And we clinked glasses.

After the first exhilarating sip of the bubbly wine, I said, 'Look, Christine, I've not really made up my mind about applying but I am certainly not ruling it out.'

She reached across the table and took my hand again. 'Gervase, I don't see all that much of you now. What is it going to be like if you have Harold's work load? Don't you really think you'll have enough on this year?'

'Yes, of course,' I replied, 'but the job won't start until next September.'

'And take Sidney. You get on really well with him as a colleague, and David as well, but what if you become their boss? They are lovely, warm, friendly people but I should imagine they can be something of a nightmare to manage. I just want you to give it some serious thought.'

'I will, I promise.' I changed the subject. 'Now, what about tomorrow? Are we still house hunting?'

CHAPTER FOUR

Willingforth Primary School resembled a prosperous, well-maintained private residence. It was set back from the main road, which ran the length of the small picturesque village, tucked behind the Norman church and the village pond. It was an imposing grey stone Georgian building with high leaded windows, each sporting a pair of white shutters, and a large oak-panelled door with brass knocker in the shape of a smiling ram's head. To the front was a small, well-tended lawn with a sundial and tubs of bright geraniums still untouched by frost. A casual visitor to the village, strolling past, would have no idea that this was a school. There was no playground or noticeboard, no noise of boisterous children.

The door opened into one large bright classroom. The walls were pale blue, the long patterned curtains at the window somewhat darker, while the high curved roof supports were painted in navy-blue and cream. In one corner, on a square of carpet, were three fat reading cushions and a small bookcase filled with picture books. On the wall above, in pride of place, was a large coloured sampler decorated with the motto 'STRAIGHT WORDS, STRAIGHT DEEDS, STRAIGHT BACKS'. The children, sitting on solid, straight-backed wooden chairs, worked at highly-polished desks complete with lids and holes for inkwells. This was a classroom like no other I had visited. The view of the dale from the classroom window was breathtaking. Acre upon acre of fields, criss-crossed by limestone walls, sloped gently upwards to a long scar of white rock, wind-scoured and craggy. In the far distance clouds oozed over the fell tops.

I was at the school very early that mild autumn day at the request of the headteacher, Miss Pilkington. I had received a blow-by-blow account of Miss Pilkington well before I had met her some two years before. Connie, my informant, had described the headteacher as 'one of the old school'. I had rather expected a dragon of a woman, with cold piercing eyes behind steel-rimmed spectacles. But I was wrong. Miss Pilkington had turned out to be a tall, extremely elegant woman, probably in her late forties. She had a streamline figure, flawless make-up and wore designer clothes. 'Miss Pilkington', I had written in my report following my first visit, 'is a teacher of high calibre.' Her lessons were well planned and organised, she had extremely good subject knowledge and had an excellent relationship with the children. Her standards were high and discipline could not have been better.

My conversation with Connie at the SDC the week before this current visit had given me enough information to know what the meeting that morning was likely to be about. Of course, I was not going to let on to Miss Pilkington that I had been discussing the situation with one of the grandparents who also happened to be the cleaner at the Staff Development Centre.

The headteacher was waiting to greet me. She was dressed in a well-cut suit, a cream silk scarf tied neatly round her neck. She looked rather pale and drawn.

'Good morning, Mr Phinn,' she said, 'it's very nice to see you again. I am so grateful that you have managed to come out so early. I really do need your advice.'

'I'm here to listen, Miss Pilkington,' I said.

'Well, shall we sit down and I'll explain. We have about twenty minutes before the children arrive.' She indicated two elegant chairs at the side of the room. 'I really do have something of a problem and I need to talk it through with somebody.' She sat stiffly on one of the chairs, clasped her hands in front of her and took a breath. I could see she was clearly very worried. 'At the beginning of the term, a new boy arrived. Terry Mossup is his name. He is being fostered by a local doctor and her husband and, from what I gather, he is from a very deprived background. I understand that there had been some abuse and there has certainly been a great deal of neglect. I would guess that he was allowed to do what he wanted and had no consistent treatment by adults and no stability in his home life. Quite frankly, Mr Phinn, I am at a loss to know what to do.'

At this point, Miss Pilkington rose from her chair and paced up and down the small space in

55

front of us. 'I've been a teacher for twenty-five years and have never ever come across a child like this one. He is just unmanageable. I never thought I would admit this to anyone but he is driving me to distraction. Most of the time he is rude, very naughty and destructive but then at other times he is totally uncommunicative and just sits there as if in a trance. At one moment he's picking on the other children, shouting out in class, refusing to do his work and then a moment later he's taking a spider that he's found and gently putting it outside. He's the only one the cat lets stroke her and he likes nothing better than feeding the birds at playtime. I've had a word with his foster parents, who must be saints to take him on, and they have asked me to persevere with him. Oh dear,' she said, swinging round to face me, 'you must think I can't cope.'

'No, not at all,' I hastily reassured her, 'please go on.'

'His foster parents don't want him to go to one of these schools that deals with disruptive pupils. They are very busy people—she's a doctor in West Challerton, and he's got an office of some sort there, too—and they would have to drive Terry in the opposite direction to the special school in Crompton if he were to go there, and then collect him again later. In any case, they feel he should feel part of this small community and be treated as just a normal little boy. Now, that is all very well, Mr Phinn,' continued Miss Pilkington, a nervous rash creeping up her neck, 'but he is not just a normal little boy and I have the other children to think about. I have already had a number of parents complaining about his behaviour and two have threatened to take their children away from Willingforth unless I . . . well, to be blunt, get rid of him.' Miss Pilkington sat back down on her chair, twisting a handkerchief nervously in her hands. 'The Chair of Governors, Canon Shepherd, is calling in to see me at lunch-time with one of the parent-governors who has asked for the boy's removal. We have an extraordinary governors' meeting this evening to decide what to do. The canon is all for giving the child a chance but the other governor, who represents the majority view on the Governing Body, is determined that Terry should go.' She paused to get a breath and looked down at her lap. When our eyes met again, I saw tears. 'I've been a teacher for many years, Mr Phinn, and I think it is fair to say that I have been dedicated to this profession. I've always believed that children deserve the very best we adults have to give, all children, even the very difficult ones. That's why I became a teacher. The boy's file made me weep. It is a catalogue of neglect, mistreatment and deprivation. I had such an advantaged life myself, with parents who loved and cherished me and expected a great deal of me. My father never raised his voice to me, let alone his hand. Terry has had a dreadful life, a cruel life, but he is so very, very difficult and, as I said, I do have the other children to think about. Oh dear, I just do not know what to do.' She fell silent at last.

I took a deep breath. 'Well,' I sighed, 'it sounds feeble, I know, Miss Pilkington, but I really don't know what to advise for the best. It would be easy for me to tell you to struggle on, that things will get better and then walk out of the door. I don't have to teach him. Like you, I don't believe that any

57

child should be put on the scrap heap, written off. We have a duty to help all children. When I started teaching, I remember the words of Sir Alec Clegg, the CEO for the West Riding of Yorkshire speaking to us at Woolley Hall College. "However damaged, ill-favoured or repellent a child is," he told us young teachers, "you have a duty to educate him." What is certain is that there is no miracle cure, no simple solution which will change Terry overnight. It sounds, however, as though the child does need some specialist help, maybe a special school, like the one in Crompton, where teachers are well equipped to deal with children like this boy. I've visited several such schools and, with a great deal of time and patience, children like Terry do get better. On the other hand, if he stays here, we could arrange for some classroom support, maybe an assistant or additional teacher.'

'You are only putting into words what I feel, I suppose,' said Miss Pilkington. 'I certainly need some help. The other teacher, Miss Bates, is away ill—I think it's stress to be frank—and I have all the children together for the time being so it's very tiring and demanding.'

'Well, I am certain we can arrange a supply teacher and get some additional help. I'll have a word with Miss Kinvara, the educational psychologist, and ask her to make a visit. She knows a great deal more than I about children with challenging behaviour.'

'Thank you, that sounds very helpful, but would it be possible, Mr Phinn, for you to stay for the morning so you can see the way Terry behaves, speak to him and then stay for the meeting at lunch-time with the governors to help us decide what to do. Will you do that?'

'Of course,' I replied, thinking to myself that I would probably be no earthly use whatsoever.

Miss Pilkington picked up the crumpled handkerchief from her lap, dabbed her nose and sniffed. At the noise of excited chatter outside, however, her back visibly straightened. 'If you'll excuse me a moment, Mr Phinn, I can hear the children arriving. I do like to welcome them each morning.' With that she left the room.

When the children had taken off their coats and changed into their indoor shoes, they sat at their desks ready for the register to be called. All, that is, except one child. He was a sharp-faced boy of about nine or ten with a scattering of freckles, wavy red hair and a tight little mouth which curved downwards. This, I guessed, was Terry.

'Come along, please, Terry,' said Miss Pilkington firmly, 'take your seat.'

'Who's he, then?' asked the child, pointing in my direction.

'That's Mr Phinn, and please don't point, it's rude.'

'Is he a copper?'

'Just take a seat will you, please, Terry,' said the teacher.

'He looks like a copper. Are you a copper?'

'Terry, will you take a seat,' repeated the teacher firmly.

'I can smell coppers a mile off.' The child slumped into a chair. 'He's either a copper or a probation officer.'

'And take what you are chewing out of your mouth, please, Terry,' said Miss Pilkington.

'Haven't finished it yet.' He looked back at me.

'I bet he is a copper.'

'Put what you are chewing in here, please, Terry,' said the teacher firmly, holding up a waste-paper basket.

The boy ambled to the front and dropped a bullet of chewing gum in the bin.

What a contrast this morning was compared to previous visits. The last time I had visited Willingforth School I had sat on that very same chair watching with great admiration an outstanding teacher. Miss Pilkington had outlined clearly to a very attentive and interested class the writing task to be undertaken and the children had got on with their work quietly and with genuine enthusiasm. Now the lesson was dominated by Terry who would not sit still, would not do as he was told nor get on with his work. The other children seemed amazingly tolerant of this demanding and disruptive child and mostly ignored him, although there were one or two who spent more time watching him than doing their own work.

When he had finally been prevailed upon to sit and put something on paper, I approached the child who looked up with an aggressive expression on his small face.

'What?' he asked, tossing back a head of wavy curls.

'May I look at your work?'

'What for?' He stared coldly at me, like a serpent.

'Because that's what I do for a living.'

'What do you do, then?'

'I'm an inspector.'

A triumphant expression came to his small face.

'I knew it! I knew you was a copper.'

'School inspector, not a police inspector.'

He made a clucking sort of noise and pushed over the paper on which he had been writing. 'It's crap,' he told me.

'Don't use that word,' I told him.

'Why?'

'Because I say so,' I said, looking him straight in the eye. I then began reading what he had written.

'I don't know why you're lookin',' he said. 'It's no good.'

'I'm sure it's not that bad,' I replied, continuing to read.

'It is. Wait till you read it. I'm rubbish at writing.' He pushed out his lower lip and clenched his eyebrows. 'Anyone can see it's crap.' I looked up. 'Rubbish,' he said.

I tried to decipher the cramped, spidery scrawl. 'What's this word?' I asked.

' "Buggered". It says, "I felt buggered." '

'I think the word you want is "jiggered",' I told him.

'No, I don't. I want "buggered".'

'Well, I am sure you can think of a much better word than that.'

'Why?' he asked, defiantly.

'That word is not a very nice word to use.'

'Mi mam uses it. What about "knackered" then?'

'That's as bad,' I said.

'Mi mam—mi real mam, that is—she uses that an' all.'

'Well, it's not really a very nice word for a boy to use,' I said feebly.

'Well, come on then, what word should I use?'

'Well, you could say that you were very tired or

61

exhausted.'

The boy gave a wry smile. 'Aye, I could I suppose, but it wouldn't sound as good as "buggered" though, would it?' He read his scrawl in a sing-song sort of voice following each word with grubby finger. ' "I got home and flopped onto t'bed. I felt tired and exhausted." That's no good, useless. "Buggered" sounds much better.'

I sighed. 'Perhaps, but it's not a word a child should use.'

'You think I'm daft, don't you?' he said suddenly. 'You think I'm thick.'

'Not at all,' I assured him. 'I think you are a bright lad but you need to behave better and not swear nor answer back.'

'What you gonna do, then, if I don't? Lock me up?' His expression was one of defiance.

'No, I'm not going to lock you up.'

'Just 'cos I speaks like this don't mean that I'm daft, you know.'

'I never said you were daft,' I told him. And he certainly was not daft. If only his obvious intelligence and quick wit could be channelled into something worthwhile, I thought to myself. 'What I can't understand is why you don't try and behave yourself?'

'Dunno really. Can't help mi'self.'

'You'd get on a lot better with people if you behaved.'

'S'pose I don't want to get on better wi' people?' he said, more ruminatively this time.

I abandoned the line of questioning. 'Shall we go through your writing and see if we can make it neater and clearer?'

'What's with the "we". Are you gonna do it for

me, then?'

'I'm going to try and help you with it.'

'Well, I don't need no help. You'll go changing all mi words.'

The child was indeed exhausting. I tried another tack. 'Do you like reading?'

'Nope.'

'Music?'

'Nope.'

'What do you like?'

'You asks a bloody lot of questions, don't you?' Before I could respond, he said, mimicking my voice, 'That's another not very nice word for a little boy to use.'

I shook my head but persevered. 'I hear you like animals.'

'Who told you that?'

'A little bird told me,' I replied.

'I'll kill that bleeding bird. That's another word I'm not supposed to use, isn't it?'

He was clearly aiming to shock, to get a reaction, but I wasn't going to play his little game. This child would surely try the patience of a saint.

'So, you do like animals?' I asked again.

'S'pose so.'

'Why do you like animals?'

He didn't answer immediately but seemed to be lost in thought. 'Because you know where you are wi' animals. They don't mess you around. They like you for what you are. Not like people. And animals don't ask a lot of bloody stupid questions either.'

'And what are you going to do when you leave school?'

'I'm going home. What are you gonna do?'

'Do you miss your last school?'

'Naw, it were crap. I was always in trouble. They picked on me.'

'Who did?'

'All of them—teachers, kids, caretaker, lollipop woman, dinner ladies. They sent me to a shrink, bit like you, in a black suit and creaky shoes, who asked a lot of bloody stupid questions. Why this and why that? And would I like to talk about it?' He stared at me with an impudent look on his face. 'He couldn't deal with me neither. Grown ups allus pretend. They say they're your friends, only trying to help you, they're all nice and kind and then they ... well ... Haven't you got owt better to do?'

'No, not really,' I replied. 'And what about here, Terry?'

'What about here?'

'Do you think they pick on you here?'

He thought for a moment, twisting his mouth to one side and cocking his head. 'Not as much,' he conceded, 'not as much.' Then as if brought out of a reverie he sat up and screwed up his writing into a tight little ball. 'That's crap.'

*   *   *

At lunchtime Canon Shepherd arrived accompanied by a whey-faced individual with a long nose, flared nostrils and a drooping Stalin-like moustache. The vicar was a small, cheerful little man, with tousled hair and flabby cheeks.

'It is very good of you to join our deliberations, Mr Phinn,' said the cleric, offering me a fleshy hand. 'I expect Miss Pilkington has explained our dilemma.'

'Not much of a dilemma as far as I'm

concerned,' said his companion. 'The lad's a bad 'un and no mistake.' This man clearly did not mince his words. 'He should be put where he won't harm himself and others.'

'That's just what we're here to discuss, Mr Gardner,' said the vicar sharply. 'I am well aware of your views.'

'And I'm well aware of yours, vicar,' retorted his companion, stroking his moustache.

'I would like to have the benefit of Mr Phinn's expertise and his advice before we make any decisions as to the future of the child.' The vicar looked expectantly in my direction and nodded. His companion regarded me seriously and continued to stroke his moustache.

'Well, Canon, he is without doubt a very difficult boy—' I began.

'We know that,' interposed the parent-governor aggressively. 'It doesn't take a genius to suss that out. We don't need *experts* from County Hall to tell us the blindingly bloody obvious. Tell us something we don't know.'

Miss Pilkington raised a hand. 'Please let Mr Phinn finish, Mr Gardner. He saw Terry in class this morning and I would like to hear his opinion.'

'He's a disturbed child, attention-seeking with a very low self-esteem and tends to react to people with this bravado. He's deeply suspicious of adults, probably because he's been let down so many times—'

'Look,' said Mr Gardner, 'I do have a business to run. We can sit here all afternoon listening to this psychobabble, about how he came from a terrible background, how he's had an awful childhood and that it's not his fault but society's, etcetera etcetera.

It's that sort of liberal hogwash that lets football hooligans—'

'Mr Gardner!' said the canon in a hard and emphatic voice. 'May I remind you that this is a church school. Our vision, our ethos, the very bedrock of our philosophy are the words of Jesus Christ, who talked about compassion, love, understanding and generosity of heart. I don't hear much of that coming from your lips this afternoon. Do you think Jesus would reject this child, turn his back on him? I think not.'

'That's all very well, vicar,' sneered Mr Gardner, his mouth tight, his face white with displeasure, 'but you don't have a child in the school. My Jill has to put up with this little demon and have *her* learning interrupted. I'm not bothered about the boy. I'm bothered about my daughter and *her* education, and I'll tell you this, my telephone has been hot with calls from parents who think as I do.' His voice suddenly softened. 'Now look, Canon, we on the Governing Body have a responsibility for the education of all the children in this school. If we decide to let this boy remain and disrupt—'

'I don't think Mr Phinn had quite finished, Mr Gardener,' interrupted the vicar coldly.

'There are two clear alternatives,' I continued quickly. 'One is for the boy to go to a special school for children with emotional and behavioural needs, like the one in Crompton. It is an excellent school and staffed with teachers who have a particular specialism in dealing with young people of this kind—'

'Now we are talking,' muttered the parent-governor.

'Alternatively,' I continued, 'you could see if

66

things get better over the next few weeks. I believe his foster parents would like him, if at all possible, to remain in the school. With support, perhaps some extra staffing and an environment where there is some stability and consistency of treatment—as he will undoubtedly get here—he may very well settle down and improve.'

The body language of the parent-governor indicated that he was about to launch into another outburst so Miss Pilkington stepped in smartly. 'I think we have to keep trying for the time being,' she said calmly. 'See how things go.'

'You mean let him stay?' demanded Mr Gardner, his moustache bristling with displeasure.

'I mean let him stay,' said Miss Pilkington. 'I am not yet prepared to be defeated.'

'Mr Phinn?' The canon turned his face in my direction.

'It is, of course, a very courageous decision,' I replied quietly, 'but if you want a personal opinion, I think it is the right one.'

*   *   *

One of the most important parts of a school inspector's job is to follow up a situation after a school visit; indeed, sometimes the visit is only the beginning of a succession of actions often involving many people. The day following my meeting at Willingforth School, I had telephoned Kath Kinvara.

Kath was one of the county educational psychologists who had worked with me on a number of courses and conferences. She always seemed to wear the same outfit: tight-fitting brown sweater, crumpled brown tweed skirt, solid brown shoes. Her thick brown hair was tied back untidily, and there was not a trace of make-up or jewellery, save for the single rope of pearls which I always felt to be totally contrary to the rest of the ensemble. She was a level-headed, down-to-earth and very amusing woman whom I had frequently consulted about children with learning difficulties, special educational needs and behavioural problems. I had spoken to her about the situation at Willingforth Primary School and she had gone there to meet Miss Pilkington and the child himself and had suggested some practical ideas and strategies in an effort to help.

Now, a couple of weeks later, I had been to a meeting in the Architects' Department about a proposed new school library and was walking along the top corridor of County Hall. I was always pleased to get out of that dark and intimidating building and back to the inspectors' cramped but friendly office. The interior of County Hall was like a museum—a silent, cool and shadowy place with long echoey corridors, high tall windows, ornate ceilings, marble figures on plinths and heavy oil paintings. Former mayors, high sheriffs, lord lieutenants, leaders of the council and dignitaries, all of them men and many of them bearded and robed, stared out of their gilt frames in solemn disapproval.

'Hi, Gervase.'

I turned and there was Kath—in her familiar garb. 'Oh hello, Kath, how are you?'

'Oh, underpaid and overworked. I hear congratulations are in order.'

'That's right.'

'You kept that close to your chest, didn't you? You never mentioned it when we were talking on the phone about Willingforth School.'

'Didn't want to mix business with pleasure.'

'Indeed, and I'm really pleased for you although I can't imagine what someone so beautiful, elegant and talented as Christine would see in you.'

'What about looks, charm, charisma, intelligence and a vibrant personality for starters?' I asked.

'Or the fat bank account. That's the reason why attractive young women go for the more mature man. Oh, and another bit of news I've just heard is that Harold Yeats is finishing.'

'That's right.'

'I thought he had a good few years to go.'

'He's fifty-nine this year,' I told her, 'and can get his pension so he's decided to retire, and who can blame him?'

'Will you be putting in for the job, then?' she asked.

'I don't know, Kath, I really don't know.'

'You ought to have a go. You can't lose anything by applying and you might regret it in later years, particularly if they appoint someone nobody likes. The Chief Psychologist who was my boss before I came to Yorkshire was a megalomaniac. He was hell to work for.'

'Well, I don't know. It's a long way off yet. Harold doesn't finish until next July. I'll just have to see.' My tone of voice must have signalled that I wanted an end to this line of discussion.

'Anyhow, I'm really pleased to have bumped into you,' she said. 'Have you got a minute?'

'Yes, of course,' I replied. I opened a door beside us and looked in. 'Shall we pop into this

69

empty committee room?' We entered a large imposing-looking ante-chamber which was dominated by a huge rectangular mahogany table around which were twelve or so straight-backed chairs. On the walls were the familiar oil paintings of solemn old men with grave expressions.

'It's about Terry Mossup, the boy at Willingforth,' explained Kath.

'Oh yes, I'd be interested to know what's happening. How's he getting on?'

'Well, there's not been any massive transformation in his behaviour but I think the situation is improving slowly. These things, I'm afraid, take time. It would be wonderful if we could work the sort of overnight miracles we see on the American films where the little rednecks are miraculously changed into angels by the caring priest. I'm afraid real life is not like that. Anyhow, Terry is still a handful. He's a very unpredictable and mixed-up little boy. His file would fill a whole shelf and be the stuff of psychological research. Poor kid, he's been knocked from pillar to post by successive "uncles" who come and live with his mum for a while and then he never sees again. His elder brothers are into drugs and crime and he's been caught on numerous occasions wandering the streets at night. Then there's his vandalising and truanting. You name it.'

'So how is Miss Pilkington coping?'

'Well, she's finding it really hard but she's digging in her heels and trying her best. She was so grateful that you were able to find a classroom assistant—and this is the good news. He's a young man who Terry has quite taken to. He's a very keen footballer and by all accounts seems to have got the

70

lad interested. Terry is a natural ball-player, I hear. Miss Bates, the other teacher, is back at work. For how long, I don't know, because she looked as if she was teetering on the brink of a nervous breakdown when I last saw her. Did you know that, after the decision to keep Terry on, one of the governors, a very aggressive, loud man—'

'I've met him. Joseph Stalin.'

'Well, he led a minor exodus. Five children left and it looks like more will follow.'

'Well, they won't find it easy to get as good a teacher as Miss Pilkington elsewhere and that's for sure,' I said, recalling the excellent lessons I had observed in the past.

'But the Chairman of Governors is not the push-over some of the other governors thought he would be,' continued Kath, fingering the pearls. 'He looks such a jolly, inoffensive little man but he's got this sort of missionary zeal and is as tenacious as Miss Pilkington. I have been really impressed by Canon Shepherd. In fact, I must tell you what happened when I was last there. Canon Shepherd goes up to Terry who was busy feeding the hamster. "Now then, Terry," he says, "how are things going?" "Bugger off, granddad!" Terry replied. Well, I had to turn away to hide my laughter. Anyway, I'm doing what I can. The thing is, Gervase, that this boy is really very bright. I gave him a non-verbal reasoning test and he scored high marks. On the mental mathematics test he also did very well. He's got a sharp little mind and a wide, if sometimes rather colourful, command of the language. Of course, his reading and written work are below average but I think the long school absences account for that. Let's just hope all this perseverance and patience pays off.'

'Yes,' I said doubtfully, 'let's hope.'

When I got back to the office I decided to give Miss Pilkington a call. She was pleased to hear from me but sounded weary and low. After I put the phone down I thought it would not be much longer before Terry was in some special unit.

*   *   *

I was just about to leave the office one cold morning three or four weeks later when the telephone rang.

'Hello, Gervase Phinn here.'

'Oh, hello, Mr Phinn, it's Miss Pilkington here, from Willingforth School.' I swallowed thickly and waited for the inevitable news. 'Could you come out when you have a free moment or are passing?'

'Yes, of course.' I took a breath.

'It's not urgent but we've been doing some poetry work and the children have produced some delightful riddles. I know that you often collect poems for the county anthology and I am sure some of the ones they have written would be ideal. Anyway, if you are in the area, you know you are always welcome.'

'How's Terry?' I asked.

'Well, why don't you come out and see for yourself?' she said.

She certainly sounded a whole lot like her old self; in fact she sounded as if she was pretty pleased with life. I immediately telephoned the school I was intending to visit that morning and put back my appointment. I was due to arrange the shortlisting of candidates for the vacant deputy headteacher post but that could wait. I just had to see what the

72

situation was like at Willingforth.

Later that morning I entered the large bright classroom to find a positively beaming Miss Pilkington. She nodded her head in the direction of a boy in the corner scratching away on a large piece of paper with a fair-haired, athletic-looking young man sitting alongside him. It was Terry and the classroom assistant.

'Children,' the headteacher said, 'could we all say "Good morning" to Mr Phinn?' There was an enthusiastic chorus of 'Good morning'. 'And may I introduce you to Mr White, our new teacher-assistant.' I learned later that Roland White was having a gap year before university and teacher-training. The young man smiled in my direction.

'Good morning,' I said.

'Now, children,' continued Miss Pilkington, 'Mr Phinn has called in to look at the lovely poetry work you have been doing.'

Terry looked up from his work and nodded. 'All right?' he shouted.

'Yes, fine. Are you?' I called back.

'Mustn't grumble,' he replied.

What was it that Kath had said, I thought to myself, about the fanciful American movies where the little rednecks were changed into model members of society by a caring priest? 'Mustn't grumble,' Terry had said. This was one of Yorkshire's most prized phrases. When asked how any Yorkshireman or woman is feeling, the speaker—whether it is in Selby or Sheffield, Doncaster or Darfield, Halifax or Huddersfield, Rotherham or Royston—is likely to reply with this time-honoured expression, 'Oh, mustn't grumble' before launching into a diatribe about the ills of the world. Connie used the phrase to maximum effect, as did Julie. Things were clearly rubbing off on the boy.

I decided to spend a little time with the rest of the children prior to approaching Terry.

'Riddles are sort of word puzzles,' explained a fresh-faced boy of about eleven, pointing to his work. 'Some are of one line, others are long and some are over nine hundred years old. We've been writing riddles of our own.' He then read out his very inventive verse:

> I'm a real square!
> Dry as dust,
> Grey as a stone,
> Paper thin and perforated.
> I may be square and full of holes,
> But in hot water my flavour bursts,
> For I am the quencher of thirsts.
> What am I?

'A teabag!' I exclaimed. 'That's brilliant.'

The next pupil was busy embellishing her poem with intricate pencil drawings as I approached. I read:

> I'm an icy blossom,
> A tiny piece of frozen paper,
> A cold white petal,
> A winter pattern.

'It's a snowflake,' she told me with a broad if rather nervous smile.

'Excellent,' I said.

Eventually I found my way to Terry's desk. 'And

have you done a riddle, Terry?' I asked.

'Yep.'

I was waiting for him to tell me it was 'crap' but he looked in his folder and produced a sheet of crumpled paper covered in the same spidery writing I had seen on my last visit. I took it from him, straightened it out and read:

> They walk all over me,
> They beat me,
> They wipe their feet on me,
> They nail me to the floor,
> They wear me out,
> They leave me to fade in the sunlight.

I was lost for words. I looked at the sharp-faced boy with wavy red hair and a tight little mouth which curved downwards. Was this about him, I thought, the neglected, mistreated child, whom adults had treated as a doormat, who had been walked over all his young life?

'Have you guessed what it is then?' he asked. He had that same defiant look in his eye.

'A carpet,' I said quietly.

'Good, isn't it?'

'It's very good.'

Miss Pilkington appeared at my side. 'Would you like to tell Mr Phinn where you went last week, Terry?'

'I had a trial game for the Fettlesham Juniors, second team. Football, you know. Don't s'pose I'll get in, but it were worth 'aving a go.'

'Go on with you, Terry,' said the young man, Roland White, who had been observing me like a school inspector himself. 'You'll be playing for one of the big clubs one day.'

The face brightened up but he tried to appear casual. 'Yeah, I bet.'

'And we've been to a farm since your last visit,' said Miss Pilkington. 'Tell Mr Phinn what you saw, Terry.'

'Pigs, we saw some pigs, big pink buggers they were—sorry, miss,' he clapped his hand over his mouth. 'I keep forgetting. Right big pigs they were, with piglets which hung on to her—you know whats.' He grinned impishly. 'And we saw some sheep.'

'And can you guess, Mr Phinn, who the farmer picked to help him get the sheep into the fold?'

'I have no idea,' I said conspiratorially.

'It was Terry.'

'Was it?' I said, sounding very impressed.

'Aye, it were,' said the boy.

'Mr Clough, the farmer, said he'd not had such a good little helper ever before. Do you know, Mr Phinn, Terry can be a really naughty boy at times but last week on our trip to the farm he was really good.'

'Mr Clough has a sheepdog called Meg,' said the boy. 'She were great. She wouldn't leave me alone, miss, would she? Kept jumping up and following me.'

'Animals really know when you like them,' I observed.

Miss Pilkington smiled. I knew what she was thinking. 'So do children.'

'And there were hens and I helped look for the eggs,' said Terry. 'And I never broke one.'

'Terry had never been to a farm before,' explained Miss Pilkington. 'He had never seen such animals close up, had you?'

'No, miss, and I want to work on a farm when I leave school.'

I thought back to my first visit and remembered what he had answered when I had asked him what he wanted to do when he left school. There had certainly been some remarkable changes since then.

'And what else did you see?' I asked.

'I saw some bulls and some 'osses and some goats and some ducks and some fuckers.'

It was as if someone had thrown a bucket of icy water over Miss Pilkington, the classroom assistant and me. We all three shot upright, spluttering audibly.

'No! No!' snapped the headteacher. 'You definitely did not see any of those, Terry Mossup!'

'I did, miss.'

'No, no, you did not! You certainly did not see any of those.'

The boy thought for a moment before replying. 'Well, Mr Clough called 'em "eff-ers" but I knew what he really meant.'

CHAPTER FIVE

One Friday afternoon in early October, I arrived at 1, Prince Regent Row in Fettlesham. The building was a tall imposing Georgian white-fronted villa enveloped with Virginia creeper, the leaves of which were magnificently crimson. There was an impressive porch with stone pillars and a heavy oak, ornately-carved door. I was here to be inspected by Mrs Cleaver-Canning—correction: the Honourable Mrs Cleaver-Canning.

Earlier that week, after a long and tiring day, I had just been finishing off in the office when Julie had popped her head around the door.

'There's someone who sounds like Mrs Savage's sister on my phone wanting to speak to you. Loud and pushy and with a plum-in-the-gob accent. Shall I tell her you've gone?'

'No, I'd better take it, Julie,' I had sighed, hoping it would not be another disgruntled parent or complaining governor. I had had several heated discussions already that day. 'Would you put it through, please?'

A few moments later a very upper-crust voice had come down the line. 'Is that Mr Gervase Phinn?'

'Speaking,' I had replied charily.

'My name is Cleaver-Canning, the Honourable Mrs Cleaver-Canning. I hear that you do talks.'

'Talks?' I repeated.

'Yes, after-dinner talks. Mrs Daphne Patterson, who is in the same Townswomen's Guild as I, attended some sort of charity event recently and said she very much enjoyed what you had to say.'

I had relaxed and leaned back in the chair. 'Oh, that's very kind of her.'

'And I'm minded to ask you to speak at my golf club, a sort of after-dinner address at our Christmas Ladies' Night function. It is short notice, I realise, but I have been let down. The Christmas evening is one of our most important and I booked—er, well, perhaps I shouldn't mention who—over a year ago and now he's gorn and let me down. Got a lucrative television offer, I believe,

78

and filming starts next month. I end my term of office as lady captain of the Totterdale and Clearwell Golf Club this December and this dinner is very important, my swan song, you know.' After a slight pause, the Hon Mrs Cleaver-Canning had continued, 'We would, of course, be prepared to make a donation to the charity you support. So, how do you feel? Can you help me out of a hole?'

'Well, yes, I think in principle I could, Mrs Cleaver-Canning, but it really depends on the date. I already have a number of evening engagements in December which is always a particularly busy time for me but if I am free, I should be delighted to join you.'

'December 16th is the date for the dinner. Do say you are free!'

I had flicked forward through my diary. 'Yes, it so happens that I am. I would be delighted to speak at your dinner.'

'Prior to making a definite booking, Mr Phinn,' the speaker had then pronounced loftily, 'I think we should meet, so I can learn something about you. I am sure you will appreciate that I am relying on the recommendation of a colleague. Daphne Patterson is rarely wrong about people but one does have to be sure. I am certain you will understand that I do need to meet you before making a firm commitment. Have a little *conversazione*, you know.'

I had had to smile. The woman wanted to vet me. 'I'm not a polished after-dinner speaker, by any means, Mrs Cleaver-Canning,' I had explained. 'I don't tell jokes or anything like that. I just talk about children and schools and some of the amusing things that have happened to me.'

'Good gracious, Mr Phinn, we don't want a comedian! This is the Totterdale and Clearwell Golf Club, not the Crompton Working Men's Club. It is a very prestigious golf club. Daphne Patterson said you were very entertaining without being vulgar and tasteless and you didn't go on for too long. That is exactly what I want. Someone who is wholesome, amusing, yes, but not long winded. We can't be doing with rambling and risqué speakers. The audience will be entirely ladies, some of whom are getting on in years, and it really would not be appropriate for the Totterdale and Clearwell to have anything ribald. The speaker last year was some sort of television personality, though I have to admit I had never heard of the man—from a soap programme, I believe—and I most certainly do not wish to renew my acquaintance with him, either. He had far too much to drink and became quite offensive. He upset a number of our ladies and he didn't know when to sit down.'

'I can assure you, Mrs Cleaver-Canning, that I do not tell rude jokes or—'

'No, no, I'm sure you don't. Now, have you your diary handy? Can you come and see me this week?'

We had arranged that I should go to see her at four o'clock that Friday afternoon which suited me well, since I could call in on my way back to the office from a school visit. And so it was that I presented myself at 1, Prince Regent Row just as the clock on Fettlesham Town Hall struck four.

I was welcomed inside by an elderly, slightly stooped man with thin wisps of sandy-grey hair and a great handlebar moustache. He looked like an ageing Biggles. I assumed this to be the old family retainer but it soon became apparent that he was

80

Mr Cleaver-Canning.

'Ah,' he said in a deep, throaty voice, 'Mr Phinn, I presume? Come in, come in. The better half is upstairs but she will be down directly. We'll go into the library, if you'd like to walk this way.' I followed the stooping figure into a room lined with bookcases set between tall sash windows, overlooking a long walled garden. The handsome cedar trees of Jubilee Park could be seen over the wall at the end. Everything exuded comfortable opulence, from the heavy velvet curtains to the thick crimson carpet, from the delicately-moulded ceiling to the deep armchairs and magazine-laden tables. 'Do take a seat. I'll just give Margot a call.'

The man shuffled off and once back in the hall he shouted up the stairs. 'Margot! Margot! Your visitor is here.'

Back came a short and impatient reply, 'I'm coming! I'm coming!' There was the sound of heavy footsteps on the stairs followed by a loud whispering from the hall. 'I do wish you wouldn't shout like that. It's not Fettlesham Market.' There was a note of sharp command in the voice.

'Yes, I know, Margot,' he replied, 'but it's a bloody long trek up those stairs and . . .'

There was another series of whispers before Biggles re-appeared, followed by an ample-bosomed, impeccably-groomed woman with pale purple hair and grey eyes so large they made her appear permanently surprised. Her mouth was a shining scarlet bow of lipstick. The Honourable Mrs Cleaver-Canning certainly commanded presence. She examined me critically like a doctor might a patient, gave a short, quick smile and proffered a fleshy hand. The air had suddenly become thick with a heady perfume.

'Mr Phinn, do take a seat. I think you have met my husband.' She waved her hand in the direction of Biggles who stood by the door like a hovering butler. 'Winco, please don't stand there like a totem pole. Put the kettle on. I am sure Mr Phinn would enjoy a cup of tea.'

'Thank you, yes,' I replied, thinking a stiff whisky at that moment would have suited me better.

'Righto,' said Mr Cleaver-Canning genially, shambling out of the room. I sat down in the nearest armchair, practically disappearing into its depths. My large companion lowered herself regally into the middle of the sofa opposite and spread herself extravagantly. 'My husband was in the RAF. Wing Commander. Called Norman but everyone calls him Winco. Now, Mr Phinn, Daphne Patterson tells me you are a school inspector. How fascinating.' The tone of voice suggested that she did not sound particularly fascinated.

'Yes, I've been an inspector now for a couple of years. Before that I was a teacher and—'

'Have you ever visited Hamilton College?' Winco had suddenly materialised at the door.

Mrs Cleaver-Canning tightened her lips and gave him a look which would curdle milk. 'Winco, I am sure Mr Phinn is not able to discuss, nor is he particularly interested in discussing, the various schools he has visited. In any case, he's probably never heard of Hamilton.' She turned to me. 'It's a minor public school in Surrey.' She turned her attention back to her husband. 'Have you made the tea?'

'Only just put the kettle on,' replied Winco. 'Anyhow, need to know what sort. Do you like Earl

Grey, Darjeeling, Ceylon, Assam, camomile, Mr Phinn, or a good old Yorkshire brew?'

'Winco,' said his wife in exasperated tones, 'just make the tea.'

'Righto,' he said good-humouredly and shuffled out of the room.

'As I was saying, Mr Phinn, it sounds a very interesting profession, a school inspector. To be frank, I find children rather exhausting and very demanding. We have nephews and nieces but we don't have any children of our own.' I could tell that by the immaculate state of the house.

'Yes, it is a very interesting profession. I get to meet a great many people, of all ages and from every background. I visit schools both in towns and the lovely Dales villages, and, on some occasions—'

'Biscuits?' Winco had appeared again at the door.

'What?' snapped his wife.

'Are we having biscuits?'

Mrs Cleaver-Canning sighed heavily and heaved her substantial bosom before pursing her cupid bow lips and replying tartly, 'Yes, Winco, I think we will have biscuits.'

'What kind?'

'Just put a selection on a plate,' she told him wearily.

'Righto,' he said amiably, disappearing out of the room once more.

'You were saying, Mr Phinn?' continued my hostess.

'Just that I get to meet a great many people and see the beautiful Yorkshire countryside.'

'And do you do a lot of talking, Mr Phinn?' continued Mrs Cleaver-Canning.

'My colleagues would say rather too much, I fear,' I replied.

My feeble attempt at a witticism fell on stony ground. 'Oh really?' She gave the short, quick little smile.

Winco appeared with a tray on which were three delicate china cups and saucers, a large silver teapot, jug and sugar bowl. There was also an enormous plate of assorted biscuits. He placed the tray on a table.

'Coasters, please, Winco,' ordered his wife, pointing to an elegant rosewood sideboard. 'Top left-hand drawer.'

Having arranged various mats on the small mahogany table, Winco proceeded to pour the tea.

'Why are there three cups?' asked his wife.

'Aren't I joining you?' Winco lifted a sandy eyebrow.

'No, you are not joining us,' she replied in low, measured tones. 'I am discussing the Christmas Ladies' Night dinner with Mr Phinn. It is golf club business. You have your errands to do.'

'Do I?'

'Yes, you know you do. Tigger has got to go to the vet. Evening surgery is at five.'

'Righto.'

'And do make sure it's the young woman vet who sees him. I have little confidence in that man.'

'Righto,' he said again, leaving the room.

Mrs Cleaver-Canning leaned forward and whispered confidentially, 'Tell me, Mr Phinn, do you drink?'

'Er, it's a little early for me, thank you,' I said.

'No, no,' she said with a fluttering laugh. 'I was wondering if, in general terms, you enjoy a drink or are you a teetotaller?'

'Yes, I like a drink, but in moderation.'

'You don't overdo it?'

'No, I don't overdo it.'

'Good, it's just that that vulgar little soap man had far too much drink for his own good and he became quite insulting. We have had a number of speakers in the past who have imbibed rather a lot.'

'Oh dear,' I said, feigning concern. 'Well, I can assure you, Mrs Cleaver-Canning, there will be nothing of that sort.'

The interrogation continued for a further thirty minutes until my hostess appeared satisfied on my suitability to speak at the Christmas Ladies' Night dinner.

'Well, that sounds most satisfactory,' she said. 'I have enjoyed our little chat and would like to confirm my invitation for you to speak. I should point out that it will be a formal affair so you will need to wear a dinner jacket.'

Before I could reply, Winco reappeared and asked: 'Where's the cat basket, Margot?'

It was time for me to leave and I made good my escape at the same time as Winco departed, carrying a small wicker basket from which emanated very cross-sounding mews.

*   *   *

Late Friday afternoons were the only times that all the inspectors were likely to be together in the office. On such occasions we could wind down, have a mug of tea, exchange incidents, and gossip and talk about the trials and tribulations of the week. We were never in a great rush and those who lived outside Fettlesham generally waited until the heavy Friday evening traffic had eased before setting off home. The exception on the team was Gerry who, having cleared her desk, was usually keen to get away.

I got back to the office from my grilling by Mrs Cleaver-Canning just after five o'clock. Sidney was in a particularly provocative frame of mind. He was standing watching Gerry as she attempted to push a set of thick folders into her briefcase.

'Do you have to be so remarkably accomplished at everything, Gerry?' Sidney asked her.

'What do you mean?' she replied, laughing.

'Well according to "The Black Death" over in the CEO's office, the pestilential Mrs Savage, in her latest poison-pen memorandum, you are the only one of us who had all the final reports, responses and guidelines completed by the end of last term and you are the only one of us who has correctly filled in her wretched engagement sheets.'

'I just like to keep on top of things, Sidney,' she told him, giving him one of her disarming Irish smiles. 'It's just the way I am. You know what I'm like.'

Actually, I thought to myself, I don't know what you are like. None of us did. In fact, Dr Geraldine Mullarkey was something of a mystery. She had everything: brains, looks, personality, a sense of humour and, during her short time as the county inspector for science and technology, she had made a very big impression. Schools were always happy to see her, the CEO had received many complimentary letters and commendations from headteachers and governors, Harold declared her reports to be models of excellence, and her training

86

courses for teachers were always vastly oversubscribed. She was an extremely pretty, slender young woman with short raven black hair, a pale, delicately-boned face and great blue eyes with long lashes, and men gazed at her with open admiration. She had been a member of the inspectors' team now for over a term but we still knew very little about her, despite Sidney's persistent probings. Gerry was a private person and kept her life outside work strictly to herself.

'Were you one of those insufferably industrious little girls at school,' Sidney now asked, 'who was top in everything, best at sports, brilliant at music, answered all the questions, got all the prizes on Speech Day? A rather prissy, precocious little missy with long plaits and a butter-wouldn't-melt-in-my-mouth expression?'

'No, not really, Sidney,' replied Gerry, cramming yet more papers into her bag. 'Quite the opposite, in fact. I think I was the bane of my teachers' lives.'

'Geraldine, how many more files are you intending to stuff into your bag?' asked Sidney.

'Oh, do leave the poor woman alone,' said David.

'I just wish to impress upon our fair colleen from County Galway that there is more to life than inspecting schools and she must appreciate that by taking home all this extra work and being amazingly industrious, we mere, weak, inadequate mortals appear somewhat less than efficient by comparison.' He gestured to his desk where an assorted heap of dog-eared files and thick folders balanced dangerously on the edge. Geraldine's desk, by contrast, was empty save for a telephone, a large pristine square of blotting paper, two small neatly-stacked piles of reports, an empty in-tray and a full out-tray.

'I can't hang around tonight, either,' I told no one in particular as I emptied the contents of my briefcase on my desk. 'I have a meeting.'

'On a Friday night!' exclaimed Sidney.

'Yes, on a Friday night,' I replied.

'Another workaholic.'

'I know why our Sidney is feeling inadequate,' said David. 'He's afraid.'

'Afraid? Afraid, pray, of what?' enquired his colleague.

'Not of what but of whom,' said David. 'You are worried about Harold's replacement. You are in a state of panic because you think we may get a martinet of a Senior Inspector who will watch your every move and get wise to your little games and ruses.'

'Little games and ruses? Whatever do you mean?'

'How, if something has nothing to do with your precious art and design, you slither and slip from the most difficult situations like an eel in a barrel of oil, wriggling your way out of anything which involves extra work.'

Sidney snorted. 'Utter rubbish! Anyway, Geraldine, I think you are overdoing it. You should slow down a bit. Work is, after all, not the be-all and end-all. In fact, I think you are looking decidedly pale. What you need is a good man.'

'Give me strength,' sighed David. 'Now he's into marriage counselling.'

'An attractive young woman like you,' continued Sidney unperturbed, 'could have your pick of dozens of panting males. I take it there is no one

88

on the scene at the moment? Perhaps someone we don't know about, tucked away in a remote cottage in the Dales?'

'Not at the moment,' replied Gerry, now clearly getting irritated by Sidney's probing. The smile had disappeared from her lips. 'I must be off.'

'No secret lover?'

'Sidney,' she said sharply, 'it really is none of your business, you know.'

'Well said,' agreed David. 'Now, leave the poor woman alone.'

Sidney merely changed tack, and directed his questions to me. 'By the way, Gervase, are you going to apply for Harold's job?'

I decided to throw the question back at him. 'Why don't you apply, Sidney?'

'No, not me. The more I view those who are at the top of the tree, the more convinced I become that I am much better off on the grass below, gently grazing, rather than being blown hither and thither by the constant winds of educational change. The very best reason for staying where I am is to look at those at the top. But you are somewhat younger, Gervase, so what about it?'

'I haven't decided yet,' I replied in such a dismissive manner that it should have given him the signal to change the subject again.

Typical of Sidney, he carried on regardless. 'You want to get on and apply,' he advised. 'You will need the extra funds—a newly-married man with an expensive wife, house and mortgage and then, of course, when the children start arriving . . .'

'I agree, you should apply, Gervase,' said Gerry as she put on her coat. 'You'd make a brilliant Senior Inspector.'

'I certainly would not go that far!' exclaimed Sidney. 'The Irish will exaggerate so. As David's much more prosaic and tiresome old Welsh grandmother would no doubt remark from her inglenook: "He would make a tidy job of it." Gervase is a reasonably personable young man, good company, has a pleasant enough manner. I'm sure he would be competent enough in the post of SI and be acceptable to we hard-working inspectors.'

'Would you mind not talking about me as if I weren't here?' I remarked.

'Yes, I think we could all live with him as Senior Inspector,' continued Sidney, oblivious to my comment. 'He is a good sort at heart, if a little stuffy at times.'

'Stuffy!' I exclaimed. 'Stuffy!'

'I wouldn't say exactly "stuffy",' David said, joining in on this completely unnecessary conversation. 'Just a trifle on the serious side perhaps, a little intense, prone to be self-critical—'

'I'm going,' I told them, rising to leave, 'before my whole character is laid out like a body on a hospital's operating table.'

'Well, I'm off, too,' Gerry said. She snatched up her bulging briefcase and headed for the door. 'Have a good weekend everyone.'

'She always rushes off, doesn't she?' said Sidney when Gerry had gone. 'Never stays for a chat or a drink after work. Very mysterious about her private life. Whatever she says, I reckon it's highly likely she has a secret man tucked away somewhere. And speaking of mystery, Gervase, pray tell us what's this clandestine meeting of yours this evening? It's not another woman, is it? You're not playing fast and loose with the affections of the Aphrodite of Winnery Nook, the delectable Miss Bentley? In fact, the more I think of it, it is highly suspect that both you and Gerry are rushing to leave the office early.'

'It is not early, Sidney, it's just not late. And if you must know, I'm meeting Sister Brendan.'

'A secret evening assignation with a nun, no less. This is getting intriguing.'

'Since Gervase has told us where he is going,' remarked David, 'it is hardly a *secret* assignation, is it? But that apart, what on earth are you doing with Sister Brendan on a Friday evening?'

'You are both as bad as each other. I am speaking at a CAFOD charity event at St Bartholomew's School.'

'CAFOD?' cried Sidney. 'CAFOD! That sounds like a prophylactic for constipation. What the devil is CAFOD?'

'Catholic Aid for Overseas Development,' I told him. 'Sister Brendan has asked me to speak to the Yorkshire Branch to raise money for the street children of South America.'

'It's very noble of you to give up a Friday evening, I must say,' commented David.

'Well, it's in a very good cause,' I replied.

'If it goes all right,' said David, 'I might just ask you to speak at my golf club dinner next year.'

I considered telling him about my invitation from Mrs Cleaver-Canning but thought better of it. Sidney was in his customary pose, leaning back in his chair, staring upwards. 'It's rather a contradiction of terms, isn't it—Yorkshire and charity? Yorkshire people, I have found, are the least charitable of people. They rarely part with

91

their money. The typical Yorkshireman, in my experience, has short arms and long pockets and lives by the Yorkshire motto of *Brasso, Inclutcho, Intacto*. There was the famous Yorkshire farmer—'

'Oh, do we have to listen to this rubbish?' sighed David, shaking his head wearily.

'No, listen,' continued Sidney, sitting up. 'This illustrates my point exactly. There was the famous Yorkshire farmer who went to place an "In Memoriam" message in the local paper following his wife's death. He wrote out exactly what he wanted to appear: "In memory of my dearly beloved wife, Ethel Braithwaite, who departed this earthly life blah blah".' He was informed that he had an extra four words included with the price, should he care to use them. Wishing to get full value for money, the parsimonious farmer agreed to the insertion of an additional four words. The "In Memoriam" message duly appeared the following week: "In memory of my dearly beloved wife, Ethel Braithwaite, who departed this life on 1st March 1955 at the age of 81 years. Much missed by her loving husband. Also tractor for sale." '

It was definitely time I left, I decided, and began to pack up my briefcase—Sidney in this sort of mood could keep going all evening.

*   *   *

It had been just after the beginning of term that Sister Brendan had telephoned.

'It's that little nun from St Bartholomew's on the phone again,' Julie had informed me. 'After something, I'll bet. She could get blood out a stone, that woman, and she has you wrapped around her little finger. You seem to go all to pieces when it comes to nuns.'

'Thank you, Julie,' I had said, taking the receiver from her hand. 'Good morning, Sister Brendan, and how are you?'

Sister Brendan, headteacher of St Bartholomew's Roman Catholic Infant School in the dour industrial town of Crompton, was a slight, finely-boned woman with small, dark eyes and a sharp beak of a nose. When I had first met her she had reminded me of a hungry blackbird out for the early worm. Her small infant school was situated near a wasteland of tall, blackened chimneys, deserted factory premises, boarded-up shops, dilapidated warehouses and row upon row of red-brick, terraced housing. The school, adjacent to the small church of St Bartholomew of Whitby, was a complete contrast. Once across the threshold, one entered another world, one which, like the little nun herself, was bright, cheerful and welcoming.

'Mr Phinn,' Sister Brendan's soft voice had come down the line, 'I have a little favour to ask.' It had taken a very short time for her to persuade me to speak at the charity fund-raising event, and that evening had now arrived.

At the entrance to St Bartholomew's School I was greeted by the local parish priest, Monsignor Leonard, his cassock as shabby and ill-fitting as usual. I had come across him on a number of occasions on my travels around the county's schools. He was a kindly and quietly-spoken man in his late fifties who relished being with the children, seeming to be endlessly interested in their education.

On previous visits, I had also met Miss

93

Fenoughty, the monsignor's housekeeper and the church organist. She was a small, round woman of indeterminate age, and was hard of hearing. On one occasion when I had heard her play the piano during school assembly, she had hammered her way up and down the keys as if there'd been no tomorrow.

'Good evening,' said Monsignor Leonard now as I approached the school entrance. 'It is so kind of you to come and speak to our little gathering.'

'Good evening, Mr Flynn,' said Miss Fenoughty, who was standing beside him. 'Not a massive turnout so far but we live in hope. It was a full hall when the last speaker spoke here. Mind you, Constance Rigby is a bit of a celebrity in flower arranging circles. Anyway, it's kind of you to come and talk to our little gathering, isn't it, Monsignor?'

The priest sighed and directed his eyes heavenwards. 'Yes, it is indeed, Miss Fenoughty.' Then he said in an undertone, 'You've taken the words right out of my mouth.'

'Good evening,' I said, shaking the priest's hand and smiling at the fussy little figure beside him.

'And it was very good of you, Mr Flynn, not to charge a fee,' continued Miss Fenoughty. 'So many of these speakers charge for their services these days, don't they, Monsignor?'

'It is extremely kind of you to give up your evening, Mr Phinn,' repeated the priest.

'I said to Monsignor Leonard,' Miss Fenoughty rattled on regardless, 'I said it's very kind of Mr Flynn to give up an evening and not to charge a fee. We can now use our funds to get a really good speaker next year, can't we, Monsignor?'

The priest looked rather embarrassed, shrugged

94

and smiled, then said quickly, obviously deciding it was time Miss Fenoughty's flow was stemmed, 'Now, Mr Phinn, no doubt Sister Brendan explained about this very worthwhile cause. The street children of South America are the most disadvantaged in the world. Abandoned by their parents to fend for themselves, they live in gutters, sewers, in cardboard boxes, they are the prey to predatory adults, the victims of corrupt police. They are the world's forgotten children. "We may be excused for not caring much about other people's children, for there are many who care very little about their own." Dr Johnson, I think, said that.'

'Dr Johnson!' Miss Fenoughty snapped. 'Don't talk to me about Dr Johnson, Monsignor. I've been waiting for my elastic stockings for four weeks now.'

'Shall we go in?' mouthed the priest. 'Sister Brendan will be wondering where we are.' He bent and barked in his housekeeper's ear. 'And, by the way, Miss Fenoughty, it's Mr Phinn, not Flynn.'

'What is?' she snapped.

The priest's voice went up an octave. 'I said, it's Mr Phinn!'

'Monsignor Leonard,' replied his housekeeper quietly but distinctly, 'there is really no need to shout. I can hear perfectly well. It is just that you mumble so.'

The evening went well and the receptive audience seemed to enjoy my talk. Afterwards, Monsignor Leonard and I joined the headteacher in her room. Sister Brendan certainly seemed well pleased, most especially with the respectable amount of money that was raised.

'Thank you so much,' she said. 'We do so appreciate it when people—'

'Monsignor Leonard! Monsignor Leonard!' Miss Fenoughty barged through the door, beckoning madly to the priest like an angry mother would to a child she wants to come in for tea. 'I need to speak to you on a matter of some urgency.'

'We were just thanking Mr Phinn—' started the priest.

'Excuse me, Mr Flynn,' Miss Fenoughty said, 'but I must drag the Monsignor away. It's imperative that I speak to him.'

The poor priest was more or less manhandled to the door by the small figure, and he threw us a baleful look as he was bundled from the room.

Sister Brendan raised her eyes to heaven. 'God grant me the courage to change what I can, the patience to endure what I cannot, and the forbearance to put up with Miss Fenoughty.'

*   *   *

On the way home, I stopped off at the late-night chemist in Fettlesham High Street. I had a slightly tickly feeling in the back of my throat and thought I might be coming down with a cold. I smiled as I entered the shop, remembering the last time I had called there. It had been after I had visited a school and had left with some 'little lodgers', as Christine had euphemistically described them. I had been extremely embarrassed having to ask for a shampoo to get rid of head lice.

The same young woman in the bright white nylon overall who had sold me the head lice medication and nit comb was serving now. She obviously recognised me. 'Not more head lice, is it?' she asked, *sotto voce*, as I approached the counter.

'No, thank goodness,' I replied. 'Just something for a cold, please. One of those lemon drinks and a bottle of aspirin should do it.'

As she selected the necessary items from the display in front of her, the pharmacist appeared from behind a glass screen. 'Dr Mullarkey?' he enquired, looking past me. I turned and there, sitting in a small alcove, was Gerry. She gave me the shocked, wide-eyed look of a shoplifter caught in the act.

'Yes, that's me,' she said, rising to take the packet from his hand. 'Hello, Gervase.'

'Hello, Gerry,' I replied.

'Give him two of these, three times a day,' said the pharmacist. 'If the condition worsens, I suggest you get in touch with your doctor, but it sounds as if it's just a bit of flu and he'll be over it in a few days.'

'That will be £3.50, please, madam,' said the shop assistant.

'Thank you,' replied Gerry, fumbling around nervously in her purse for the right amount. Before I could enquire after the health of the 'him', she pushed the money into the assistant's hand, gave me a quickly vanishing smile and said, 'Must be off. Have a lovely weekend.'

Perhaps Sidney was right, I thought to myself. Perhaps she does have a secret lover tucked away somewhere deep in the Dales after all. It was certainly very mysterious, very mysterious indeed.

CHAPTER SIX

The scenery in the Yorkshire Dales, without doubt, includes some of the most varied and stunning in the British Isles. The county may not embrace within its sprawling borders the vast magnificence of the Scottish Highlands or the towering grandeur of Snowdonia but there is a particular beauty in each of the diverse landscapes. There is a breathtaking beauty in the hay meadows of Wensleydale and Swaledale where buttercup and clover blaze along the valley bottoms. There is a simple pastoral beauty in the close-cropped sheep pastures of Ribblesdale, smooth and soft as a billiard table, where rock rose and mountain pansy flourish. This is a land of contrasts: of dark, scattered woodland creeping up the steep slopes, soaring fellsides leading to vast empty moors, great rocky wind-scoured crags, bubbling becks leading into curling rivers, vast swathes of crimson heather and golden bracken on the turn.

With each season this vast, beautiful landscape changes dramatically but it is in winter that the most spectacular transformation takes place. It is then that the multicoloured canvas of pale green fields and dark fells, twisting roads and miles of silvered walls, cluttered farmsteads and stone cottages, squat churches and ancient inns are enveloped in one endless white covering, and a strange, colourless world stroked by silence emerges.

It was a bright, cold morning, a week before the schools broke up for the Christmas holidays, and I was scheduled to visit two small schools. There were flurries of snow in the air as I drove out along Fettlesham High Street but by the time I had reached the open road great flakes started to fall thick and fast. Soon the snow began to settle in bitter earnest and in no time it was draping the branches of the skeletal trees, lacing the hedgerows, covering walls and roofs. The rays of a watery winter sun pierced the high feathery clouds making the snow glow a golden pink. The scene was magical.

I crawled up the narrow road to St Helen's, a tiny Church of England school nestling in a fold of the dale, wondering if it would be passable later when I was due to go on to my next appointment. The small, stone school served the village of Kirby Crighton and neighbouring Kirby Ruston, as well as a few children from the US air base at Ribbon Bank. The last time I had visited the school it had been on a mild autumn afternoon. Gone now were the brilliant colours, the golden lustre of the trees, the thick carpet of yellow and orange leaves and the rusty bracken slopes. Now it was a patchwork of white, criss-crossed with the dark walls.

The interior of the school was warm and welcoming. A tall Christmas tree stood in one corner of the classroom, festooned with coloured lights and decorations; a large rustic crib was set in the opposite corner. Every wall was covered with children's Christmas paintings in reds and greens and golds. There were snowmen and reindeer, plum puddings and fir trees, Father Christmases and carol singers and some delightful silhouettes showing the journey of Mary and Joseph to Bethlehem.

Mrs Smith, the headteacher, was more than surprised to see me. 'My goodness, Mr Phinn,' she said as I entered the classroom, brushing flakes of snow off my coat, 'I really didn't think you would venture out here in this weather. I hope you get back to Fettlesham. You don't want to be stranded out here.'

'It was not too bad when I started,' I explained, 'but if it doesn't ease off, Mrs Smith, I'll go back and fix another time to visit.'

The snow, however, did soon stop so I decided to stay and carry out the inspection as planned. It was nearly lunchtime by the time I had heard the children read and looked though their books, examined the teachers' development planning and lesson notes, studied the test scores and the mark books and observed two lessons.

'Well, things are fine, Mrs Smith,' I told the headteacher. 'No major worries that I can see. I'll get the full written report off to you before the end of the week.'

'That's reassuring, Mr Phinn,' said the headteacher. 'Now, I wonder, if you have the time, perhaps you would like to see our Nativity. We're performing it for parents later this afternoon in the village hall and are having one last run through to iron out any creases, so to speak. An objective view would be very much appreciated.'

'I should love to stay,' I said.

While the children put on their costumes, I helped push the desks and chairs to the back of the classroom, to leave a large space in the front. Then, having ensconced myself on the teacher's chair at the far side of the room, I sat back to see yet another performance of surely the most famous and poignant stories of all time. This would be the fourth Nativity play I had seen in a fortnight and each had been quite different from the last. I wondered if this one was going to be as memorable as the others.

*   *   *

The highlight of the evening in the first Nativity play of this Christmas season had been the Annunciation. Mary, a pretty little thing of about six or seven, had been busy bustling about the stage, wiping and dusting, when the Angel of the Lord had appeared stage right. The heavenly spirit had been a tall, self-conscious boy with a plain, pale face and sticking-out ears. He had been dressed in a flowing white robe, large paper wings and sported a crooked tinsel halo. Having wiped his nose on his sleeve, he had glanced around suspiciously and had sidled up to Mary, as a dodgy market trader might to see if you were interested in buying something from 'under the counter'.

'Who are you?' Mary had asked sharply, putting down her duster and placing her hands on her hips. This had not been the quietly-spoken, gentle-natured Mary I had been used to.

'I'm the Angel Gabriel,' the boy had replied with a dead-pan expression and in a flat voice.

'Well, what do you want?'

'Are you Mary?'

'Yes.'

'I come with tidings of great joy.'

'What?'

'I've got some good news.'

'What is it?'

101

'You're having a baby.'

'I'm not.'

'You are.'

'Who says?'

'God, and He sent me to tell you.'

'Well, I don't know nothing about this.'

'And it will be a boy and He will become great and be called—er, um—' The boy stalled for a moment. 'Ah—called Son of the Most High, the King of Kings. He will rule for ever and His reign will have no end.'

'What if it's a girl?'

'It won't be.'

'You don't know, it might be.'

'It won't, 'cos God knows about these things.'

'Oh.'

'And you must call it Jesus.'

'I don't like the name Jesus. Can I call him something else?'

'No.'

'What about Gavin?'

'No,' the angel had snapped. 'You have to call it Jesus. Otherwise you don't get it.'

'All right then,' Mary had agreed.

'And look after it.'

'I don't know what I'm going to tell Joseph,' the little girl had said, putting on a worried expression and picking up her duster.

'Tell him it's God's.'

'OK,' Mary had said, smiling for the first time.

When the Angel of the Lord had departed Joseph had entered. He had been a cheeky-faced little boy dressed in a brown woollen dressing gown, thick blue socks and a multi-coloured towel over his head, held in place by the inevitable elastic

102

belt with a snake clasp.

'Hello, Mary,' he had said cheerfully.

'Oh hello, Joseph,' Mary had replied.

'Have you had a good day?'

'Yes, pretty good,' she had told him, nodding theatrically.

'Have you anything to tell me?'

There had been a slight pause before she had replied. 'I am having a baby—oh, and it's not yours.'

The audience had laughed and clapped at this, leaving the two small children rather bewildered.

The highlight of the second Nativity play had been after the entrance of the Three Kings. Someone had really gone to town on the costumes for the little boys who came in clutching their gifts tightly. They were resplendent in gold and silver outfits, topped by large bejewelled crowns that shone brilliantly under the stage lights.

'I am the King of the North,' said one little boy, kneeling before the manger and laying down a brightly wrapped box. 'I bring you gold.'

'I am the King of the South,' said the second, kneeling before the manger and laying down a large coloured jar. 'I bring you myrrh.'

'I am the King of the East,' said the third and smallest child, kneeling before the manger and laying down a silver bowl. 'And Frank sent this.'

In the third play, Joseph, a rather fat boy dressed in a Mexican poncho and a towel over his head, had not looked entirely happy when he too heard the news of the imminent arrival of the baby.

'Are you sure about this?' he had asked, an anxious expression suffusing his little face.

'Course I'm sure!' Mary had replied. 'An Angel

103

of the Lord told me.'

'Are you sure it was an angel?'

'Course, I'm sure. Her name was Gabrielle.'

At this, I remembered that the school was very big on equal opportunities.

'I think I'm going faint,' Joseph had sighed.

'Pull yourself together. It's great news. Angel Gabrielle told me not to be frightened.'

'I must admit that I'm dead worried about this, Mary,' Joseph had confided, shaking his head solemnly. 'It's come as a big shock.'

'There's nothing to worry about, silly. Everything will be all right.'

'I suppose we'll have to get married then.'

'S'pose so.'

'Are you sure you're having a baby, Mary?' Joseph had persisted.

'Yes, I've told you, and we're going to call him Jesus and he will be the best baby in the whole wide world and we will love him very, very much and take care of him.'

Joseph had nodded but had not looked too happy. 'All right then,' he had sighed.

How many young couples, I had thought to myself that afternoon as I watched the small children act out their play, had been in that situation?

*   *   *

Now at St Helen's, the Christmas play was staged rather differently. Mrs Smith explained that she had asked the children to write the different parts of the Christmas story in their own words and four of the best readers would read the narrative while

104

the other children mimed the actions.

Mary sat centre stage, staring innocently into space. The first little reader began the story: 'Long, long ago there was a girl called Mary and she lived in a little white house with a flat roof.' Then the angel appeared, a large boy wearing what looked like part of a sheet with a hole cut in it for his head. He stretched out his arms dramatically as the reader continued: 'One day, God sent an angel and he told Mary she was going to have a very special baby boy and His name would be Jesus.' The angel looked heavenwards. 'When the angel went back up to God, he said, "Mary did what I said, God. She is calling Him Jesus, just as you told me to tell her."'

A beaming little boy with red cheeks strode into the scene and positioned himself behind Mary who was still gazing serenely into the middle distance. He put a parcel on the floor, then placed his hand on Mary's shoulder and stroked her fair hair.

A second reader took over: 'In a town called Naz'reth, there was an old man called Joseph and he was a carpenter.' The angel appeared again and stretched out his arms. 'God sent an angel to him as well and told him to marry Mary. So Joseph asked Mary to marry him and she said, "Yes please," and soon expected the baby. Joseph came home from work and he bought Mary some baby clothes and a big box of chocolates.' Joseph bent down, picked up the parcel and dumped it in Mary's lap.

Three children shuffled on, followed by a fourth smaller child carrying a toy sheep. The reader continued: 'In the fields there were these shepherds looking after their sheep.' The angel appeared again and stretched out his arms. 'The angel went to see them as well. When they saw this great shining light, they were really, really scared. "Ooooh—er, ooooh—er," they went. "What's that?" "Don't be frightened," said the angel. "I bring you tidings of great joy. Today, a little baby boy will be born and you have to go and see Him." "Righto," said the shepherds.'

Three more children appeared, staring upwards and pointing, at which stage a rather large girl pushed the second reader out of the way, and started to read: 'The three kings were very rich and they wore beautiful clothes and had these crowns and things. They looked at the stars every night. One night one of the kings said, "Hey up, what's that up there, then?" "What?" said the other kings. "That up there in the sky? I've not seen a star like that one." The star sparkled and glittered in the blue sky. "You know what?" said another king. "It means there's a new baby king been born. Shall we go and see Him?" "All right."'

The narrator continued: 'They shouted to their wives: "Wives! Wives! Go and get some presents for the baby king. We're off to Beth'lem to see Him." "OK," said the wives.

The three kings wandered around for a moment before miming knocking at a door. An aggressive-looking boy, with short spiky hair and a front tooth missing, emerged, holding a plastic sword. He stuck out his chin and glowered. 'The three kings came to this big palace,' continued the reader. 'It was covered in expensive jewels and had a golden roof and a silver door. They could hear this blasting music. They knocked on the door and a man called Herod answered the door. "What do you want?" he shouted at them. "We are looking for the new baby king." "Well, he's not here!" said Herod. "And shift those camels. They can't stay there." He waved his sword about and said, "Clear off!" Herod was not a very nice man at all.'

At this point, the reader was replaced by a small boy in trousers too big for him. Mary and Joseph reappeared, pulling behind them a cardboard donkey on small wheels; it had a straw tail and very large, polystyrene ears. 'Mary and Joseph went to Beth'lem on a donkey,' piped the small reader, 'but there was no room in the inn so they had to stay in a barn round the back. Mary had her little baby and she wrapped Him up nice and warm and kissed Him and called Him Jesus, just as God had told her to.'

Children began to enter slowly and gather around the baby. 'And from the hills came the shepherds and from Herod's palace came the three kings following a big star, and they all loved baby Jesus. He was small and cuddly and He laughed. "Why is He laughing?" asked the shepherds. "Because God's tickling Him," said Mary.'

Last of all came the little shepherd boy and he laid the toy sheep before the manger. 'And they sang a lullaby for the baby Jesus, and everyone was happy,' read the small boy. The whole area was now filled with children singing 'Away in a Manger' in clear, high voices.

When the carol finished, I sat for a moment and looked around me: the children's faces were glowing with pleasure, Mrs Smith was wiping away a tear, the lights of the fir tree winked and twinkled, and the walls were ablaze with the colours of Christmas. Through the classroom window a pale sun cast a translucent light and the whole world gleamed silver. This was indeed something spiritual.

*   *   *

My afternoon appointment was at Highcopse County Primary School, and was a follow-up visit. I had inspected the school over a year earlier and written a substantial report with many recommendations. I was there now to see if the issues I had identified had been addressed. On my last visit I had noted that the children's speaking and listening was good, the reading sound but the range of writing narrow and the standard barely satisfactory.

The first part of the afternoon I spent examining the teachers' lesson plans and mark books before looking at samples of the children's written work. Things had certainly got better and at afternoon playtime Mrs Peterson, the headteacher, smiled broadly when I told her there had been significant improvements in the standard of writing.

'Well, Mr Phinn, that's the best Christmas present I could have wished for. I am so pleased. I hope that you find the same in the infants. Mrs Dunn has been working extremely hard since your last visit to get things up to scratch.'

'By the way, where's Oliver today?' I asked. On my previous visit, I had met Oliver, a remarkably articulate boy but somewhat accident-prone, like the time when a wax crayon became lodged in his ear.

'You notice how quiet it's been then?' said the headteacher. 'He's in the pantomime at the

Fettlesham Little Theatre this afternoon, the matinée performance, no doubt putting his considerable acting talents to good use.' There was a hint of sarcasm in her voice.

'Any more accidents?' I enquired.

'Need you ask! Only last week he managed to get a sensitive part of his anatomy caught in his zip.' Mrs Peterson did not elaborate on the last and most memorable accident. She merely sighed and gave me a knowing look.

'So he's in a pantomime this week?'

'He is. He's playing the part of the cat in the Thornthwaite Thespians' production of *Dick Whittington* and, knowing Oliver, he'll steal the show. His costume is a minefield of zips. I said to Mrs Dunn when I saw it that he'd have been better off with buttons because if he's not careful it'll be a neutered cat that turns back to London with Dick Whittington.'

For the remainder of the afternoon I joined the infant class in a large, well-equipped room with colourful Christmas displays. Dominating the room was an old-fashioned teacher's desk in heavy pine with a hard-backed chair tucked underneath. The infants' teacher, Mrs Dunn, was dressed in a dark blue cardigan and dark brown skirt. Her grey hair was stretched back across her head and small dark eyes blinked nervously behind large frames. I had not been greatly impressed with this teacher when I had first observed her lessons the year before and my report had not been a good one.

I found to my surprise that things had improved vastly and was able to reassure a very worried Mrs Dunn before I packed my papers away in my briefcase, ready to depart.

109

'Tom's been a great influence, of course,' she told me, a brief smile playing on her thin lips.

'Tom?'

'My partner.' Mrs Dunn smiled. 'I'd been on my own for a good few years since my husband died and then I met Tom on one of Mr Clamp's wonderful art courses. He's very creative is Tom, been a real inspiration.'

'Well, I am very pleased,' I told her. 'I'll be sending in a report later this week. Well, goodbye, Mrs Dunn, and have a pleasant and restful Christmas.'

As I made for the door, however, the teacher called out to me. 'Mr Phinn, we have about ten minutes left before going-home time. It would be very nice if you could read the children a little of the Christmas story. They have been listening to a couple of pages each day this week and we are up to where Mary and Joseph arrive in Bethlehem.'

'Well,' I murmured, not expecting such a request but hardly in a position to refuse, 'I suppose I could. I must leave immediately at the end of school, however, since I have an engagement this evening and must get home to change.'

'Oh, that would be splendid. I am sure the children will enjoy hearing another voice.' Mrs Dunn clapped her hands together smartly. 'All onto the carpet now, quickly and quietly, please. Thomas, will you not do that to Bethany's hair and, John, leave the Christmas lights alone. Come along, Simon, you're a real little slowcoach this afternoon.'

When the children were settled, had crossed their legs and folded their arms, and were sitting up straight with their eyes to the front, Mrs Dunn

110

introduced me. 'Today, as a special treat, Mr Phinn is going to read a little more of our story, a story we all know but love to hear again and again at Christmas time.'

I opened the large crimson-covered book, smiled at the sea of faces before me and read, 'Now, children, it was a cold winter night when Mary and Joseph arrived in Bethlehem many, many years ago. Joseph walked ahead, holding up his lamp to light the way—'

'Didn't he have a torch?' asked a small girl with a Christmas ribbon in her hair.

'No, Briony, he did not have a torch,' Mrs Dunn told her. 'There were no torches in those days, were there, Mr Phinn?'

'No, no torches,' I said. I knew from experience that telling stories to children of this age usually ended up as more interruption than story. 'Mary was on an old donkey which walked oh so slowly. I think he knew he was carrying a precious cargo—'

'Did it have bells on?' Briony asked.

'No, it didn't have bells on.'

'The donkey I rode at Blackpool in the summer had bells on.'

'Briony!' said Mrs Dunn sharply 'Come over here and sit on my knee, please. I have asked you before not to shout out. It spoils the story for everyone else.' As Briony scrambled over the small bodies which surrounded her, Mrs Dunn told her, 'Mary's donkey did not have bells on because it wasn't a seaside donkey, was it, Mr Phinn?'

'No,' I said wearily, and returned to the book. 'Now Mary, who was riding on the old gentle donkey, knew she was going to have her baby very soon. She was very excited but also felt very tired

111

for she and Joseph had travelled far—'

A small freckled boy, who had been perfectly still and attentive until this moment, raised a hand, waved it in the air and called out, 'Mr Phinn! Mr Phinn! My Auntie Jackie felt tired when she was having a baby. She had swollen ankles as well and a bad back. She said it was the last baby she was going to have because—'

'Thomas, just listen, please,' said Mrs Dunn. 'We want to hear about baby Jesus, not about your Auntie Jackie's baby, don't we, Mr Phinn?'

'We do,' I said, and struggled on. 'Mary and Joseph had been travelling for many miles and when they got to Bethlehem there was nowhere for them to stay. They looked everywhere but there was no room, not even at the inn.' I glanced up to see Briony sitting quietly on Mrs Dunn's knee, her thumb stuck firmly in her little mouth. 'The innkeeper told them that there was a stable and they could stay there. Mary had her baby and wrapped Him in swaddling clothes and laid Him in a manger. And high above, in the clear sky, a great star shone above them. And all around them were the animals, the ox and the ass—'

'What's an ass, Mr Phinn?' called out Thomas.

'It's a donkey,' I said.

'I wouldn't like to sleep with a donkey!' cried Briony, coming to life again on her vantage point on Mrs Dunn's knee. 'The ones in Blackpool are really smelly.'

'This was a very nice donkey,' said Mrs Dunn, 'wasn't it, Mr Phinn?'

'Yes, Mrs Dunn,' I replied, hearing with great relief the bell for the end of school. 'It was an exceptionally nice donkey.'

112

'And did *this* one have bells on?' asked Briony, as she scrambled off Mrs Dunn's knee.

'No, I don't think so,' said Mrs Dunn, straightening her skirt. 'What do you think, Mr Phinn?'

I had had enough of Mrs Dunn and her constant referring questions back to me. I fleetingly thought of her new partner, Tom, and decided he must be a veritable saint. 'I think perhaps this donkey did wear bells, Mrs Dunn. Now, I really must be off so I can get back in daylight and before it starts to snow again,' and I left the dowdiiy-dressed teacher to stem the flow of questions from Briony who was now demanding to know what sort of bells they were.

*　　　*　　　*

Two days after I had been checked out by Mrs Cleaver-Canning, I had received a letter from her, written on pale, embossed and scented paper, confirming the invitation to speak at the golf club dinner. She had suggested—and it was clear from the tone of the suggestion that there was little point in arguing—that I should leave my car at 1, Prince Regent Row, and Winco would drive us both down in the Mercedes. I was not at all sorry about this since the morning's snow, which had melted a little during the day, had frozen and the roads were lethally icy.

I arrived at the elegant Georgian house, now denuded of its crimson covering, at the appointed hour, parked my car in the drive and scrunched across the gravel to the impressive porch with the stone pillars. In the middle of the ornately-carved front door hung a vast wreath of holly, ivy and bright red ribbons.

I was welcomed again by Winco. 'Ah,' he said in his deep, throaty voice, 'Mr Phinn. Come in, come in. Nasty weather, isn't it? The better half is upstairs and will be down in a moment. We'll go into the drawing-room, if you'd like to come this way.'

Above the marble fireplace of the sumptuously-furnished room I now entered hung a huge portrait in oils of a heavily be-medalled and be-plumed cavalry officer who bore an unnerving resemblance to the lady of the house.

'That's Margot's two or three times great-grandfather General Sir George Sabine Augustus Cleaver-Bolling in his uniform of Colonel of the 12th Royal Lancers. Impressive looking chap, isn't he?'

'Yes, indeed,' I said, staring up at the self-important looking man, mounted on a rearing horse.

'Brought the Cleaver hyphen with her when she married me. Didn't fancy plain old Canning. Anyway, do sit down. I'll just give Margot a call.' Winco shuffled off and once in the hall shouted up the stairs, 'Margot! Margot! Mr Phinn's here.'

Back came the predictable short and impatient reply, 'I'm coming! I'm coming!' Then came the barked instruction, 'Start the car up, Winco, will you, and get it warm.'

'Already warm and waiting,' he called back.

I wandered round the room in wonderment at the sumptuousness of it all. On a table was a selection of photographs in elaborate silver frames. A plump, curly-headed girl with large eyes and pouting lips posed with a pony. Various severe-looking old men and women, all in black, stared out with disapproving expressions. In pride of place was a black and white picture of a handsome, dashing young RAF officer, with a head of wavy hair, a bristling moustache and an infectious grin. It was the younger Winco. He wore the ribbon of the Distinguished Flying Cross.

There was the sound of heavy footsteps on the stairs, followed by a whispering outside the door. 'I have asked you, Winco, on so many occasions, not to shout up the stairs.' Then the Honourable Mrs Cleaver-Canning entered the drawing-room looking—well, magnificent. She was dressed in an amazing black, low-cut dress that she filled out abundantly and which made her great bosom bulge. She dripped with jewellery.

'Ah, Mr Phinn, how very nice to see you.' She turned regally to Winco who was hovering at the door. 'Haven't you changed yet?'

'I'm not going, am I?'

'Well, not to the dinner, you're not, but you are driving us there and you can't very well take us looking like the gardener. Put on your blazer and flannels. But get us a sherry first, will you, Winco? Amontillado, Mr Phinn?'

'Yes, thank you.'

'Righto,' Winco said jovially and ambled out of the room, returning a moment later with two glasses of sherry on a small silver salver. He then departed to get changed.

'It's a dreadful night,' remarked Mrs Cleaver-Canning. 'I just hope Winco takes care. Once he gets behind the wheel he thinks he's in a cockpit. The roads are offly slippery at this time of year. So

115

dangerous.'

She was speaking of the man who no doubt had faced a wing of Messerschmitts, guns blazing; who had scrambled into the cockpit of his Hurricane or Spitfire four, five, six times a week, risking life and limb; who flew lonely dawn patrols, knowing that behind every bank of clouds enemy aircraft could be waiting. I sipped my sherry and stared at the formidable woman in black. Enemy aircraft must have been a bit of a breeze compared to her, I thought to myself.

Shortly, Winco appeared, smart in a dark blue blazer, flannels and RAF tie.

'Right,' stated Mrs C-C, 'I think we are ready. Shall we go, Mr Phinn?'

I did not believe what next came out of my mouth. 'Righto,' I said, following her to the door.

*   *   *

The Totterdale and Clearwell Golf Club was packed with about a hundred or so obviously well-heeled women. I let my gaze sweep across the figures and felt my heart lurch. Why on earth had I agreed to this? I asked myself. The only man there. However, I did not have time to dwell on this since Mrs C-C introduced me to the ladies of her committee. I made small-talk with Mrs Daphne Patterson, who had recommended me as a speaker in the first place, until the Master of Ceremonies 'banged up' and announced, 'Dinner is now served, if you would like to make your way to the dining-room.'

After everyone had wended their way into the adjoining dining-room, I followed Mrs Cleaver-

Canning as she made her queenly progress to the middle of the top table where she stood and faced the chattering throng. She did not need to speak. She stood as though posing for a photograph, her commanding stare flicking over the guests until their voices fell away and she had secured their full attention.

'Please be seated, ladies,' she said authoritatively, 'and gentleman,' she simpered. After we had settled ourselves, she continued: 'Welcome to our Christmas Ladies' Night and may I wish you all the compliments of this very special season. May I also welcome our principal guest and speaker, Mr Gervase Phinn, whom we shall be hearing from later. Mr Phinn has waived a personal fee, which is very generous of him, and will be donating the cheque to a charity close to his heart.' There was a flutter of applause. 'I'm not exactly aware what it is, but it has something to do with child prostitution in South America.'

'To prevent it rather than promote it,' I muttered under my breath.

The dinner was a very convivial affair. Mrs C-C, who sat on my left, proved to be a surprisingly interesting dinner companion after she had imbibed a good few glasses of wine. Between mouthfuls of melon and prawn cocktail, poached breast of guinea-fowl and lemon mousse, all of which she tucked into with relish, she told me about the golf club, which had a distinctive history, and gave an entertaining description of the various activities which had taken place during the previous year.

She was half way through demolishing a mince pie when she said, 'We do like our speaker to present the balls.'

'The balls?'

'Yes, if you wouldn't mind. You can do it before you speak. It's not too arduous a task. We always ask our guest speaker to present the balls. It's a bit of a tradition in the club.'

'What balls would these be?' I enquired, imagining some sort of esoteric ceremony.

'The golf balls there,' and she pointed to a pile of boxes on a nearby side-table. 'We award the cups, shields and medals at the annual Christmas dinner to the winners of the year's competitions. I, as the lady captain, dispense these, but a presentation box of golf balls is given to the oldest member, the newest member and the member who has spent most time this year on the greens. We like to give them something as a small token and to encourage them.'

'I see,' I replied. 'Well, y es, certainly I'll make the presentation.'

'As I have said,' she continued after another hearty quaff of wine, 'we ask our guest speaker to do the honours. Everyone looks forward to the presentation, although that vulgar little actor who spoke last year and consumed far too much alcohol for his own good, made a disgraceful exhibition of himself and used the occasion to make some very tasteless and lav—, er, lavi—, ah, lascivious observations.'

As I watched the waiter re-charge her wine glass for the third or fourth time the words 'pot', 'kettle' and 'black' immediately came to mind. 'I should be delighted to present your balls,' I said—and then wished I hadn't.

Mrs Hills, the lady captain-elect, sat on my right

and also proved to be an interesting and informative dinner companion. I learned that she was a woman of property and she gave me some excellent advice on where to look for houses and the best estate agents to contact.

'I have four cottages,' she informed me. 'A couple on the coast at Robin Hood's Bay and two more here in Totterdale, just north of Fangbeck Bridge in the village of Hawthwaite.'

'You don't want to sell one of them by any chance, do you?' I asked.

'No, no,' she replied. 'They are a precious source of income and, anyway, I couldn't part with them. They've been in the family for years and years. Old aunts and uncles died and I sort of accumulated them. But one of the cottages in Hawthwaite might be free to rent soon. Have you thought of renting until you find somewhere you want and can afford?'

'It may come to that, but we would really like to start married life in a house of our own. I expect we will end up in a modern semi in Fettlesham,' I said. 'It's so beautiful here in Totterdale, isn't it? I think it has some of the most magnificent views in the entire county. My fiancée and I have looked for property here but it is so expensive.'

'It's in the National Park, you see, so there are strict regulations on the building of anything new, and conversions have to follow very stringent rules. It's a whole lot cheaper to the north of Crompton or at Ribsdyke. You ought to try there.'

My thoughts, however, were still on Totterdale. 'Actually, I have an idea one of my colleagues lives somewhere in Totterdale and she rents a cottage.'

'Oh yes?'

'Geraldine Mullarkey. I don't know whether you know her but—'

'Well, well, well!' Mrs Hills interrupted. 'What a coincidence!'

'You *do* know her?'

'Of course I know her. She's one of my tenants in Hawthwaite. Delightful young woman. But I didn't know she was in your line of work. I thought she must be a medical doctor. She's never in during the day and keeps herself very much to herself when she is at home. So she's a school inspector, is she?'

'Yes, Geraldine and I actually share an office in Fettlesham.'

'I imagined she worked in the hospital there,' said my companion.

'Oh no,' I replied.

'Well, I couldn't hope for a better tenant. She's so pleasant and friendly, she's done wonders with the garden, and the inside is like a palace. I've only called a couple of times because, as I said, she is a very private person.'

'She's like that at work. Very friendly and conscientious and her desk is the tidiest, without a doubt.'

'And her little boy is a poppet, isn't he?'

I'm sure my mouth fell open. 'I'm sorry, what did you say?'

'Dr Mullarkey's little boy, Jamie. I said he was a poppet.'

'Little boy?'

'Yes, her son, Jamie. You surely knew she had a little boy?'

'Yes, yes, of course,' I replied, trying to conceal the shock of the revelation. 'I'd just for the moment

120

forgotten his name. Jamie, that's right. How old is Jamie now, then?'

'He must be three, nearly four, because he starts in the nursery next year. He's such a good little boy and as bright as a button. I know this because my sister's girl is the child-minder in the village, and she loves him to bits. I don't know anything about Dr Mullarkey's husband except I think he works abroad.'

My head was in a whirl, and I had to escape. 'I wonder if you would excuse me for a moment, Mrs Hills, I need to wash my hands before my speech.' I began to push back my chair.

'Getting a few butterflies, Mr Phinn?' she teased. 'You mustn't worry about your audience. The lady members are always very appreciative. They won't eat you. Mind you, there were more than a few eyebrows raised when the man from the television soap stood up last year.'

'Don't mention that odious man,' snapped Mrs Cleaver-Canning, turning towards us. Then she added, 'Hurry back, Mr Phinn, it's almost time to present your balls.'

'I'll not be long,' I said and dashed for the Gents.

'Ladies!' boomed Mrs Cleaver-Canning behind me. 'There will be the Loyal Toast in five minutes, then a comfort break and after that we will start the proceedings.'

In the Gents, I tried to come to terms with the bombshell which had just landed. Geraldine had a child! She had never breathed a word, not a word to any of us. None of us in the office had had an inkling. And what about her husband or partner? Did he work abroad or was she divorced, separated, a widow? Why was she so secretive? But

121

now I thought about it, things did make more sense. She was always evasive about where she lived. 'Somewhere in the wilds,' she would say. She had never mentioned anything about her life before she had become a school inspector, or her interests outside the office. There were the times when she had looked anxiously at her watch if a meeting had continued past six o'clock as if she were late for some appointment—she had obviously been keen to collect her little boy from the child-minder. She never stayed in the office for the usual badinage at the end of the day and only attended speech days or evening functions like school plays and concerts when she had to; I suppose she found it hard to find a baby-sitter. When I had had that chance meeting with her in the chemist earlier in the term, the tablets had been for her little boy and not for some mysterious lover as I had imagined. Then there were her questions about the most appropriate books to buy for young children. It all made sense now. But why had she never said anything? Why the mystery? Well, I decided, if she wanted to keep Jamie a secret, so be it. I wouldn't spill the beans.

I was too preoccupied with the news of Gerry's secret life to feel nervous about the rest of the evening. Following the presentation of the balls and the trophies, I stood and spoke for twenty minutes and received a very warm reception, probably because a great deal of alcohol had been consumed and my audience were in Christmas good-humour. Clutching a generous cheque for CAFOD, I clambered into a beautifully warm car to be chauffeured back to 1, Prince Regent Row by Winco. The lady captain of the Totterdale and

Clearwell Golf Club slumped in the back, breathing like a hippopotamus which had remained too long underwater. She was rather worse for wear.

'I hope you haven't been winking, drinco,' she remarked. 'It'sh very icy and we don't want an accident and all end up in hopsital. So take your time and go shlowly.'

'Righto!' replied the Wing Commander, pushing his foot down on the accelerator pedal and skidding out of the car park.

CHAPTER SEVEN

Standing outside the Foxton School office was a small boy of about six or seven. It was clear that he was in trouble for he held his head down so far his chin rested upon his chest. His hands were clasped behind his back and he remained motionless in an attempt to be as inconspicuous as possible. However, as I approached, he glanced up furtively before thrusting his head back down again.

'Hello,' I said.

'Hey up,' he mumbled, not looking up.

'You look to me as if you're in trouble.'

'I am,' he replied, still staring at the floor. 'I've been sent out to cool off.'

'Cool off?' I repeated.

'I can only go back when I've cooled off,' he said.

'And have you cooled off?' I asked him.

'Not yet,' he mumbled.

'And what have you been up to?' I asked.

The small boy relaxed a little, sniffed, wiped his nose on the back of his hand and looked up at me.

'We're not supposed to speak to strange-looking men.'

'I'm not really a stranger,' I told him, tapping the large square badge on my lapel. 'I'm a school inspector.'

The child's bottom lip started to tremble. 'I don't mean to do it,' he moaned. 'I only learnt how to do it yesterday and now I can't stop miself.' He sniffed noisily. 'I'd stop if I could, but I can't.'

'Whatever have you been doing?' I asked, rather intrigued.

'I can't tell you,' he replied mournfully, his eyes now brimming with tears.

'That's all right,' I reassured him. 'You don't need to tell me if you don't want to, but I won't be angry with you if you do.' The small boy replied by giving me an enormous wink. 'So are you going to tell me what you were sent out of the classroom for?' I persisted. He winked again in the same exaggerated manner. 'Aren't you going to tell me?' He winked a third time, contorting his face as if he had a mouth full of vinegar. 'Go on, tell me what you have been doing,' I urged. By this time I was desperate to know.

'I've been doing that,' he replied pointing at a squinting eye. 'I've been winking.'

'Winking?' I chuckled. 'Well, that doesn't sound too bad.'

'Mrs Smart doesn't think it's funny,' he told me in a stage whisper. 'She went bananas. She said she was sick and tired of me winking at her all morning, so she sent me out to cool off.'

'I see.'

'I just can't stop winking, you see. I've only just learnt how to do it and now I can't stop miself. I just keeps on winking all the time.'

'Oh dear,' I said, trying to keep a straight face. 'Bit of a problem that, isn't it?'

'Are you Becky's granddad?' he asked suddenly.

'No,' I replied. 'I told you, I'm a school inspector.'

'You could be Becky's granddad as well.'

'Well, I'm afraid I'm not.'

'He's coming in this morning is Becky's granddad. He's dead old but he used to be a referee. He's going to take us for football after playtime. Mrs Smart says that if I haven't cooled off before break, I can't play.' He sniffed again, and the nose-wipe with the back of his hand seemed an automatic follow up.

'Well, you had better stop winking then,' I told him.

'It's not that easy,' sighed the boy. 'I've tried but I just can't. I wish I'd never learnt how to do it.' I was about to make my presence known by pressing the buzzer at the reception desk when the small boy asked, 'Can you wink then, mester?'

'I can,' I replied.

'Can you?'

'I can wink with both eyes. Like this.' I went down on my haunches so I was on a level with him and proceeded to demonstrate how it was possible to perform a double wink. I was blinking and winking madly and screwing up my face like someone with tear gas in his eyes when the frosted glass on the window of the school office slid back sharply.

'Is there anyone there?' a disembodied voice floated into the air above us. 'Justin, who are you talking to?'

125

'Oh yes, yes,' I spluttered, springing upright like a puppet which had just had its strings yanked. 'I'm the school inspector.'

'Indeed?' she said, eyeing me suspiciously and looking unconvinced as to the authenticity of this statement.

'Mr Phinn,' I elaborated. 'From the Education Office in Fettlesham. Here to see Mrs Smart.'

'Oh, yes, Mr Phinn,' she replied. 'The headteacher is expecting you. She's teaching at the moment but asked me to send you down to the classroom when you arrived. I see you have met our Justin.' The secretary popped her head through the hatch the better to see the recalcitrant pupil. 'Now then, Justin Heath, have you cooled off?'

'Not really, miss. I was getting cooler but then mester here was showing me how to wink with two eyes.'

'Mr Phinn!' exclaimed the school secretary, and all I could do was look up at the ceiling, and whistle gently.

'Well, you had better return to your lesson anyway. It's nearly playtime.'

'Yes, miss.'

'Perhaps Mr Phinn will take you back down with him to Mrs Smart's classroom.'

'Yes, miss.'

'You can show him the way.'

'Yes, miss.'

'And no more winking.'

'No miss, I'll try,' said the child.

The secretary gave me a look as if to say, 'And don't you go encouraging him any more, either.'

On the way down the corridor, I felt a sticky

little hand slip into mine. By the time we were approaching Mrs Smart's classroom, the little boy was swinging his arm, and mine, backwards and forwards.

'Justin,' I said, 'I don't mind you holding my hand, but cut out the swinging. OK?'

'Sorry, but I can't seem to stop miself from doing that, either.'

Mrs Smart, a plump woman in a shapeless knitted suit and sporting a rope of very large yellow beads, put on a theatrically disapproving expression when she caught sight of me entering the classroom with the little boy in tow.

'Oh,' she announced, 'I see our little winker has returned. Come along in, Mr Phinn. Justin, you go and sit down and let that be the end of your winking. And if I see you doing it again this morning, you will face the wall.'

'Yes, miss,' replied the boy, scurrying to his seat.

'Do you know, Mr Phinn, we've had Justin winking away all morning and distracting the entire class. I looked round at the children at one point and found he had set them all off. It was like teaching a flock of owls with conjunctivitis.'

'Oh dear,' I said, having to restrain myself from bursting out laughing.

'Well, anyway, it's very pleasant to have you with us this morning. Shall we all say a nice "Good morning" to Mr Phinn, children?'

'Good morning, Mr Phinn,' chanted the class obediently.

'If you would like to take a seat,' continued Mrs Smart, 'we'll get on with the lesson. We're doing the tenses, Mr Phinn—past, present and future.'

I found myself a chair in the corner of the room.

'Now,' the teacher said, tapping a list on the blackboard with a ruler, 'today I talk, present tense, tomorrow I shall talk, future tense, yesterday I talked, past tense.' She stared in Justin's direction, seemingly daring him to wink. 'Today I look, tomorrow I shall look, yesterday I looked. Very often we add "ed" to the end of the verb in the present tense to change it into the past tense but sometimes this is not the case. For example: today I sing, tomorrow I shall sing, yesterday I sang. Today I run, tomorrow I shall run, yesterday I ran. Now, I want you all to think of a really good verb which, when it changes into the past tense, does *not* have an "ed" on the end. Thinking caps on, please.'

After a moment, while the children variously scribbled on pieces of paper, or just sucked the ends of their pencils and gazed up around the room, Mrs Smart said, 'Yes, Alice. Have you got an interesting verb for us?'

'Miss, catch,' the girl shouted out.

'Let's say it in full shall we, Alice? Today I catch, tomorrow I shall catch, yesterday I caught. Good. Come on, then, Ross, I can see your hand waving in the air.'

A little fair-headed boy took a hearty breath before announcing: 'Today I fly, tomorrow I shall fly, yesterday I flew.'

'That was a very good one, Ross. Well done. Now, let me see. Who shall I pick? What about you, Joanna?'

'Today I write, tomorrow I shall write, yesterday I wrote,' chanted the girl confidently.

'We are getting some lovely verbs,' chortled the teacher. 'Now who else has one?' Mrs Smart looked round the room and I saw her eyes come to

128

rest on Justin.

'What about you, Justin? Have you an interesting verb for us?'

'I can't think of one, miss,' he replied.

'Well, try.'

The child thought for a moment before saying loudly, 'Today I wink, tomorrow I shall wink, yesterday I wank.'

Mrs Smart gasped and spluttered like a fish out of water. She took a deep deep breath, like a swimmer preparing to plunge into the pool, and her eyes grew wide and wild. 'Winked!' she said slowly and with tight restraint. 'Today I wink, tomorrow I shall wink, yesterday I W-I-N-K-E-D!' and she spelled out the last word with heavy emphasis.

Little Justin stared at her mutely. The teacher then clapped her hands smartly and plucked up a stick of chalk. 'Everyone! Put your pencils down for a moment and look this way.' She turned to the blackboard and wrote a series of words in large letters, sounding them out loudly and distinctly at the same time. 'Today I wink, tomorrow I shall wink, yesterday I *winked*. Let's all say it.' The class chanted the sentences in sing-song tones.

'Today I blink,' continued Mrs Smart, her face and neck suffused in crimson, 'tomorrow I shall blink, yesterday I blinked.' The children dutifully repeated the phrases.

At morning break, I sat with Mrs Smart in her room. She continued to wear a determined expression and her blotchy red neck still betrayed traces of the nervous rash. She fingered the rope of yellow beads without appearing to realise she was doing so.

'I wish I had never ever started to teach them about tenses,' she told me, clutching the beads. 'Especially with you being here. I mean, I nearly died when he came out with that word.'

'We all do it, Mrs Smart,' I said, trying to put her at her ease.

'I beg your pardon, Mr Phinn?' she gasped a second time.

'What I mean,' I replied, beginning to turn her shade of red, 'is that we all apply our knowledge, if you see what I mean.'

'No, I don't see what you mean,' said Mrs Smart, her eyes as wide as chapel hat pegs.

'It's a tricky and troublesome business—'

'What is?' she interrupted.

'The English tense system,' I attempted to explain. 'Actually, all Justin was doing was making a reasonable guess. Sink, past tense sank, stink, past tense stank, shrink, past tense shrank, wink past tense—'

'Winked!' she interposed quickly.

'You see, Mrs Smart,' I explained, 'the child is employing a rule which applies to a similar word. Actually, it was pretty astute of him. It's called linguistic extrapolation, you know.'

'I don't care what it is called, Mr Phinn,' asserted the teacher, huffing and puffing and fingering the beads, 'he's not doing any extrapolating in *my* classroom!'

*   *   *

As I was driving back to Fettlesham at the end of the morning, I was thinking of Justin and was reminded of other occasions when pupils had been

130

in trouble with their teachers. There was the one bright spark, of about the same age, who had been sent to the headteacher by the crossing patrol warden for throwing a piece of hard mud at another child. The infant, far from being remorseful, had told the headteacher that he had not intended to hurt the other child, he had been merely trying to attract his attention. The headteacher, unconvinced, had told the child to sit in her room and, as a punishment, to write out several times the very convoluted sentence: 'Rather than throwing a piece of hard mud at another child, which is a very dangerous thing to do, I could communicate with him by . . .' She had asked the child to think about what he had done and complete the sentence. Several minutes later, the miscreant had presented her with a series of somewhat lop-sided lines which read: 'Rather than throwing a piece of hard mud at another child, which is a very dangerous thing to do, I could communicate with him by letter, postcard, phone, carrier pigeon or smoke signals.'

There was another memorable occasion when a pupil's response had compelled me to smile. In the corridor outside a classroom of a very prestigious secondary school had stood an extremely smartly turned-out young man, his school uniform immaculate.

'Have you been sent out?' I had asked him.

'Yes, sir,' the student had replied, with no trace of embarrassment or discomfiture.

'And why is that?'

'Gross insolence, sir,' he had replied seriously.

'Gross insolence?' I had repeated, thinking that his crime must have indeed been heinous.

'Yes, sir.'

'Whatever did you say?'

'Well, it wasn't so much what I said, sir,' he had replied, 'it was more what I wrote.'

'And what did you write?'

'We were asked to compose an essay entitled, "Imagine you are a new born baby, and describe your first week in the world".'

What a ridiculous essay to set a class of fifteen-year-old boys, I had thought. 'I see,' I had remarked.

'And I did as I was asked,' the boy had continued, 'and wrote three sides on the topic.'

'And what did you write?' I had asked again.

'Glug, glug, glug, glug, glug,' he had replied without a trace of a smile.

*   *   *

The afternoon following the winker episode, the full team of inspectors was in the Staff Development Centre, giving Harold feedback on one of the endless Ministry of Education initiatives which were sent to try our patience.

'Colleagues,' said Harold, 'you have worked extremely hard and I am very grateful. I can put all this together in the next couple of days and get it off to the Ministry before Christmas.'

'Since we have done such a sterling job of work, Harold,' I said, 'and as a small token of your gratitude, may we have the remainder of the afternoon off to complete our Christmas shopping?'

'I'm afraid not, Gervase. There is a lot to get through. In addition, I have asked Mrs Savage to join our meeting later on. There are a number of items on the agenda which involve her.'

'Oh dear, oh dear,' I groaned, 'that's the Christmas spirit out of the window.'

'That has certainly taken the shine off proceedings and no mistake,' said David. 'It has completely and utterly spoilt the rest of my day. I have avoided that woman assiduously this term, dodged her memos, eluded her telephone calls, evaded her wretched forms and escaped having to meet her and now I am dragooned into spending an afternoon with her. Any Christmas spirit I had has quite drained away.'

'David,' said Gerry, laughing, 'this is a time of peace and goodwill to all.'

'I am happy to dispense peace and goodwill to everyone with the exception of that woman,' replied David, screwing up his face.

'Hear, hear,' I added.

'I really do think you are being a little unkind to Mrs Savage,' said Harold. 'I know she can be rather difficult and sometimes somewhat short with people, but she is a colleague and I do hope you will all show her, at the very least, some common courtesy when she arrives.'

'I'm surprised she can find the time to join us,' remarked Sidney. 'She must be missing the matinée performance in the pantomime in which she stars as the Wicked Stepmother or is it the Wicked Witch this year?'

'You are all being very childish about this,' said Harold crossly.

'No, Harold,' cried Sidney, 'that woman is impossible. She's so unpleasant, she would get threatening telephone calls from the Samaritans.'

'She is definitely getting worse,' I said.

133

'Incidentally, Harold, how's her romance with Dr Gore?'

Before he could answer, Sidney jumped in. 'Can you imagine her as Mrs CEO? She would, no doubt, adopt a pretentious double-barrelled name, calling herself Mrs Savage-Gore and be even more insufferable, self-opinionated, patronising and all-round disagreeable.'

'Don't hold back, Sidney,' said Gerry, shaking with laughter. 'Why don't you tell us all what you really think about Mrs Savage?'

'There's nothing afoot on that score from what I can tell,' reported Harold. 'I think when you saw Dr Gore and Mrs Savage at the end of the summer term, Gervase, it was merely a boss taking his assistant out for dinner to thank her for all her hard work.'

'Thank her for all her hard work!' exclaimed David. 'And what hard work would this be then?' He put on his spectacles and peered across the table. 'As far as meaningless phrases and unpronounceable gobbets of jargon the Ministry is so fond of using, you need go no further than Mrs Savage's memoranda. I mean—'

'I thought you said you were very adept at dodging her memos,' remarked Sidney.

'Have you two ever thought of becoming a comedy double act?' asked Harold. Before my colleagues could reply, he stood and headed for the door. 'Let's have lunch.'

*   *   *

'This morning,' said Sidney, 'I received yet another frightful Christmas card from some unknown

134

person.' We were sitting in the staff lounge having a cup of tea and a break while Harold sorted out his papers and made some urgent telephone calls before the start of the final session. 'Every year I receive these awful cards from people who apparently know me but I have no idea who they are. I might well dispense with the whole tiresome business of sending Christmas cards.'

'You sound like Scrooge, Sidney,' Gerry told him. 'I like getting cards. It's part of Christmas.'

'So do I,' I agreed. 'I even got a card from the estate agent, signed by all the staff. I reckoned it was rather thoughtful.'

'You got a card from the estate agents,' Sidney told me, 'because they'll try every means to inveigle you into stumping up thousands of pounds for a mound of rubble they euphemistically call a "desirable residence". Anyway, how is the house hunting going?'

'Oh, we've looked at a few places. Christine and I have our heart set on an old country cottage with a view but they are so expensive.'

'You live in an old cottage, don't you, Gerry?' said Sidney, availing himself of the opportunity to do a little probing.

'Yes, I do,' she replied without elaborating.

'In Bartondale, isn't it?'

'Totterdale,' she replied.

'Oh, Totterdale. It's very picturesque up there,' said Sidney, 'and not an arm and leg away from Fettlesham. Are there any cottages for sale in Totterdale, then?' When no one answered, he persevered. 'Geraldine?'

'I'm sorry, Sidney,' she said, 'were you talking to me?'

'I was asking if there were any cottages for sale in Totterdale? You could have the Phinns as neighbours.'

'Oh, very few come on the market,' she replied defensively. 'It's rather a pricey area. I rent mine.' She changed the subject quickly. 'On the question of whether or not to send Christmas cards, I shall certainly be sending them but it is just a question of finding the time to write them.'

'Well I, for once, agree with Sidney,' said David. 'It's become merely a wearisome ritual every Christmas to send cards to people you haven't seen for years and are not likely to ever see again. And the majority of cards are expensive and hideous to boot.'

I had had just about enough of the carping duo and knew just how to shut the two of them up. I winked conspiratorially at Gerry.

'Oh, I don't know. The one from Dr Gore, I thought, was particularly tasteful this year,' I said casually.

'You got one from Dr Gore?' demanded David in a startled voice.

'Yes, exceptionally large and impressive.'

'You received a card from our esteemed leader?' asked Sidney. 'Really?'

'Yes,' I replied, 'didn't you?' In time-honoured tradition, I crossed my fingers as I told my tiny white lie.

'Well, no,' said Sidney. 'I did not.' He was obviously rather affronted.

'Neither did I,' said David.

'Perhaps he's trying to tell you something,' remarked Gerry, attempting to keep a straight face.

'Did you get a card from Dr Gore, too,

Geraldine?' asked David.

'I thought everyone got one,' she replied, smiling sweetly. 'Mine was very artistic—a superb view across a snow-covered dale and the thoughtful message inside was—'

'Superb view, thoughtful message,' repeated Sidney.

'This is most upsetting,' said David. 'Why should he send a card to Gervase and Geraldine and not to us? After all, they're relative newcomers in the department.'

'I thought the two of you considered the whole idea of sending cards was a waste of time,' I said smugly.

'I bet it was that harridan, that ghastly Mrs Savage, who just crossed us off Dr Gore's list,' snorted Sidney.

'Well, if you won't fill in your weekly reports,' I began but was interrupted by Connie making a sudden entrance.

'Good afternoon,' she said, scrutinising the room for any mess.

'Good afternoon, Connie,' we all chorused.

'I thought I'd let you know, my step-ladders have materialised.'

'Materialised?' I said. 'I didn't know they were missing.'

'Yes, they disappeared from the store-room. At first, I thought Mr Clamp had taken them to do his arty displays.'

'Would I do such a thing, Connie?' said Sidney, pretending to be affronted.

'Yes,' said Connie sharply. 'Then I thought it might be Mr Pritchard using them for his PE classes.'

David raised his hand to his face in mock horror. 'I would never do anything of the sort.'

'Yes, you would, Mr Pritchard. You did last year. Anyway, the steps have materialised.'

'Really!' exclaimed Sidney. 'Materialising step-ladders! Did they appear to you in some sort of miracle?'

Connie threw him a dark look.

'Where were they?' I asked.

'The maintenance men used them when they were pruning the creeper on the fence at the back. Just took them out of the store without a by-your-leave and then left them out. Propped up on the wall at the back, they were. I do wish folks would put things back where they found them.'

'I am sure you impressed this upon them, Connie,' said Sidney, 'in your usual indefatigable way.'

'Do you know, Mr Clamp, I can never make head nor tail of what you are on about half the time. It's all double Dutch to me.'

'Where has plain English gone?' said David. 'Where is the language of Chaucer and Shakespeare and Oscar Wilde?'

'Anyway,' continued Connie, 'they'll not be walking off with my step-ladders again. I've put a lock and chain around them.'

'A little drastic, Connie,' observed Sidney. 'Isn't there a law about chaining people up?'

'The ladders!' snapped Connie.

'How's your father?' I asked, reckoning it wise to change the subject.

'Not too good, I'm afraid. They're keeping him in hospital for the time being. I went to see his doctor to talk about what we ought to do when he comes out. He was about as much use as a chocolate teapot. I don't think we'll see Dad at home for Christmas.'

'If there's anything we can do, Connie,' said Gerry, 'let us know. You might want running in to the hospital, some shopping, that sort of thing.'

'Thanks, but I've got my Ted and my daughter, Tricia. Thank you for offering anyway. I really came in to tell Dr Yeats that that Mrs Savage has arrived from County Hall and she's waiting in the meeting room. I had to tell her to park her car away from my entrance again. If looks could kill, I'd be six foot under. People just don't read notices.'

'Dr Yeats is making a few telephone calls,' I said, getting to my feet. 'I'll tell him she's arrived.'

'Colleagues!' cried Sidney, jumping up as if he had sat on something sharp. 'Let us face the enemy. Once more unto the breach, dear friends, once more! Stiffen the sinews, conjure up the blood, disguise fair nature with hard-favoured rage. Cry God for Harold, Yorkshire and Dr Gore!'

'Double Dutch,' mumbled Connie shaking her head. 'Double Dutch.'

*   *   *

Mrs Savage was standing stiffly by the window with an expression of icy imperturbability when we entered. She wore an expensive navy blue blazer with gold buttons over a tailored stone-coloured dress, silk scarf at her neck and the usual assortment of heavy jewellery. Her make-up was impeccable and not a hair was out of place. She turned slowly to face Harold, with a clash of bracelets and a false smile.

'Ah, Dr Yeats,' she said.

'Mrs Savage,' said Harold, giving her a great toothy grin. 'It is good of you to join us. Do take a seat. Would you like some coffee?'

'No, thank you,' she replied loftily. 'I only drink herbal tea.'

'Well, I don't think Connie runs to that at the Centre. Shall we make a start then?' We all sat at the large square table with Harold alone on one side. He smoothed his hair, shuffled some papers and took out his pen. 'Right, well, the first item on the agenda this afternoon is—'

'Before we begin, Dr Yeats,' said Mrs Savage, picking up a large brown envelope that was on the table in front of her, 'I have brought with me the short-list for the post of Senior Inspector. The CEO and the Sub-Committee have whittled down the large and very impressive number of applicants for the post to ten and Dr Gore has asked if you would cast your eye over them and give him your views before he makes the final selection. We will be calling five for interview in the New Year.' She was careful to avoid looking at me.

There had been no need for Mrs Savage to have brought along the applications and to make such a public show of the whole thing. She could have easily given them to Harold much more discreetly but I knew her little game. She was no doubt aware that I had applied for the post and was wanting me to know that it had attracted a wide and high-quality field and that I stood little chance. After a lot of soul-searching and late-night conversations with Christine, I had decided to go ahead and put in an application.

140

'Thank you, Mrs Savage,' said Harold, reaching over and plucking the envelope from her hand. I could see that he was far from pleased with her little ploy.

'And I don't need to impress upon you, Dr Yeats, that the contents of that envelope are strictly private and confidential.'

Harold stared at her for a moment with his large watery blue eyes before replying.

'No, Mrs Savage, you do not have to impress that upon me. I am fully aware of the procedures regarding the appointment of staff. Now, let us look at the first item on the agenda—secretarial support.' His gaze remained on Mrs Savage. 'As you are aware, Dr Mullarkey swelled our ranks last term and this has resulted in a great deal of additional paper work for Julie to deal with. It has added an extra and unacceptably heavy load on our secretary and—'

'May I stop you there one moment, Dr Yeats,' said Mrs Savage, swivelling a large ring round one of her fingers. 'The young woman in your office is not designated as a secretary. She is a clerical assistant.'

'No matter what you call her, we refer to her as our secretary,' said Harold firmly. 'For all intents and purposes, Julie does the work of a secretary— and more. Anyway, we did, as you know, have some temporary help initially from an agency but the young woman secured a permanent post and we are now in need of someone else to help out.'

Mrs Savage smiled. It was not a pleasant smile. 'I am afraid the on-going strategic situation in the education department, Dr Yeats, is that we have, at present, a serious clerical personnel establishment

141

shortfall.'

'A what?' asked Sidney, sitting bolt upright in his chair.

'I said,' repeated Mrs Savage, speaking slowly and distinctly, 'a serious clerical personnel establishment shortfall.'

'Not enough staff,' explained David.

'This was the direct result of necessary downsizing some years ago.'

'Downsizing?' said Sidney.

'Sacking,' explained David.

'We are now looking to enhance our staffing complement.'

'Employ some more people,' said David.

'So, what you are saying, Mrs Savage,' I said, trying not to laugh, 'is that you recognise that we are understaffed and you are going to sort out another secretary for us.'

'Clerical assistant,' corrected Mrs Savage.

'You can call the person whatever you like, Mrs Savage,' said David. 'All we need is someone to help Julie type reports, deal with the post, arrange appointments, deal with the telephone queries, photocopy materials for our courses, do the filing and make the odd cup of coffee.'

'I think you have made your point, Mr Pritchard,' said Mrs Savage. 'I shall see what I can do.'

'It is pretty urgent, Mrs Savage,' said David.

'I cannot, at this stage, promise anything, Mr Pritchard,' replied Mrs Savage casually. 'As I have just said, I shall see what I can do.'

'Well, is it possible for you to do it sooner rather than later?' I said. 'Julie has a real backlog which none of us wants carried on into the new term.'

Mrs Savage eyed me acidly. 'Mr Phinn,' she said, 'I shall endeavour, as I keep saying, to see what I can do.'

'Let's move on,' said Harold. The smile had disappeared from his face. 'The next item on the agenda is the Fettlesham Show.' There was a series of audible sighs and groans from around the table. 'Yes, yes, I know, but it is fast coming around again and we all have to pull our weight.'

'Harold,' said Sidney, 'the Fettlesham Show is an opportunity for farmers, landowners, local shopkeepers and craftsmen, and all manner of people involved in rural life to spend a week mounting displays and exhibitions, but why do we, as educationalists, have to be a part of this? It is nothing whatsoever to do with inspecting schools.'

'We go through the reasons every year, Sidney,' began Harold wearily but was, once more, interrupted by Mrs Savage.

'If I may, Dr Yeats,' interposed Mrs Savage. 'Dr Gore is very keen that the Education Department is represented at the show, as it has been for many years now. Education is always in the public eye and it gives us an opportunity to set out our stall, tell the general public what we are about, answer questions and give information about the schools and colleges in the county. It is an excellent public relations exercise for us.'

'Do you know, Mrs Savage,' said David, 'you have mentioned the words "us" and "we" several times, but I should point out that it is *this* team which has to do all the work. Dr Yeats has to man that wretched Education Tent all day, and I and my colleagues have all the exhibitions to mount.'

'May I remind you, Mr Pritchard,' said Mrs

143

Savage tartly, 'that there are some of us who work extremely hard behind the scenes dealing with all the administration.'

'And what administration would this be?' enquired Sidney.

'Look, this is getting us nowhere,' broke in Harold. 'I asked Gervase to collect together a few initial suggestions, Mrs Savage, and you will be pleased to hear that we will be organising the various exhibitions of children's work. However, I cannot, at this stage, promise very much more.'

'Dr Gore is particularly keen,' said Mrs Savage as if she had not heard, 'that this year we have a significant presence. Last year, it was a very small-scale contribution on our part compared with previous years. The art competition was, for some unaccountable reason, cancelled.'

'I can account for that, Mrs Savage, if you have five hours,' remarked Sidney.

'The sports events did not take place,' she continued blithely.

'With good reason,' said David.

'And the poetry competition was judged by some local poet rather than you, Mr Phinn.'

'Which can be fully explained,' I said.

'Now this year, Dr Gore hopes that all the activities of previous years, and indeed more, will be up and running, in addition of course to our advisory desk in the Education Tent. I shall, of course, be co-ordinating everything and if Dr Gore is in agreement, I should be only too happy to join you, Dr Yeats, in the tent on the day and give what help and support I can.' I smothered a grin as I saw Harold wince. 'I am sure that Dr Gore and I can rely on the inspectors to give this matter their full

144

and immediate attention.' Mrs Savage sat back in her chair, apparently finished.

Harold thought for a moment, stroked his chin and nodded sagaciously. 'The competition judging has always proved to be a little contentious. However, we will discuss it.' He thought for a moment. 'As you are aware, Mrs Savage, we have a vast amount of work on at the moment and there is, of course, the extra and unacceptably heavy load on our secretary.' He smiled, displaying his set of large white teeth. 'We shall have to see what we can do.'

The remainder of the afternoon, in which we discussed a whole range of tedious matters, seemed to drag interminably.

At six o'clock, Connie popped her head around the door. She had abandoned her pink nylon overall in favour of a large grey duffel coat with fur-trimmed hood, thick woollen scarf tied in an enormous knot under her chin and short green boots. She looked like an Eskimo. 'How long are you going to be?' she asked bluntly.

'Nearly finished, Connie,' said Harold.

'I'm locking up in ten minutes,' she told him. 'I'm just doing my rounds.'

'We won't be long now, Connie,' said Harold.

'It's getting very icy tonight so be careful on the path. I've put some salt and sand down but it's still very slippery. It's cold enough to freeze the flippers off an Arctic penguin out there.' Connie disappeared only to return a moment later. 'Oh, and whose is that fancy red sports car out the front?' She knew very well who the owner of the sports car was since she had asked the owner to remove it on many occasions.

'It's mine,' said Mrs Savage coldly. 'You may recall that you asked me earlier to park it well away from your entrance which I did. Is there something else?'

'Well, you've left your lights on,' said Connie.

'I sincerely hope you haven't got a flat battery, Mrs Savage,' said Sidney with mock concern in his voice. 'That *would* spoil your evening.'

CHAPTER EIGHT

It was the first week back after the Christmas break and the office was unusually quiet. Sidney was directing an art course at the Staff Development Centre, David was on a conference for mathematics inspectors, Harold was closeted with Dr Gore, no doubt discussing arrangements for the interviews for the Senior Inspector's post, and Julie was nowhere to be seen. So there was only Gerry and me in the office. I had not seen her alone since I had heard the news about her extended family at the golf club dinner before Christmas.

'So what sort of Christmas did you have?' she asked, looking up from her papers.

'Oh, rather more hectic than last year,' I replied. 'I spent a few days with Christine's parents in Shipley, meeting all the relations and doing the rounds of friends and neighbours, before going to my parents for Boxing Day and then we had a weekend to ourselves in Settle. We went to the same excellent hotel as we went to last Christmas— it is really comfortable and has marvellous food so we decided to go back. We walked for miles and spent hours discussing weddings and honeymoons and houses.'

'Of course, it's only a few months to go now before the big day, isn't it? Have you decided where you're going to live yet?'

'Well, Christine lives at home at the moment and I'm still in that poky little flat here in Fettlesham above the Rumbling Tum. I certainly won't miss the smell of chips wafting up the stairs every day and the noise of lorries off-loading in the High Street late at night and in the early hours of the morning. We really want somewhere in easy reach of both her school and County Hall. Ribsdyke is quite nice, Willingforth is lovely but expensive, Mertonbeck is a possibility but a bit out of the way. I really like Totterdale where you live but the houses are expensive and hard to come by. When the weather improves, we intend looking seriously.'

'What sort of house have you in mind?'

'Ideally, we'd like that small country cottage in honey-coloured stone with roses around the door, the one you see on postcards, with uninterrupted views of open countryside. Everybody else wants it, too, I'm afraid. We've got a mass of brochures from the estate agents and just love one particular cottage in Hawksrill but it is being sold at auction and one never knows what they will fetch. I expect we'll end up in a modern box on an estate in Fettlesham. I think that's the only place we'll be able to afford.'

'What about the job, have you heard anything about that? If you got the Senior Inspector's job, you would be able to afford more.'

'Not a thing. Harold says that the CEO will be sending out the letters inviting candidates for

147

interview this week, so I should know before Friday. I don't hold out a lot of hope after what Mrs Savage said. Of course, Harold hasn't said a word, just keeps staring at me inscrutably. In fact, the main reason for calling in this morning was to see if there was any news.'

When I saw that Gerry had not returned to her work, but was staring pensively out of the window, I asked, 'What about you, did you have a nice Christmas?'

'Yes, I did, thanks. Pretty quiet but very pleasant.' As usual, she wasn't giving much away.

'Did you go back to Ireland?'

'No, I stayed here.'

'By yourself?'

'Yes, well, no, I had friends round and . . . I had some family over. Gervase, you haven't seen the note Harold sent around about the Fettlesham Show, have you? I've put it down somewhere and can't lay my hands on it.'

'It's right there under your nose,' I said, pointing to the green memorandum that could not be missed.

'Oh, yes. I'm actually looking forward to taking part in the Fettlesham Show. I thought I'd get a group of students to demonstrate some practical technology work, perhaps mount an exhibition of children's writing and drawings on wildlife, animal conservation, that sort of thing. What do you think?'

Gerry clearly wanted to keep off the subject of what she had done over Christmas so I decided to probe no more. 'Sounds good,' I said, 'but I would go easy on the animal conservation bit. This is a fox-hunting and grouse-shooting county, you know, and there's some wildlife many of the locals are not very keen on preserving—pigeons and rooks, moles and rats, for example. I once made the great mistake of reading a Beatrix Potter story to group of infants most of whom lived on farms. "What a pity it would be if Mr McGregor caught poor little Peter Rabbit," I told them. It went down like a lead balloon. "Rabbits!" said one little lad. "We shoot 'em!"'

'I'll remember that,' said Gerry, laughing.

The clattering on the stairs signalled the imminent arrival of Julie. She entered a moment later with such a broad smile on her face that she resembled some manic clown.

'I could kiss that darling man!' she exclaimed. 'I could squeeze him to death. I don't know what he said to Mrs Savage but Dr Yeats is a miracle worker.'

'Someone's in a good mood,' said Gerry.

'That's because I've got an assistant to help me with all the paperwork and, wait for it—it's a he, a chap! He can type, file, do everything.'

'Wow!' laughed Gerry. 'A man!'

'Yes, there are more and more male secretaries, you know. I've not got him all to myself, mind. He's spending half his time with the psychologists downstairs and half his time with me up here. His name's Frank. You know, of all the people who have dealings with that dreadful woman, Dr Yeats is the best. He has her eating out of his hands.'

'It's called charm and patience,' said Gerry. 'Usually a highly successful formula.'

'I don't care what it's called. He's got me an assistant. Now, who's for a cup of coffee?'

'No, thanks, Julie,' I said, rising to go, 'I have a

full day in schools today so must be off. Actually, I only called in to see if there was any news on the interviews and to shift some of the paperwork. I'll be in tomorrow early. There's that course outline to finish, if you can get around to it today. It is pretty urgent, I'm afraid.'

'No worries,' replied Julie. 'I shall give it to Frank.'

*   *   *

Sister Brendan saw my car pull up outside her office window and moments later was at the entrance waiting to greet me.

'Good morning, Mr Phinn,' she said cheerfully, ushering me into the school.

'Good morning, Sister.'

'And have you had a restful Christmas?'

'Yes, indeed, and what about you?'

'Lovely. Now, I've put you with Mrs Webb and the juniors first thing. Then after morning playtime, you're with me and the little ones. Is that acceptable to you?'

'That's fine. And how *is* Mrs Webb?'

The last time I had inspected St Bartholomew's Roman Catholic Infants School in industrial Crompton, Mrs Webb had been absent. She had been on a guided tour of the Holy Land, called 'Walking in the Footsteps of Jesus', when she had fallen down a pothole and broken a leg. Monsignor Leonard had remarked to Sister later that had Mrs Webb been sensible and worn sandals, such as Jesus might have worn, she would not have found herself hospitalised in Jerusalem.

'I'm afraid her leg is still not right,' said Sister,

150

'but I have to say that Mrs Webb is a woman of great faith and fortitude. She is going on another pilgrimage this year, to Lourdes. She's not only a woman of great faith and fortitude, you know, Mr Phinn, she's also something of a martyr. Miss Fenoughty has signed up for the trip as well and Mrs Webb has agreed to sit next to her on the coach. I cannot imagine a worse penance than spending a long coach journey through France with deaf Miss Fenoughty at my side. I know it sounds uncharitable, but Miss Fenoughty would try the patience of a saint.'

Mrs Webb was waiting for me: she was a prim, red-faced woman with small quizzical eyes and sported a thick brown elastic stocking on one leg. Her classroom was bright and cheerful, the walls covered with glossy travel posters. In pride of place, on a small table at the front of the room, stood two plaster statues with small vases of fresh flowers before them. One statue was of the Virgin Mary, draped in a pale blue cloak and wearing a golden crown. She had large blue eyes and a gentle smile. The other was of Jesus who I noticed wore very substantial footwear, the sort of sandals that would stand up to the potholes of the Holy Land.

I spent an interesting time with Mrs Webb's junior class who were busy writing little poems on paper cut-outs of footsteps.

'Later, I shall type out all the poems and make a small anthology which the children can take home to their parents. I shall mount the original footsteps along the wall and call the display "Walking in the Footsteps of the Poet".'

I was tempted to say, 'Rather safer than "Walking in the Footsteps of Jesus"' but thought

151

better of it. Watching the teacher limping from desk to desk and recalling the account of her ill-fated journey to Jerusalem, I thought this rather an incongruous task to set the children.

For the remainder of the morning I joined the infants. They were busy painting, showing all the confidence and enthusiasm that only very young children and very experienced artists can do. At such a young age, children are totally uninhibited in their painting. They depict the world as a bright, bold, happy place full of round, pink, smiling faces, houses like smiling boxes and blue trees. They splash on colours with abandon, making great swirling curves and huge blobs with their brushes, they spatter and daub, smudge and smear and produce the most wonderful creations.

'Tell me about this,' I said to Mary, a small girl with a round saucer face. Her drawing depicted a brightly coloured, egg-like figure with long spidery fingers, kneeling before what looked like an immense coloured lake with tiny rocks, bits of driftwood and floating weed in it.

'It's someone saying a prayer,' explained the child.

'I see,' I said. 'And is this a lake?'

'No, that's the sick,' little Mary replied, dipping her brush into a large pot of mustard-coloured paint. 'She's saying a prayer for the sick.'

The next child I encountered, a serious-faced girl with more paint on herself than on the large piece of paper in front of her, had drawn what I thought was a snake. The long, multi-coloured creature curled and twisted across the page like a writhing serpent from a fairy story. It was a small masterpiece with intricate patterning and delightful

152

detail.

'That's a very colourful snake,' I commented.

'It's not a snake,' the child told me, putting down her brush and folding her little arms across her chest. 'It's a road.'

'It looks like a snake to me.'

'Well, it's not. It's a road. I know 'cos I painted it.'

'Ah, yes, I can see now,' I had said tactfully. 'Is it a magic road?'

'No.'

'It looks like a magic road to me.'

'Well, it isn't,' said the child. 'It's an ordinary road.'

'But it's full of greens and reds and blues. It, looks like a magic road. Perhaps it leads to an ice palace beyond the ragged clouds where the Snow Queen lives.'

The child observed me for a moment. 'It's an ordinary road and doesn't lead to any ice palace.'

'Why all the colours?' I asked, intrigued.

Her finger traced the curve of the road. 'Those are the diamonds and those the rubies and those are the emeralds,' she explained.

'It *is* a magic road!' I teased.

'No, it's not,' the child replied, 'it's a "jewel" carriageway.'

Having delivered another very positive report to Sister Brendan on what I had observed that morning, I discussed some of the children I had met. When I brought up Mary and her prayer for the sick, an enigmatic smile came to the nun's face.

'Ah yes,' said the nun, 'the very mention of that child's name always makes me recall a funny incident when I put my foot well and truly in it with

153

her father. I was travelling by train from York to Liverpool just after Mary had started here. The carriage was one of those old-fashioned ones where three people sit facing each other. I happened to choose a carriage full of businessmen on their way to work. The conversation stopped immediately I got in. Nuns often have that effect on people. They are either terrified of us or see us as soft touches for money. Anyhow, every man stood to offer me his seat but I was quite content to sit on the last seat, in the middle of one side. The conversation resumed but stuck to trivial topics like the weather and the amount of traffic on the roads. The man I was facing looked very familiar, much like Mr Ryan, Mary's father. He seemed to recognise me, too, because he kept smiling. After a while I thought I had better say something so I leaned towards him and said, "I have an idea you're the father of one of my children." Well, you could have cut the atmosphere with a knife.'

* * *

The afternoon visit to Tarncliffe Primary School was to see a probationary teacher. During their first year in the profession, teachers are carefully assessed and monitored and have to pass a period of induction. Part of my brief was to visit newly-qualified teachers in the county a number of times during the year, observe them teach and examine their lesson plans, schemes of work and record keeping. If everything was deemed satisfactory they passed. If not, the teacher could be referred for another year, or failed.

Tarncliffe Primary School was tucked between

the village shop and the grey brick Primitive Methodist chapel and didn't resemble a school at all. From the pavement, the door opened directly onto one large classroom and curious passers-by would often peer through the leaded windows to observe the pupils at work. On one occasion an elderly couple had walked in, thinking it was a café, in search of a pot of tea for two and a toasted teacake.

The headteacher, Miss Drayton, was one of those permanently optimistic and cheerful people whom nothing and no one seemed to dishearten or discourage. She was a totally dedicated teacher who ran an excellent school. Her former assistant, Mrs Standish, had retired the previous term and a new member of staff, Mr Hornchurch, had been appointed. My visit that afternoon was to assess the new teacher's competency. Prior to meeting Mr Hornchurch and observing his teaching, I sat with Miss Drayton in her small office to discuss his progress.

'Well, Mr Phinn,' she said, smiling, 'I've either got someone who will turn out to be brilliant or someone who will be a millstone about my neck. I knew it would be a bit of a risk when we made the appointment but Mr Hornchurch had something about him, something you couldn't put your finger on, that convinced me he would make an outstanding teacher. He just stood out from the rest who applied for the job. He's an enthusiast for a start, and I like enthusiasts because they get children to be enthusiastic. He's also very hard working and spends hours outside school time, organising trips, coaching the football team, getting together a group to go carol singing and much

much more. Standards in English and mathematics have soared since he started, and the children are book-mad.'

'He sounds amazing,' I said. 'What's the downside?'

'Well, to be perfectly blunt, he's eccentric. That's the only word for him. He's idiosyncratic, unpredictable, untidy and sometimes infuriating. He does the most brilliant thing one minute, like the project on astronomy when he had the whole class and their parents sitting in the playground in the middle of the night staring at the stars and identifying all the constellations. Then the following week he took the children on a school trip to the Wildlife Centre at Willowbank and failed to notice one child climbing into the pond area. After the child had got home and had his tea, he had been sent upstairs to get ready for bed. His mother discovered him sitting in the bath, surrounded by bubble suds, with a baby penguin paddling away merrily in there with him.'

Something told me that Miss Drayton rather admired Mr Hornchurch's idiosyncrasies, and relished recounting them.

'Yes, indeed,' she continued, 'I shall be very interested in your assessment of him.'

Dividing the one large room was a wooden partition with the infants, in the charge of Miss Drayton, in one half and the juniors with Mr Hornchurch in the other. The infant classroom was neat, clean and orderly with everything in its proper place. Walking through into Mr Hornchurch's classroom was like entering a completely different world. It was like an exotic junk shop—a mass of clutter and colour. There were boxes of every conceivable shape and size stacked in a corner, huge abstract art posters and paintings covering the walls, piles of books, a basket of footballs and cricket equipment, a trestle table full of interesting-looking objects. It was like a scene from *The Old Curiosity Shop*. In the centre of this confusion was Mr Hornchurch, lounging back against the teacher's desk, with his pupils sitting at theirs, watching him intently. He was a tall, pale-faced man in his early twenties, with an explosion of wild, woolly hair and a permanently startled expression.

'Do come in, Mr Phinn, and find a chair if you can. This is Mr Phinn, children, and he's a school inspector. Here to see if I'm any good as a teacher. That's right, Mr Phinn, isn't it? So, if he asks you what sort of teacher I am, you all have to tell him that I am absolutely brilliant. Now, sitting up straight, eyes front, everyone listening, please.'

I climbed over boxes and stacks of books, negotiated the basket of sports equipment, and found a chair tucked away in the corner next to the trestle table. While Mr Hornchurch was settling the children, I had an opportunity to look at the objects on the table. There were birds' skulls, old tins, bits of pottery, coins, little brass figures, curiously-shaped pebbles, fossils and shells, faded feathers, dried flowers, rusty keys—a fascinating pot-pourri of objects.

'I've taught the children something about the qualities of a good story, Mr Phinn,' the teacher explained to me. 'About the need for clear structure, a gripping opening paragraph, intriguing ending, authentic characterisation, significant detail, figurative language, imagery, etc. We've read and discussed some really interesting and descriptive extracts and I've now asked them to attempt something similar, something really colourful and vibrant and full of atmosphere. OK, OK, let's get on.'

It sounded to me far too advanced for the children in the class but I was in for a surprise. The lesson I observed was one of the best I had ever seen. The pupils were encouraged to give their opinions, and each contribution was evaluated by the teacher who constantly challenged the children to justify their points of view.

'How would you have felt if you had been the person in this story, Monty?' he asked. 'What do you think I meant in this sentence, Mandy?' 'Can you explain why this character decides to do this, Lucy?'

The children then began writing their own stories and the quality of the writing that I saw as I walked round was remarkably good. Child after child produced work of a high standard. One boy, who frequently consulted his dictionary before scribbling away, passed his paper over for me to see. 'We've all been asked to write a descriptive paragraph in a different genre,' he explained.

'Genre?' I repeated.

'You know, different varieties of writing—science fiction, mystery, adventure, historical. I've written a ghost story.' Not only was the boy's piece extremely vivid, it was also neat and accurate.

'Are you really a school inspector?' asked the boy when I had finished reading it, and had congratulated him.

'Yes, I am.'

'And are you really here to see if Mr Hornchurch is a good teacher?'

I tried to evade the question. 'Well, I'm really interested in how well you pupils are doing.'

'But you have to do a report on him?'

'I don't discuss teachers with pupils,' I explained, 'but I do report on the lesson, yes.'

'Well he's a really good teacher and I'm not saying that because he told us to. I didn't much enjoy school before this year. I never used to like reading and writing and now I do. I can read better, my mum can now read my writing, and my mental arithmetic is miles better.'

'I'm pleased to hear it,' I said.

'This year, we've been to castles and museums, the fire station and a wildlife centre, all sorts of interesting places. School was all right before Mr Hornchurch came, but now it's brilliant.'

I quizzed the boy about the books he had read, his knowledge of grammar and punctuation, tested his spelling, asked him what he knew about history and geography and about the amount of homework he received. He was obviously receiving a broad, balanced and appropriate education.

'Mr Hornchurch is . . .' He paused for a moment as if struggling to find the right words. 'Well, he's different, you know, not like lots of teachers . . . he's a bit . . . well, different, but he's really good. Do you know what I mean?'

'Yes,' I replied, 'I know what you mean.'

Towards the end of the afternoon Mr Hornchurch instructed the children to put away their folders, which they did without a murmur, and to sit up straight. He then climbed onto his desk, crossed his legs and, much to my amazement, proceeded to place a large cardboard box on his head which had been adapted to resemble a

159

television set. There was a cut away square (the screen) and various felt blobs (the knobs).

'Will someone please turn me on?' he asked pleasantly.

One of the boys came to the front and made a clicking sound as he 'turned him on'.

'Hello, children,' began the teacher in the voice of the storyteller. 'Welcome to the world of the story. My story today is about the child who could not cry. Once, many, many years ago . . .'

Along with the entire class, I sat completely transfixed as Mr Hornchurch related a captivating folk tale, using a range of accents. When the story ended, the same boy came to the front and 'turned him off'.

What was I going to say to this wildly eccentric but obviously very talented young teacher? I thought to myself. His classroom was a mess, the lesson plans were scrappy, his planning virtually non-existent and the record system of no practical use at all. And yet the standard of education was high, the range of work wide and challenging and the quality of the teaching quite outstanding.

'You see, Mr Phinn,' explained the teacher after the children had filed out of the classroom to make their way home, 'children these days live in a television culture. The average eleven-year-old, you know, watches thirty hours of television a week. We've got to get them to read, haven't we, but more importantly to encourage them to become life-long readers and enjoy books. I find that if I pretend to be a television set, lift the text from the page so to speak, the children listen better.' I was lost for words. 'So how was my lesson then, Mr Phinn?' he asked. 'Will I do?'

160

'Before I give you the feedback on the lesson, Mr Hornchurch,' I began, 'perhaps you might remove the box.'

*   *   *

When I arrived back in the office that afternoon, Julie popped her head round the door and told me Harold wanted to see me as soon as I got back.

I knew it was going to be news about the interviews and whether I had been shortlisted or not. I felt terribly nervous and spent a few moments unpacking my briefcase in order to calm myself.

Harold looked up as I entered. 'Ah, Gervase, yes, do come in. I am glad—er, good that we have been able to find a time to talk. Er, have you had a good day today?'

'Thank you, yes,' I replied. I could see by his expression and tell by his uncharacteristic fumbling for words that he was about to tell me that I had not been put on the shortlist.

'I'm not on the shortlist, am I?' I said.

'I'm afraid not,' he replied.

'Oh,' was all I could muster up to say.

'Dr Gore will, no doubt, be having a personal word with you but wanted me to break the news. The fact is, as Mrs Savage was at excruciating pains to point out at our last full meeting, the calibre of applicant for this position has been particularly high and all have considerably more experience than you. You have only been a school inspector a little over two years and Dr Gore and the Education Sub-Committee felt you needed more time in the job before you can aspire to a senior

161

position of this kind.' Harold rubbed the side of his nose with a forefinger. 'I have to say, Gervase, that I agree with them.'

'I see.'

'You are only a relatively young man and have a long career ahead. I expect you are very disappointed with this news but your time will come. I really feel you have a field marshal's baton in your knapsack.'

'Thanks, Harold,' I said quietly. 'I thought it was a bit of a long shot when I sent in the application. I suppose, deep down, I knew I'd have little chance for the reasons you've just given. I just felt it was worth a try.'

'As I'm sure you know,' continued Harold, 'Dr Gore values your work highly, as I do, so don't be too downhearted. If I may be quite blunt, we often learn more from our failures than from our successes. The other point you should know is that the Sub-Committee felt that the inspectorate would benefit from an outside appointment.'

'I see.'

'To be frank, Gervase—and this is my personal opinion—I think you will have quite enough on this year what with your wedding and setting up a new home, without having to manage the team which is not an easy job, as well you know. There are endless meetings, late nights and weekends away from home. Not the sort of life-style for a newly-married man. I did think, when you said you were applying, of having a quiet word with you but decided not to in case it discouraged you.'

'So, what are the five candidates like?' I asked. 'Or aren't you allowed to say?'

'No, I'm not in a position to say anything at this

stage. You, along with the rest of the team, will be meeting the shortlisted candidates later this month when they come for interview. I won't be directly involved in the appointment this time. That will be done by Dr Gore and the Sub-Committee but we will all have the opportunity of meeting the candidates prior to the interviews when they will be shown around. All I can tell you is that, as I said, the field is very good. All the applicants are in senior positions at the moment, all are well qualified and have substantial experience—perhaps this might make you feel a little better, knowing the competition you were up against. Don't let this get you down. Your time will surely come.'

'Thanks, Harold,' I said. Then, attempting to push the disappointment to the back of my mind, I asked, 'Do you have a few more minutes? There is another matter I wanted your advice on.'

'Of course. Fire away.'

Driving back to the office that afternoon, I had realised I was in a considerable dilemma over what to do about young Mr Hornchurch. All the things he should have had in place were simply not there: clear planning, detailed documentation, careful record-keeping, an orderly classroom—and yet his results were well above average, his teaching was very good, and the children were making excellent progress in their work; above all, they were all immensely motivated.

Harold sat hunched over his desk, his head cupped in his large hands, listening intently as I described my visit to Tarncliffe School. When I had finished, he steepled his fingers in the familiar fashion, and said, 'I've come across this sort of teacher before and they are the devil's own job to

163

deal with, but the bottom line is this. Do the children in his care get a good education? I think it's as simple as that. Are his lessons interesting, challenging, broadly based? Does he thoroughly know the subjects he teaches, and does he develop the children's knowledge, skills and understanding of them? Does he achieve high standards, have good discipline, mark children's books carefully and constructively? If he is doing all that, then he is doing more than many. The most important thing, Gervase, as you well know, is the teaching, not the paperwork or the neatness of his classroom. Everything pales into insignificance compared with the quality and effectiveness of the teaching. You can have the most efficient, well-organised, meticulously tidy teacher but if he can't teach then he might as well pack his briefcase and go home.'

I nodded. Would I ever be as wise an inspector as Harold? I thought.

'You see, Gervase, we don't want a profession of clones. Teachers are as different as any other professionals. Look at our office and how different we all are. I know for a fact that my successor will be very different from me. He or she will want to make changes, stamp a new identity on things, highlight different priorities. I know also that I shall be remembered, affectionately, I hope, for a few weeks and then forgotten. Life will go on. None of us is indispensable. We are all different and that is what makes the world so interesting. You and David and Geraldine might think at times that I'm a little easy on Sidney, putting up with his comments, letting him climb on his bandwagons and ramble on about his likes and dislikes. Well, Sidney is like your Mr Hornchurch. He can be the bane of one's life—unpredictable, short-tempered, mercurial, full of schemes and projects and mad ideas—but, deep down, I know he is passionate about his subject, about education and about children. You cannot stifle that creativity. Sidney's an enthusiast and we need enthusiasts in education. That's why I put up with his constant badinage, his moods and his idiosyncrasies, because I know the calibre of the man and how effective he really is. To confine and cramp that sort of personality would destroy so much good. He needs channelling, he requires a light touch on the tiller, not a heavy hand on his shoulder. Had you been successful and taken over from me, handling Sidney would have been no easy matter, as my successor will soon discover. So I would say to this young man at Tarncliffe: "You are in many ways an exceptional teacher but you have to conform to some extent. Tidy up your room, plan your lessons better so people like us can see what the pupils have been doing, keep records so parents can see what progress their children are making, but, above all, continue to be imaginative, enthusiastic—and different."'

On my way back to the main office, I decided that no new Senior Inspector could ever be quite as understanding and tolerant as Harold. I was so deep in thought that I bumped into a young man carrying a stack of files. He looked as if he had walked straight out of a fashion magazine.

'Hi!' he said. 'I'm Frank.'

'Gervase Phinn,' I said. 'Pleased to meet you.'

'Ah, Mr Phinn—you'll find the course outline you wanted typing on your desk. Anything else just pop in my in-tray. See you later.'

With that, he headed down the stairs, whistling.

*   *   *

When I got back to the office, my three colleagues had returned from their various school visits and, presumably primed by Julie as to my whereabouts, were hanging around to hear my news.

'Well?' asked Sidney.

'No, I'm not on the shortlist,' I replied, slumping into my chair and sighing.

'Oh, that's tough,' said Gerry, and came over and placed a hand on my arm. 'I'm really sorry.'

'Yes, a damn shame,' said David. 'Did Harold give a reason?'

'Not enough experience,' I replied.

'Well, that's true enough,' said Sidney. 'You've not been in the job five minutes.'

'That's right,' said David, 'put your extensive and sensitive counselling skills to good use, and make a man feel better. He wants some sympathy and understanding, not you telling him that he shouldn't have applied in the first place.'

'In actual fact, it was I who encouraged Gervase to go for the job. I think he would have made a pretty good Senior Inspector but, it has to be admitted, he is inexperienced. Anyway, it's not the end of the world, is it? He might have changed had he become our boss—all serious and demanding and full of his own importance. I'm sure your old Welsh grandmother would say to him if she were here, which I am thankful that she is not, that it is probably for the best.'

'She would almost certainly have said,' David reposted, '"If you get knocked to the floor, pick yourself up, dust yourself down and start all over again." '

'She could have made a mint writing lyrics for Hollywood musicals, your old Welsh grandmother,' said Sidney. 'Ah! I think I detect a small smile on our colleague's face,' he continued, looking over at me.

'You know, Gervase, life's problems are all relative,' said David, taking off his spectacles which was a sure sign that I was going to hear one of his homilies. 'Take my friend, Owen Wynn-Jones. Highly successful doctor, JP, captain of the golf club this year, president of the Fettlesham Rotary Club. Got everything going for him and then he receives this letter from his daughter, Bronwen, who's at a top-class girls' independent boarding school in Wales. "Dear Daddy", she wrote. "I think you should sit down before you read on." No parent wants to receive a letter starting like that, I can tell you. "I'm pregnant," she wrote. "In fact, I'm expecting twins." Owen, of course, was devastated, completely devastated. "Do you remember when I hurt my ankle playing lacrosse and went to hospital," continued his daughter, "and the headmistress wrote to say I had to stay in overnight? Well, that's when I met Shane. He was coming out of the Drug Rehabilitation Unit and we got talking and I fell in love with him. It was love at first sight." Anyhow, the girl goes on to tell poor old Owen that this Shane is the father of the twins, that people don't take to him because of his aggressive appearance—shaven head, facial tattoos and extensive body piercing etc. And it got worse. She wrote that he was trying to kick his heroin addiction and had an imminent court appearance for burglary. Owen, by this time, was a quivering wreck. "I want so much for you and Mummy to meet him before his court case," continued Bronwen, "and come to love him as I do, because he will probably be sent back to prison. What I would really like is for us to get married and have the reception at the golf club with all our family and friends." It couldn't get much worse could it?' said David, looking at each one of us in turn. '"I hope you still love me, Daddy," she ended. "Much love, Bronwen." Well, of course, old Owen was near to collapse at this stage. Then his eye caught a small PTO at the bottom of the page. He turned over and found an additional sentence. "All of what I have just told you is complete and utter rubbish," his daughter had written, "but I've failed my exams again and want you to get things in perspective."'

*   *   *

As soon as the other inspectors had gone home, I telephoned Christine at Winnery Nook School.

'I'm really quite relieved,' she said. 'I think we will both have more than enough on our plates this year without the extra pressures of a new job.'

'Yes, I know, that's what you said before, and it's what Harold has just said.'

'You're not too disappointed, are you, darling?'

'Well, I am a bit. I thought I might have got an interview at the very least. It's a bit of a knock to my ego, isn't it? Not even called for interview. I just hope Harold's successor is as easy to work for and as supportive as he's been.'

'As you know, I'm stuck here this evening for a governors' meeting, but it should be finished by eight-thirty. Why don't I take you out then and you can drown your sorrows?' After a moment, when I didn't answer, she said, 'Gervase, are you still there?'

'Yes, I'm still here.'

'So, shall we go for a drink?'

'Yes, all right.'

'Well, you don't sound all that enthusiastic,' she chided. 'Cheer up! It's not the end of the world. Incidentally, I went round to the estate agent's at lunchtime, and have got some interesting brochures to show you.'

'OK.'

'Our dream cottage might be amongst them, darling.'

'Yes, of course.'

'With honey-coloured stone walls and a grey slate roof—and roses round the door and a view across the dale.' She was trying so very hard to cheer me up.

'Sorry, Christine,' I said, snapping out of it. 'I must sound a real misery guts. Of course, we'll go out tonight and forget all about the job.'

'Fine, see you at the school at about eight-thirty, then.'

'Oh, and there was something else,' I told her.

'Oh dear,' sighed Christine. 'This sounds ominous. What is it?'

'I love you,' I said.

'Aaah,' Christine said softly, and put down the telephone.

169

CHAPTER NINE

The Lady Cavendish High School for Girls was built at the end of the last century, paid for by an industrialist who had accumulated his enormous wealth through the wool industry and who wanted to leave his mark in the world. Sir Cosmo Cavendish, who had had little formal education himself but had a real talent for making money, had endowed a boys' grammar school which he had named after himself; a few years later, he had funded a girls' high school which took his wife's name. Like the boys' school, the girls' High was a vast over-decorated pile with red-brick towers and turrets, parallel rows of sightless mullioned windows and distinctly lacked charm. I was there to spend a day with David and Gerry inspecting the core subjects of English, mathematics and science. When Harold had notified the headmistress of our impending visit, she had been less than enthusiastic, so we were not expecting a particularly warm welcome.

The walk up to the main building from the visitors' car park was exceptionally pleasant that bright morning in late February and I was in excellent spirits. I was quickly getting over my disappointment about the Senior Inspector's post and was determined to remain optimistic about the future. After all, in less than two months Christine and I would be married. On that sunny morning all seemed right with the world. The air was fresh, the sun warm on my face, the sky vast and blue; the almond trees just outside the car park were

170

speckled with a delicate blossom, and I noticed clumps of daffodil leaves were pushing up through the grass bordering the carefully combed gravel path.

I paused at the large dull-bronze statue of the school's founder, identical to the one which dominated the entrance to the boys' school. Sir Cosmo stood on a large plinth, hands on hips, legs apart and chin jutting out as if to say to the world: 'Now then, look at me. I am somebody to be reckoned with.' The statue was so enormously vulgar that it was obvious Sir Cosmo had been a man with a pathological desire to be in the public eye and to be remembered. The effect of coming face-to-face with the imposing figure was rather diminished at this particular moment, for, perched on the monumental head, was a fat pigeon pecking at a piece of bread in its claw.

The entrance to the school, through a great archway shaped like a yawning mouth, was forbidding. Stone steps rose between baroque pillars to a heavy oak double door the size of which would not have disgraced a cathedral. The reception area was cool and silent and smelt unpleasantly of disinfectant, lavender floor polish and school dinners. There seemed to be a great deal of wood everywhere: heavy, dark-panelled walls, a well-worn but highly polished wood-block floor, and long wooden shelves on which huge silver cups and shields were displayed, together with ranks of photographs of stern headmistresses in black gowns and rows of unsmiling girls; all these were set in identical heavy wooden frames. A forest must have fallen to furnish the school, I thought to myself.

171

I pressed the buzzer on the reception desk and a moment later the frosted glass slid back slowly and I faced an elderly woman with thin bloodless lips and a fuzz of white hair.

'Good morning. May I help you?' she asked.

'Good morning,' I replied. 'My name is Mr Phinn and I'm from the Education Office.'

'Is the headmistress expecting you?'

'Indeed she is,' I replied.

The woman ran a long finger down a register before her. 'Ah, yes, here you are, Mr Phinn, right at the bottom of my list. Would you take a seat and I will tell Miss Bronson's secretary you have arrived.'

A minute later I followed the secretary's respectfully hurrying footsteps along a narrow, green-tiled corridor with its curiously pervasive smell of dust. A flood of white sunlight poured through a high window, slanting in long bars across the musty air and onto the floor. The woman made no effort to engage me in conversation.

'It's a lovely day,' I remarked finally.

'Yes, it is,' she replied, stepping ahead purposefully.

Up a long curving staircase with highly-polished mahogany banisters and stone steps we went and then down another narrow, green-tiled corridor.

'I wonder if I might wash my hands,' I said.

She stopped in her tracks and turned to face me. 'Yes, of course,' she replied stiffly. 'There's a cloakroom just off the corridor here.' She gestured down yet another corridor. 'I'll wait here.'

The cloakroom was just that, a small room with a row of black metal pegs along the wall, two large cupboards and a washbasin. There was no lavatory. I emerged a moment later and informed the secretary, with not a little embarrassment, that it was a lavatory I really wanted.

'Oh,' she said, rather taken aback, 'well, if it was the lavatory you needed you should have said.' She shook her head and made a sort of clucking noise. 'We will have to return to the reception area. There's only the girls' lavatories up here.' Off she set again, her heels clicking on the wooden floor. 'I do wish people would make themselves clear,' she sighed as she headed down the stairs with me in pursuit.

Following my ablutions and another journey through the labyrinth and up the stairs, I was shown into the headmistress's study—a large, opulent room, panelled in light oak and carpeted and curtained in deepest blue. A bookcase, which covered one entire wall, was crammed with dull-covered volumes and dominating the whole area was a huge roll-top desk, behind which Miss Bronson was sitting magisterially with her hands clasped before her. David and Gerry were perched facing her on uncomfortable mahogany chairs with high arm rests and looked like naughty children in front of the headteacher for misbehaving. There was an empty chair next to them.

Miss Bronson rose to greet me. She was a thin, slightly stooped woman with a pale indrawn face, narrow dark eyes and thick iron-grey hair cut in a bob. A voluminous black gown was draped around her shoulders. 'Do come in, Mr Phinn,' she said in a very upper-class accent.

'Good morning,' I said, reaching forward to shake a small cold hand. I smiled and nodded at David and Gerry.

'We now have the full complement,' announced

the headmistress. 'I am not sure what the collective noun is for school inspectors. Perhaps you, as the English specialist, might enlighten me, Mr Phinn. A "threat" of inspectors, maybe?' She gave me a watery smile, revealing a remarkably fine set of even teeth. 'Would you like to have a seat and we can talk about the day, briefly I should say, because I have to take the morning assembly in ten minutes or so.'

'I was just explaining to Miss Bronson before you arrived, Mr Phinn,' said David, 'that we are hoping to observe a range of lessons in the course of the day, evaluate the teaching, look at the students' books and folders and present a combined written report to reach the school within the next few days.'

Miss Bronson listened to him with a kind of half-amused detachment before leaning forward and responding. 'And I was endeavouring to enquire of Mr Pritchard what exactly is the purpose of this visit. You are aware, Mr Phinn, as I am sure your two colleagues are as well, that we achieve the very best results in the county and we have done so for a number of years. Indeed, we are one of the most academically successful schools nationally and there is a ridiculously long waiting list of gels wishing to come here. Ninety-nine per cent pass rate last year. Twenty-four gels went up to Oxford or Cambridge and the great majority of the rest went on to higher education elsewhere. We beat all the local independent schools into a cocked hat and are quietly confident that this performance will be replicated this coming summer.'

'Yes, indeed, Miss Bronson, I am fully aware of the excellent results,' I said.

'And as I was also explaining to your colleagues, Mr Phinn,' she continued, giving a sigh which expressed both impatience and amusement, 'when the gels start here, they get a good grinding—'

'I'm sorry?' I said, startled.

'We give the gels a good grinding.'

'Ah yes, a good grounding,' I repeated, trying to keep a straight face.

'That's what I said, a good grinding in the basics and then we develop their abilities and aptitudes, enabling them to reach their full potential. Gels are sent to this school in order that, by dint of our solid and rigorous teaching, by discipline of mind and body, by the example and unstinting support of my staff, they may develop into the very best type of woman: confident, independent, strong-minded, honest and fair. Because of our reputation and our outstanding results, I think it would be reasonable to extrapolate that the teaching is of the very best at this school. The parents are highly satisfied with the calibre of my teaching staff, the governors are more than happy and the gels, I am sure you will discover, find their lessons both challenging and interesting.' A shaft of sunlight fell across her pale face and gave it the appearance of wax.

'It is important, don't you think, Miss Bronson,' said Gerry, 'to have an outside, objective view of things—an external audit if you like—to see how things are going?' The headmistress looked pensive but did not reply. Gerry continued, 'We are in a position, since we visit many schools and observe a great deal of good practice, to advise and support teachers and help them improve their teaching.'

The headmistress's expression remained one of detached interest, like that of a connoisseur glancing down an unfamiliar wine list. 'I have to be honest, Dr Mullarkey,' she replied in her quietly commanding voice, 'and I say this without, I hope, giving any offence, I really do feel that school inspectors would be more usefully employed visiting failing schools and giving the benefit of their advice and support to the unfortunate teachers who have to struggle with recalcitrant and disaffected adolescents, instead of spending their time telling me something which I'm sure I already know.'

'It is possible, Miss Bronson,' I said, 'that the girls here succeed in spite of less than satisfactory teaching.'

The headmistress slowly transferred her stare from Gerry to me. She looked me full in the face, not angrily but with an intense and overpowering gaze. 'Less than satisfactory teaching?' she said in her quiet, controlled tone of voice. 'By that, I imagine you mean poor teaching. I think if you were to say to my Chairman of Governors that there is poor teaching at Lady Cavendish's, Mr Phinn, it would have a similar effect as announcing that God did not exist in sixteenth-century Spain.'

'I am not for one minute suggesting that there *is* poor teaching at this school, Miss Bronson,' I said, shifting uneasily on the unyielding mahogany chair, 'but it is quite conceivable to have a weak teacher who gets excellent results because her students are intelligent, motivated and ambitious and come from massively supportive homes.'

Miss Bronson sat for a moment in thoughtful silence and then smiled, displaying her splendid set of very white teeth. She fixed me with a sceptical look. 'Don't imagine for a moment that teaching

176

the able pupil is an easy task. The bright gel can be as difficult, awkward and demanding as any other gel, often more so. She has a sharp, enquiring mind and often will argue and present her views quite forcefully. The bright gel does not suffer poor teachers gladly, I can assure you of that. It is also a popular misconception that those who attend a grammar school can be taught by cardboard representations of teachers because they are intelligent, well behaved, keen and committed. Pupils need to be taught whether they are of high academic ability or not.' I opened my mouth to continue the discussion but caught David's eye and thought better of it. I gave Miss Bronson my fullest and most charming of smiles. She glanced at her wristwatch. 'We could debate this endlessly, but time is getting on. As a county school I am obliged to grant you entry, so discussion of the rights and wrongs of your visit is merely academic. I just felt I ought to make my views plain. I believe I lead and manage a first-rate staff of teachers and I know their strengths and weaknesses intimately. It would be a poor headteacher who did not.' Miss Bronson stood and collected some papers and the Bible which were on her desk. 'My secretary will give you each a programme of lessons for the day. Perhaps you might like to join me for tea at four o'clock to share your deliberations. Now, I am taking assembly and I would very much like you to join me on the stage so I can introduce you to the staff and to the gels.'

With that, the headmistress swept around the desk, her gown billowing and undulating about her ankles, and marched for the door.

The school hall, a vast barn of a room, with a

mock hammerbeam roof, a gallery and an imposing stage, was packed from front to back with girls. All were dressed immaculately in identical white blouses, bottle-green pinafore dresses with bright yellow sashes and thick brown stockings. Around the sides of the hall were the sentinel staff wearing black gowns and sober expressions.

The whole congregation stood in complete silence as Miss Bronson, with considerable dignity, strode down the central aisle, her black gown flapping behind her, climbed the steps to the stage and strode purposefully to the large wooden lectern. Gerry, David and I followed her at a cracking pace, down the aisle, up the steps and onto the stage where we stood, somewhat embarrassed, at the side.

'Good morning, school,' said the headmistress in a loud, commanding voice.

'Good morning, Miss Bronson,' the girls and staff responded equally loudly.

'Before I begin this morning's assembly, gels, I should like to introduce three important visitors to our school.' She turned in our direction and gestured with a wave of her hand. 'This is Dr Mullarkey, Mr Pritchard and Mr Phinn. They are inspectors.' She paused for effect. 'They are school inspectors and they will be with us for the day, joining lessons, talking to you about your work and scrutinising your books. I would like them to depart . . .' she paused, 'with a very favourable impression of the students of the Lady Cavendish High School, which has a deserved reputation for high academic standards, outstanding sporting achievements and excellent dramatic productions.' She had to get that in, I thought to myself. Miss Bronson gave a smug

178

smile; she was obviously feeling quite pleased with herself. She continued: 'Should the inspectors ask you anything, I am certain that you will answer them in your usual clear, confident and courteous manner, befitting the students at Lady Cavendish's, and should they look lost . . .' she paused again, 'I am sure you will be able to tell them where to go.' Just what sort of day were we in for? I thought. 'You may sit,' ordered the headmistress.

The girls, as if some invisible lever had been pulled, sat in one perfect synchronised movement. The three of us remained standing prominently at the edge of the stage like spare parts, not knowing what to do with our hands or where to look. The eyes of the entire school were focused on us.

'I feel as if I'm part of some school production standing here,' whispered David out of the corner of his mouth. 'Could we get off the stage, do you think?'

Before I could respond, Miss Bronson shuffled her papers and opened the Bible. 'Now, our assembly this morning . . .' she began, and then caught sight of the three of us standing like totem poles.

'Oh, I'm sorry,' she said. 'Could we have three chairs for the school inspectors?'

Her request was followed immediately by three hearty cheers of 'Hip, hip, hooray!'

*   *   *

The first lesson of the day I attended was with Miss Bridges, the Head of the English Faculty, who was taking the fifth form for poetry. From the earlier conversation with the headmistress, I was rather

179

expecting a frosty welcome but found the very opposite. Miss Bridges, a woman not dissimilar to the headteacher in looks and bearing, welcomed me like a long-lost friend and shook my hand vigorously as soon I was through the door to her classroom.

'Now, girls,' she said to the class with jovial earnestness, 'we are very fortunate to have with us this morning Mr Phinn, whom you will remember seeing on the stage earlier and who is something of an expert on English.' She turned and beamed at me. 'It is a real pleasure to have you with us, Mr Phinn, and we do hope that you will join in our discussions of the poems we are studying.'

'Good morning,' I said. 'I'll sit at the back, if I may.'

'Wherever suits you, Mr Phinn,' said the teacher. 'Go whither you wish. Just make yourself comfortable. It will be most interesting, will it not, girls, to have a male perspective on our reflections?'

'Yes, Miss Bridges,' chorused the class.

'Now,' said the teacher brightly, 'Rebecca, perhaps you could give Mr Phinn a précis of what we have been doing.'

A tall girl with long dark brown locks tied back neatly in a pony-tail, turned to face me. 'Over the year, we have been reading and discussing the poems in the anthology which we have to study for our exam this coming June. We have covered sections on "Childhood", "Friendship", "Hopes and Dreams", "Sons and Daughters" and now we are on the final section called "Reminiscences".'

'Thank you, Rebecca,' said Miss Bridges. 'Take over please, Ruth.'

Another smart young woman turned to face me. 'We have all been asked by Miss Bridges to select one of the poems from the last section and do a presentation on it. We have read all the poems through in class and, with one or two exceptions, we all found them very dull and dreary. Most of them are about death. Miss Bridges said she has seen more life and laughter at a state funeral, didn't you, miss?'

The teacher gave a small embarrassed smile.

'I suppose the examiners think that such poems will encourage deeper study and greater discussion than lighter verse,' I hazarded. 'More to get your teeth into.'

'Amusing poems can have depth and lead to interesting discussions,' retorted the girl. 'Don't you think?'

I was reminded of the headmistress's earlier words about the students having sharp, enquiring minds and their predilection for arguing and presenting their views quite forcefully. 'Yes, indeed they can,' I conceded and decided to keep a low profile from then on.

'So most of the poems we have looked at,' continued the pupil, flicking through the book on her desk, 'are pretty depressing. There's "Come not when I am dead", a really morbid poem by Alfred, Lord Tennyson, a rather over-rated poet in our opinion. Then there's "Death of a Recluse" by George Darley, for whom death seems to be a way of life. "Lament for the Death of Thomas Davis" by Samuel Ferguson, an Irish writer who succeeds in lowering our spirits to the point of suicide. And "A Poison Tree" by William Blake. Not a barrel of laughs. None of us have picked these because they were universally unpopular.'

'"Has picked", Ruth. Don't forget "none" takes

the singular,' chided Miss Bridges.

'Sorry, miss,' said Ruth.

'All the poems, with the exception of four, were written by men, all of whom are dead,' said the girl at the next desk. 'I don't understand why examiners choose such depressing writers. Why can't they put in some funny poems, like Ruth said, by poets who are still alive? People of our age enjoy amusing poems. Death is the last thing on your minds when you are sixteen.'

'Young people have aspirations,' said Miss Bridges philosophically, 'old people have memories. The young have dreams, the old have visions. It has been ever thus.'

'Young people never think about death, though, Miss Bridges,' said another pupil. 'Old people think about little else. My grandma is forever talking about the fact she's well past her three score years and ten.'

'Tell Mr Phinn, Sarah, what we are doing today,' prompted the teacher. I could tell that she felt the discussion was leading us away from the point of the lesson.

'We have all chosen a poem that we liked and we have been asked to learn it,' continued the girl. 'We have to say why we chose it, what we like about it, what parts we did not understand and then be prepared to answer some questions.'

'Do you feel that is a reasonable activity, Mr Phinn?' asked the teacher.

'Yes, certainly I do,' I replied, genuinely looking forward to what promised to be a most interesting lesson. So often I sit at the back of a classroom listening to the teacher dominating the lesson with a very passive group of pupils not confident enough

182

to challenge a view or offer a personal opinion. It would be quite a change, I thought to myself, to hear the students doing the lion's share of the talking and, from what I had heard so far, I imagined that they would have quite a bit to say. I could tell that these pupils would, as the Yorkshire saying goes, 'not be backwards in coming forwards'.

'Now, Bethany,' said Miss Bridges, 'I think it is your turn, so if you would like to tell us all about the poem you have chosen?'

A small girl, sandy-haired with saucer eyes behind green-framed glasses went to the front of the room. 'Well it's one of the more depressing ones, Miss Bridges, I'm afraid, but I really like it. Actually, it made me cry. It's called "Requiescat" and it's simple and poignant, has a gentle rhythm and very effective rhymes. It's by Oscar Wilde.'

'Most people think of Oscar Wilde as a very flamboyant figure,' said the teacher, 'with his fancy clothes and green carnation in his buttonhole, the author of witty plays like *The Importance of Being Earnest*, but he could write some very melancholy poems and this is one. Off you go then, Bethany.'

'I suppose some people might think this poem is very sentimental,' said the girl, 'but Oscar Wilde wrote it when he was only thirteen years old, just after his little sister, Isola, had died of a fever. So, here goes. "Requiescat" by Oscar Wilde.' The girl then recited the poem in a slow, soft tone of voice, ending, a few moments later, with:

> Peace, peace, she cannot hear
> Lyre or sonnet,
> All my life's buried here,
> Heap earth upon it.

There followed an animated and intelligent discussion of the poem, in which the whole class joined, the teacher occasionally interrupting to clarify a point, ask a probing question, challenge a view or offer a comment. She was positive, encouraging, good humoured and moved the discussion along at a good pace.

The next student had picked an equally melancholy piece of verse, 'Requiem' by Robert Louis Stevenson. She recited it with superb timing:

> Under the wide and starry sky,
> Dig the grave and let me lie.
> Glad did I live and gladly die,
> And I laid me down with a will.
>
> This is the verse you grave for me:
> 'Here he lies where he longed to be;
> Home is the sailor, home from sea,
> And the hunter home from the hill.'

'And what do you understand by that line, "And I laid me down with a will"?' asked the teacher. 'A bit tricky, that. Any ideas?'

A very studious-looking young woman at the front raised a hand. 'The line is ambiguous, isn't it, Miss Bridges?' she said.

'I think I would agree there, Daisy,' said the teacher. 'Would you like to hazard a guess as to its meaning?'

'It could mean that he had a determination to die, an intention to give up, in a way welcoming death after an interesting and fulfilling life. Some people when they get old and tired feel that they are ready to die. I remember my great-grandmother reached ninety just after my great-grandpa had died. She just lost the will to live after that, and a couple of weeks later died herself. She told my mother that she was going to see George—that was my grandpa's name—turned her face to the wall and just closed her eyes. She never feared death. There was nothing medically wrong with her—she just felt it was time for her to go. She "laid herself down with a will". It might mean this. It might, on the other hand, have a literal meaning, that he was actually buried with his will, with his last will and testament placed in the coffin with him. Perhaps he had a sense of humour and by taking the will with him had the last laugh on those hoping to inherit all his money.'

'It's an original speculation, certainly, Daisy,' remarked the teacher.

'It would mean, Miss Bridges,' added the girl, 'that he died intestate.'

The girl at the next desk to me pulled a face, leaned over in my direction and remarked, 'Don't they have horrible names for men's diseases?'

I was busy trying to suppress my laughter when I heard my name mentioned and sat up smartly like a chastised schoolboy. 'I don't think we can let Mr Phinn leave,' said Miss Bridges with a twinkle in her dark eyes, 'without reading a poem himself or perhaps reciting one he has learnt by heart. Have you a favourite poem, Mr Phinn, one that you could share with us and tell us why you like it?'

'I do have a favourite poem,' I replied, 'but I am afraid it's another sad one. When I recall it, I remember my old English teacher, Miss Wainwright. It was her favourite poem and she introduced us to it in the sixth form.' All faces turned in my direction as I recited 'She dwelt among th' untrodden ways' by Wordsworth.

'Beautifully spoken, Mr Phinn, if I may say so. I wonder if someone told you that Wordsworth is my very favourite poet, too. I was telling the girls that good poetry is so wonderful to read and listen to and write themselves but it tends to have very bad press. When I was at school it was drummed into our unwilling heads and we never related it to the real world. It was about elves and daffodils and written by rather insipid lank-haired men in velvet jackets, dying consumptive deaths on *chaises longues*. It was only when I met a remarkable teacher in the sixth form, Miss Ruddock, who sounds rather like your Miss Wainwright, Mr Phinn, that the magic door of poetry was opened for me. Yes, hearing Wordsworth impresses upon us that the real world was his concern and he described it more accurately and more powerfully than most other poets.'

Miss Bridges glanced at her watch. 'Well, we near the end of our lesson, so I need to give you some notes to add to those of your own and set the homework. One thing that comes through very clearly in all these poems, for me, is the need for these poets to tell those who come afterwards about a much-loved person, whether it be little Isola with her "bright golden hair" or Lucy "whom there were none to praise". They have in a sense immortalised them. They will live forever and be read about for many years to come.' She paused for a moment and then said rather wistfully, 'I suppose, in one sense, we all would like to be remembered.'

186

Listening to that diminutive woman in the long brown skirt and white blouse that bright February morning with the sunlight streaming though the small window, I was back in the classroom of my own English teacher, remembering her warmth, intelligence and commitment. It had been my unquestionable good fortune to have been taught by Miss Wainwright, I thought to myself, to have had my mind stretched, my aspirations raised and my love of poetry developed. In thinking of her at that moment and recalling all the things she did for me, she was in a sense in that classroom with us.

*   *   *

For the remainder of the day I watched one excellent English lesson after another. I saw Shakespeare acted with confidence and vitality by the younger pupils, I listened with rapt interest as the third form pupils debated the pros and cons of fox-hunting—and, considering the countryside which lay not far from the school, wasn't at all surprised when the pro lobby won by a large margin—and I joined in a lively discussion with the sixth form on changes in the English language. Just before the end of the school day, I visited the library to inspect the range of books there. The wood-panelled room, with cosy alcoves where the older students were working quietly, was crammed with tomes from floor to ceiling.

'May I ask what you are doing?' I asked three girls almost hidden behind a tower of books.

'Yes, of course,' one of the students replied. She was a round, jolly-looking girl with curly red hair. 'You're the inspector, aren't you?'

'I am indeed,' I replied.

'We're working on an "A" level history essay about Marie Antoinette,' the student told me. 'I don't know whether you know anything about her?'

'Not a great deal,' I admitted. 'Only that she was reputed to have said, when she heard the people were without bread, "Let them eat cake." She was quite a cruel woman by the sound of her.'

'I think she has been misjudged,' the girl informed me, smiling. 'It's rather sad to be remembered for that comment which she probably never said anyway. We have been reading her last letter to her sister, Elizabeth, just before her execution and it paints a very different picture. It tells of someone who was very brave, resigned to her fate, a loving mother. You know, I think that at the end she achieves true greatness. Her life changed overnight from incredible luxury and power to poverty and degradation. I suppose it was far worse for her to be locked up away from her children, without food, water or clean clothes because she had had so much.'

'I never knew she was imprisoned,' I said. 'I thought she went to the guillotine with her husband.'

'No, no, they humiliated her first, locked her up, mocked her, treated her dreadfully but she was proud and courageous, right to the end when she climbed the steps to the guillotine. She was paraded through the streets of Paris in a cart to be beheaded—a quite pathetic figure in a dirty starched bonnet with a shaven head and red cheeks.'

'What does she say in the letter?' I asked, intrigued.

'She is writing to her sister, asking her to take care of her children, pleading with her to remind her son to always remember their father's last words about not seeking to avenge their deaths. She comes across so unlike the callous woman who was supposed to have said, "Let them eat cake." As I said, I suspect she never said that anyway. The main themes in the letter, and it's true for all the other aristocrats in prison waiting to be executed, are concern for her family, asking forgiveness from God for past sins and pleas for her not to be forgotten.'

'You like history, don't you?'

'Yes,' replied the girl. 'I think it's because Miss Johnson, our teacher, brings it to life. We learn not just about people's lives but about their feelings, thoughts, motives, often through what they wrote.'

'So what is the point of studying history, would you say?'

'They say the best way of predicting the future is to study the past.'

'And what lessons do you think we learn from history?' I asked.

'That people haven't changed,' the girl replied without a second thought.

'And what about the school? Do you feel you are receiving a good education?'

'It's a brilliant school,' replied the girl simply. 'I'm sure you've discovered that today.'

*   *   *

Miss Bronson sat behind her large roll-top desk with David, Gerry and myself facing her on the hard chairs. We must have looked like the three

189

monkeys—hear no evil, see no evil, speak no evil. It was four o'clock and we were there to give the headmistress the benefit of our 'deliberations'.

'Well, Miss Bronson,' David began, peering through his spectacles at his small black notebook, 'in summary, the mathematics faculty is highly successful, achieves excellent results and covers the examination syllabuses well. There is a need for more up-to-date text books and the rooms are somewhat drab but generally things are in a very good state.'

'And the teaching?' enquired the headmistress.

'Excellent,' replied David simply.

'The science faculty, too, is highly successful and achieves first-rate results,' said Gerry. 'It is well managed and the teachers work well as a team. There is, however, a need for extra resources, particularly on the technology side and the laboratories need some modernisation.'

'And the teaching?' enquired the headmistress again.

'Excellent,' said Gerry.

'The English faculty is also highly successful and achieves very good results,' I said. I saw the corner of the headmistress's mouth twist into a slight smile. 'And before you enquire, Miss Bronson, the teaching is also excellent.'

'Well, that is all very reassuring. The staff, from what I have heard, tell me that you have been most pleasant and professional and the gels, I gather, have found you friendly and interested. I am sure there are areas which we need to improve—one always strives to be even better—and I look forward to receiving your full and detailed written reports. I cannot guarantee that your recommendations, if they involve a deal of money, can be implemented but we shall certainly consider them. Of course, if the county were able to finance new mathematics text books and extra resources in science . . .' She left the sentence unfinished and showed her set of magnificent white teeth.

*   *   *

On my way down the path to the car park a short while later, I paused for a moment beneath the towering statue of Sir Cosmo. The fat pigeon I had observed earlier on the monumental head pecking at a piece of bread, now had a mate. The two birds sat gently cooing and preening on the shoulders of the imposing figure. Poor Sir Cosmo, he looked rather more of a pigeon fancier or a circus performer than a powerful magnate. As I looked up at him, I thought of Miss Bridges' words: 'I suppose, in one sense, we all would like to be remembered.' Miss Wainwright and Miss Bridges might not have had poems written about them or statues erected in their memory, but they would live on in the hearts and the minds of those whom they had taught.

CHAPTER TEN

When the call arrived from Mrs Savage summoning me to Dr Gore's office, I had a shrewd idea what the meeting would be about. Following my conversation with Harold concerning the appointment of the new Senior Inspector, I had rather expected to be called to see the Chief Education Officer but it had been so long in coming I had begun to think that it would never happen.

Mrs Savage got up from behind her large computer-covered desk as I entered her domain. She was wearing another expensive outfit in reds and greens, was liberally bedecked in an assortment of heavy jewellery and her hair was gathered up on top of her head in carefully arranged curls, held in place by a metal comb. She looked positively biblical.

'Good morning, Mr Phinn. Dr Gore is expecting you,' she said, and crossed the room to open the door into the CEO's office. She gestured me to enter Dr Gore's large office with the great glass-fronted bookcase full of leather-bound tomes, comfortable chairs and the director's huge mahogany desk.

'Come along in, Gervase,' said the CEO. Mrs Savage stood back but remained in the room, looking expectantly at Dr Gore. 'That will be all, Brenda, thank you,' said the CEO. 'And I don't wish to be disturbed.'

'What about the telephone call you are expecting from Councillor Peterson?' enquired Mrs Savage.

'If he calls, tell him I shall ring him later.'

'And remember you must get in touch with Lord Marrick regarding tomorrow's interviews. I did say that you would—'

The CEO cut her short. 'Brenda,' he said slowly and distinctly as if speaking to a naughty child, 'I do not want to be disturbed.'

'Very well,' said Mrs Savage, sweeping out of the

room with a swirl of multicoloured silk and a jangle of jewellery.

Dr Gore waited until the door was closed before confiding, 'She is very well meaning but sometimes a trifle over-zealous.' I could think of many words to describe Mrs Savage, I thought to myself, but 'well meaning' did not readily spring to mind. 'Do sit down, Gervase.' The CEO smiled a rather unnerving, thin-lipped smile and stared intently at me for a moment over the top of his gold-framed spectacles. I shuffled nervously in my chair. 'Thank you for coming to see me. First of all, how is Miss Bentley? What an ideal couple you will make. When is the happy day?'

'Christine is well, thank you,' I replied, 'and our wedding is on April 15th.'

'Good, good,' he murmured. 'Nothing nicer than a spring wedding. Not long to go now.'

'No,' I replied, wishing he would get to the point.

'And have you got yourselves fixed up with a house yet?'

'No, not yet. We've seen a cottage in Hawksrill but I think it's a bit out of our price range. It comes up for auction soon but I fear it will go for far more than the asking price.'

'Well, you never know. Nice part of the world up there. Very picturesque.'

'Yes, it's very pleasant.'

Polite conversation over with, the CEO leaned forward, steepled his long fingers and rested his elbows on the desk. 'Now, I have asked you to pop in because there is something I would like to talk to you about.'

'Yes,' I replied, 'I had an idea you might.'

'Tomorrow, Dr Yeats's successor will be

appointed and I wanted to have a word with you about your unsuccessful application. I intended speaking to you before now but life is so frenetic, isn't it, and we have all been so very busy, haven't we? However, I know that Dr Yeats has had a word with you.'

'Yes, he has,' I replied.

'I am sure that you must be very disappointed but, you know, both Dr Yeats and I feel it was a little soon for you to put in for such a post. We both feel that you lack the necessary experience and expertise at present to take on the role of team leader. In time, I have no doubt you will become a senior inspector and, should a vacancy arise in a few years' time, I would most certainly welcome an application.'

'I see,' I replied. 'Well, thank you for explaining things, Dr Gore. I am very grateful.'

I really did not want to go over my unsuccessful application yet again. I had had post-mortems with Christine and Harold and Sidney and David and my parents and countless others who had heard the news. I heartily wished I had listened to Christine in the first place and not put in for the wretched job. I just wanted to get on with my life and put the whole sorry business behind me.

'Perhaps it would have been sensible if you had had a word with me before you submitted an application. I would like to think I am approachable enough for that.'

'Yes, of course you are,' I replied, wishing that the interview would reach a speedy conclusion.

Dr Gore stroked his chin and leaned further back in his chair. 'I want staff in the Education Department to feel they can come and talk to me at any time. That if they ever want to have a little chat about anything, anything at all, they know where I am.'

'Yes, I appreciate that, Dr Gore.' When would either of us, I thought, bearing in mind the 'frenetic' and 'busy' lives we both led, have the time for 'a little chat'? Apart from anything, there was the small matter of getting past Mrs Savage without an appointment; it would be harder than getting past a scrap-yard Rottweiler.

'You see, Gervase, I don't want people to think I'm this remote figure up here in my ivory tower, out of touch with people. I want everyone in the Education Department, this team of ours—and that's what I think we are, a team working together with a shared vision and core values—to feel that they can share their ideas, concerns and aspirations with me and that their contributions are valued. That is what good leadership and management is all about.' I smiled to myself. Dr Gore had clearly been on a management course in the not-too-distant past. 'So, if in future there are things you want to discuss, well, my office has an open door.'

'Thank you, Dr Gore,' I said, 'I'll remember that.' I prayed that this would be the end of his homily.

'Good, good,' he said, smiling like a hungry vampire about to sink its teeth into a helpless victim. 'You will appreciate also that we do need some fresh blood.'

'I'm sorry?'

'We need someone to take us forward, meet the constant challenges facing us in education and manage a talented, if rather unusual and sometimes a little prickly, team of school

195

inspectors. So, I hope you are not too disappointed with our decision not to call you for interview and understand the reasons for rejecting your application.'

'No, not at all. I mean, yes. I mean, no, I'm not too devastated and, yes, I understand your decision.'

'Good, good,' he murmured. I got up to go, desperate to get out of the office, but he continued: 'Now, there is another matter with which I hope you are in a position to help out.'

I sat down again. I just knew what was coming next. I could tell by the way he smiled, steepled his fingers again and stared over his glasses.

'Now, Gervase, I have a little job for you.'

*   *   *

The interviews for the Senior Inspector post were held the following day. All the inspectors were in early and gathered in the larger office for a cup of coffee. Harold was looking very smart in a charcoal-grey suit, white shirt, highly-polished shoes and carrying a black, leather-covered clipboard. He looked as nervous as a candidate for the job, pacing up and down the office like a caged animal.

'Harold,' sighed Sidney, 'I would be most grateful if you would refrain from wandering around like a lost soul or, if you must, do it in your own office. You are putting us all on edge. And I wish you would dispense with that ridiculous black clipboard—you look as if you are about to measure someone up for a coffin.'

Harold was clearly not taking much notice. He stopped pacing, however, and glanced at his wristwatch, rubbed his chin and looked abstractedly into the middle distance.

'What time are the candidates arriving, Harold?' I asked.

'I'm sorry,' said Harold, 'did you say something, Gervase?'

'What time are the candidates arriving?' I repeated.

'Oh, not until nine. Interviews begin at nine-thirty. I think I'll drive up to the SDC, though, to make sure everything is ready.'

'But it's not eight o' clock yet,' said Sidney. 'Connie will still be buffing up her brasses, swabbing her floors, wiping her surfaces and poking into every conceivable orifice with that fearsome feather duster of hers.'

'Someone might arrive a bit early,' said Harold thoughtfully. 'I'd better go, just to be on the safe side.'

'What are the candidates like?' I asked.

'Well, it's a little difficult to say, really. Of the five up for interview, three are men and two are women. All are very well qualified and in senior positions already in the educational world. It's an excellent field.'

'What are they like as people though, Harold?' asked David. 'Are they personable, pleasant, congenial, easy to get along with? Have they a sense of humour? Are they people people or systems people?'

'I'm not psychic, David,' replied Harold, chuckling. 'I haven't met any of them yet. I'm only going on what was on their application forms which seemed to me to be first rate. Of course, I cannot go into details contained in their references.'

197

'But you must have got a feel for them,' said Sidney. 'A gut reaction.'

'Look, I am not on the interview panel, so it is irrelevant what I think or feel. My function today is merely to make sure things go smoothly. I'm not directly involved.'

'You were when I was interviewed,' observed Gerry.

'Ah, yes, but because this is for my replacement, Dr Gore feels that it would not be appropriate for me to attend. He has consulted me, of course, and I had a say in the shortlisting. The full Education Sub-Committee will be present at the interviews so I think there are quite enough people involved.'

'Will they have to go through what I had to endure?' asked Gerry. 'The formal presentation, interviews, sociometric, psychological and personality tests, informal conversations with all sorts of people? It really was a nightmare.'

'Yes, they will, I'm afraid. It is a long and rigorous process but we do want to get the best person for the post, don't we?' Harold glanced self-consciously in my direction and coloured a little before continuing. 'Now, I hope that you will all be at the SDC at about five-thirty when we should know who my successor is and you will have the opportunity of meeting him or her.'

I had an early appointment some way away so I walked with Harold to the cars. 'It will be strange not having you around,' I said. 'I hope your successor will be as helpful and supportive as you have been.'

'Oh, I'm sure he or she will be. Did Dr Gore have a word with you, by the way?'

'Yes, he did,' I replied, recalling the conversation

I had had with the CEO the previous day and wondering if the new Senior Inspector would be someone with whom we could 'share our ideas, concerns and aspirations'. As I strolled with Harold across the formal gardens in front of County Hall I had a feeling that things would not be quite as happy in the office when he had retired. I would find out soon enough whether my premonition would turn out to be true or not.

*   *   *

I arrived at the Staff Development Centre a little after five to find Connie and Mrs Savage outside the kitchen in heated conversation. Connie, attired in her usual bright pink overall and with arms folded tightly over her chest, was facing her adversary with an expression of distaste. Mrs Savage was wearing a magnificent scarlet dress into which she looked as if she had been poured. The assortment of heavy silver jewellery which was draped everywhere was jangling as usual. The pink and scarlet duo clashed horribly, as, obviously, did their opinions.

'Look,' Connie was saying, 'I knock off at five o'clock. I've been here since the crack of dawn and I don't get paid for stopping on, pandering to the likes of all these councillors and officials. I've been in and out, up and down like a fiddler's elbow all day, taking them in refreshments and I don't know what. They must have bladders like air balloons the tea and coffee them lot have consummated. And biscuits. They are like gannets, the lot of them.'

'I am only asking you to provide one further tray of refreshments, not to lay on a running buffet for a hundred people,' said Mrs Savage tartly. 'It sounds a perfectly reasonable request to me.'

'Yes, well, it might do to you, because you're not the one what has to do it,' retorted Connie undeterred. 'There's all them in the interview room and then there's the candidates waiting outside and now all the inspectors are arriving. I bought six bottles of gold top and four packets of Garibaldi biscuits this morning and now there's nothing, not a crumb to be had.'

Mrs Savage caught sight of me approaching. 'Ah, Mr Phinn, perhaps you can persuade the janitor here—'

'Excuse me!' snapped Connie, 'I am no janitor. I'm the Centre Caretaker.'

Mrs Savage sucked in her breath and screwed up her face as if she had something unpleasant in her mouth. 'I am attempting to get the caretaker here to provide some tea and biscuits for the interview panel but she is most reluctant to do so.'

'And I've just told her that I knock off at five and it's ten past now and there's no biscuits or milk left. I have a bus to catch and a home to go to.'

'Well, perhaps you could pop down to the shops and get some milk and biscuits before you depart,' said Mrs Savage.

'I'm doing no popping down to no shops. Only place I'm popping to is home.' With that Connie took off her pink overall, hung it behind the kitchen door, put on her outdoor coat and marched off down the corridor.

'I shall, of course, be mentioning this altercation to Dr Gore,' shouted Mrs Savage after the departing figure.

'You can tell the Queen of Tonga, for all I care,'

200

yelled back Connie without turning her head. 'I'm off home.'

'The woman is impossible!' Mrs Savage told me with a twist of the mouth. 'I don't intend to be spoken to like that by a cleaner. I shall be referring the matter to Dr Gore first thing in the morning.'

'Actually, Mrs Savage, Connie does a very good job here at the Centre.'

'That's as may be, Mr Phinn,' said Mrs Savage, bristling like an angry cat, 'but that is no excuse for such outrageously ill-mannered behaviour.'

I decided to change the subject. 'I gather that the interviews haven't finished yet,' I said.

'Well, the interviews themselves have,' said Mrs Savage, regaining her composure, 'but the panel is still deliberating. Some of the presentations ran over and then one candidate, having gone all the way through the interview and sat the various tests and done his presentation, withdrew. He gave no reason, I gather, just pulled out. Dr Gore was extremely disconcerted. I have never seen him quite so angry. Now, I've got to go back in and tell him that there are no more refreshments.' She waited for a reply but when it was not forthcoming, continued in a much sweeter tone of voice. 'I think it will be some time before the panel has made up its mind, so I wonder, Mr Phinn . . .'

I knew what was coming next. 'I'll go and get some milk,' I said before she could complete the sentence.

'Oh, thank you,' she said. 'That is *most* kind of you. I would, of course, go myself but Dr Gore does like me to be on hand at all times. He does tend to rely very heavily upon me.' There was an enigmatic smile playing on her lips. 'Oh, and some biscuits, too—chocolate digestive, I think. The ones the caretaker provided tasted like cardboard.'

Connie was waiting at the bus stop when I drove out of the Centre. I pulled into the kerb. 'Come on, get in, Connie, I'll give you a lift.'

She climbed in next to me. 'Thanks, Mr Phinn, you're a real gentleman. But don't take me home, I'm a fair way out of town.' She put on the seat belt. 'In fact, to tell the truth, I wasn't going home. If you could take me to the High Street, I can walk to my bingo from there.'

'Righto!' I said, in my best Winco-style.

'You weren't long at the Centre. Have they picked somebody then?'

'No, I'm on a commission to get the milk and biscuits,' I replied.

'Huh!' she snorted. 'Well, I wouldn't do it. It wouldn't hurt Lady High and Mighty to get on her bike and go to the shops. All she's done all day is swan around the Centre, on those high heels, in that fancy outfit and the dynamite earrings, looking important and pretending to be busy. She'd be overdressed if she was going to the Buckingham Palace Garden Party. She wants to watch it, walking round like something out of a jeweller's window. Fall over and she'd have difficulty getting up with all that metal on her. She's like a gramophone record which has got the needle stuck. "Oh yes, Dr Gore", "Oh no, Dr Gore." She's about as much use as a pulled tooth, as my father used to say.'

'I forgot to ask you, Connie,' I said, 'how is your father?'

She was quiet for a moment and stared down at her lap. 'He died,' she said quietly.

'Oh, I am sorry, Connie,' I replied. 'I didn't know.'

'We had his funeral last week.'

'I thought he was on the mend.'

'Well, he'd come out of hospital, seemed to pick up a bit, much like his old self, then he had another stroke, more serious this time. He lingered for a bit but then we lost him. Mind you, he'd started having conversations with his brother who was killed in the war, and he thought I was my mother at one point. I think he was losing some of his facilities.' She was silent for a moment, then sniffed and shook her head. 'It was a lovely service and that young vicar, I've got to hand it to him, was wonderful. I've not always seen eye-to-eye with him, what with his jeans and his motorbike blocking my entrance, but my goodness he was good. Gave a beautiful sermon about Dad and how he had served his king and country and how there ought to be more people in the world like him. Lucy, my little granddaughter read a poem called "Granddad" which she wrote special and we had all his favourite hymns: "Fight the Good Fight", "Onward Christian Soldiers", "To be a Pilgrim". It was lovely.'

'Well, I'm very sorry, Connie. He was a remarkable man, by all accounts.'

'He had his moments, did Dad. He could be as stubborn as a limpet on a rock but he was a marvellous father. Kept his sense of humour right up to the end. "Live in hope," he said, "and die in casualty." Oh, I will miss him.'

'You never get over losing a parent.'

'We had him cremated. Well, it's more environmentally friendly, isn't it? That's what my Ted said. I drew the line, though, at a cardboard

203

coffin. I wanted him to go out in style. He always liked a bit of a ceremony.'

'So everything went off all right, then?'

'Yes, but we was worried about the crematorium because of what happened at my mum's funeral.'

'What happened there?' I asked.

'Well, it was a couple of winters back, just before you started and, oh, it was bitter. I've never known such a raw wind. The path up to the crematorium was like an ice rink. We were slipping and skidding, slithering and sliding, hanging on to each other for dear life. My Auntie Dot nearly went full length. She could have broken a leg or worse. You'd have thought they'd have put some ashes down, wouldn't you?' I didn't say anything. 'Then the music was all mixed up. It was a right fandango. You can have modern music there, you know, at the crematorium. It doesn't have to be religious or anything like that. When everything's been said, this little curtain comes across to hide the coffin, and they play some tune or other. Some have quite happy ones. I remember my neighbour having "Look on the Bright Side of Life" when her husband died. Well, my mother was called Sally and always loved Gracie Fields. She's a bit before your time. Singer from Lancashire, but I don't hold that against her. My mother used to love all her films and had all her records so we thought it would be nice for her to go out to "Sally", you know, the Gracie Fields' number, "Sally, Sally, pride of our alley, You're more than the whole world to me."'

'That's nice,' I said.

'It would have been if she'd have got it.'

'What happened?'

'They played the wrong track, didn't they? The curtains closed with Gracie Fields singing, "Wish me luck as you wave me goodbye".' I had to bite my tongue to stop myself laughing. 'So I said to my Ted, I said, "You must check that Dad has the right tune." He loved Frank Sinatra so we thought a good exit would be Frankie singing "I did it my way".'

'Very appropriate,' I said.

'So I told Ted to check with the man on the tape recorder. After all, I didn't want Dad disappearing to "Smoke gets in your eyes".'

This time, I couldn't help myself but luckily was able to turn my laughter into a sort of spluttery cough. I was relieved that we reached the High Street at that moment, and Connie asked me to stop.

'Well, let me know if there's anything I can do, Connie,' I said.

'Thanks, but it's all sorted out now.' She put her hand on the door handle but sat there for a moment. 'I hear you put in for Dr Yeats's job then?'

'Yes,' I replied.

'It'll take a big man to fill his shoes.'

'Yes, it will,' I agreed.

'Salt of the earth is Dr Yeats, a real gentleman. So, why didn't they interview you, then?' she asked bluntly.

'It's not really a question I can answer, Connie. You would have to ask those who did the shortlisting. I suppose they thought I hadn't the experience.'

'I think you would have done a good job myself,' she said, nodding.

'Thank you, Connie, that's very kind of you.'

'You mustn't get too down. As my old dad said to me when I failed my eleven-plus examination: "When one door closes, another shuts."' She climbed from the car, then bent for a parting piece of advice. 'And you make sure you let Lady Hoity Toity make the tea. Mind you, she probably doesn't know the difference between a teapot and a bedpan.'

When I arrived back at the SDC with the milk and biscuits, my three colleagues had arrived and were sitting in the staff lounge.

'It's not like you to be late, Gervase,' said Gerry, glancing at the clock on the wall. 'It's nearly six.'

'I've been on an errand,' I explained. 'We had run out of milk.'

'They're certainly taking their time,' said Sidney. 'They've been rattling and prattling on all day. You would think that by now they could have arrived at a decision. The trouble is, you see, people who sit on these interview panels have one thing in common—too much time on their hands and verbal diarrhoea.'

'Isn't that two?' asked David.

'Isn't what two?' demanded Sidney.

'Two things in common: "too much time on their hands" *and* "verbal diarrhoea".'

Sidney sighed heavily. 'I really do despair of people who like the sound of their own voices.'

'I'm saying nothing,' I remarked.

'Are you going to bid for the house in Hawksrill then, Gervase?' asked Gerry.

'Yes,' I said, reaching into my briefcase and pulling out the estate agent's brochure. 'So long as we get a positive surveyor's report, we will bid. It will be a complete waste of time, I'm sure, because it is bound to go miles beyond what we can afford. But it will give us some practice at bidding in an auction.'

Sidney plucked it from my hands and read: 'A beautiful listed cottage in a delightful position overlooking a watercolour landscape near the picture-postcard Dales village of Hawksrill. The ground floor partially and tastefully modernised and decorated. The upper floor would benefit from further attention. Entrance hall, cloakroom, living room, kitchen, two bedrooms. Small mature garden to front, magnificent view across open countryside to rear.'

'Sounds lovely,' said Gerry.

'Sounds full of estate agent's fanciful language,' said Sidney. 'You have to read between the lines, Gervase. When they say "small compact garden to front", they mean a window box. When they say "in need of modernisation", they mean a ruin. If they say "would benefit from an extra bathroom", they mean it has an earth closet. This is what they really should have said about this property: "The previous owner of Peewit Cottage, an incontinent hermit who suffered from a twisted sense of humour, hence the name—the bird, pewit, only having the one 'e'—let it go to rack and ruin. The crumbling pile is at the end of a rough muddy track, well trodden by herds of smelly cattle and flocks of lazy sheep. Those looking for a primitive and lonely life will relish the absence of a toilet, mains electricity or gas, central heating and running water but there are lovely views beyond the power station and grain silos." '

'Very droll,' I remarked. 'And "pewit" with one

"e" is only a variation on the double-e spelling. I know that because it happened to be in a crossword last week. But don't worry, Sidney, we're having a thorough survey,' I told him.

'I'm not in the least worried, dear boy. It's you and Christine who need to worry. You never stop shelling out money when you buy an old house. You want a smart apartment or a modern town house in Fettlesham, in walking distance of the office. Anyway, who's doing the survey? Dr Livingstone, I presume. It must be uncharted territory up there. No one would find it except an intrepid explorer.'

'Oh, I wish they would hurry up,' sighed David. 'Some of us have homes to go to.'

'Go and reconnoitre will you, Gerry,' said Sidney, 'and get Connie to rustle us up a cup of tea on the way back.'

'Connie's gone,' I told him. 'She went nearly an hour ago.'

'And you can rustle up your own cup of tea, Sidney,' said Gerry.

'I shall,' said Sidney springing to his feet, 'and, being such a good-natured fellow, I shall bring one back for my slothful colleagues.'

When he had gone David shook his head wearily. 'I really don't know what the new Senior Inspector will make of Sidney. I hope he has a strong constitution, a bizarre sense of humour and the patience of Job.' It was the kettle calling the pot black, I thought to myself.

Sidney returned five minutes later with the tea. 'It looks as if they're finished,' he said conspiratorially as he set down the tray. 'They are all standing about looking pleased with themselves and shaking hands. I think I have seen everything now. I have just passed Mrs Savage pushing a trolley like a tea lady down the corridor back to the kitchen. I asked her if she had a new job. Her face was a picture, well, not really a picture, more of a gargoyle.'

'Did you see who they appointed?' asked Gerry.

Before Sidney could respond, the door opened and Harold breezed in rubbing his large hands together and with a great toothy smile on his face. 'Colleagues,' he boomed, 'may I introduce you to my successor! This is Mr Simon Carter.'

*   *   *

'Well, I rather took to him,' said Sidney the next morning in the office. We were discussing the Senior Inspector designate. 'I was very pleasantly surprised with Mr Simon Carter. He seems a most amiable and positive sort of chap and he certainly had a lot about him. What is more, he was most interested in the work I have been doing in art and design. Asked me all about my projects, courses and exhibitions. He was genuinely interested, I could tell.'

'Yes,' added David, nodding. 'I have to agree for once, Sidney. He seems like a good sort. I've met him before, of course. I recognised him as soon as he walked through the door. He was a keynote speaker on a mathematics conference I attended a couple of years back—his subject is maths, you know—and he was excellent, very well organised, knowledgeable and interesting. He went down really well with the delegates. I think he'll be a real asset to the team.'

'Well, it's a great relief to know we have somebody reasonable,' said Sidney, leaning back in his chair and scrutinising the ceiling. 'I feel a whole lot better now. It will not be the same, of course, without Harold but life goes on and this fellow seems a pretty good egg.' Sidney looked over in my direction. 'You are very quiet, Gervase. How did you find our Mr Carter?'

'I liked him,' I replied. 'He certainly seemed a very friendly man, as you say, and keen to know all about us and, from what he said, he has plenty of ideas for various initiatives. I think he'll be good.'

'And, of course,' said Sidney mischievously, 'he's relatively young as well, intelligent, quite good-looking and he isn't married. Play your cards right, Geraldine, and you could be in with a chance. Now, that *would* be interesting.'

Gerry grimaced and shook her head. 'And completely out of the question, Sidney,' she replied. 'So don't start getting any ideas. Mr Carter is definitely not my type.'

'And what *is* your type?' asked Sidney.

'Well, let's just say not Mr Simon Carter.'

'Do I take it you are less than impressed with our new SI?' asked David.

'No, I am impressed. He seemed smooth, good-humoured and very positive about everything and everybody,' she replied. 'He certainly knows the right things to say and how to make a good impression.'

'But you do have some reservations?' I commented.

'I shall keep an open mind about him, Gervase,' answered Gerry. 'I am a scientist after all. I shall give you my opinion after he's been in the job for a few weeks.'

'I don't think you liked him, did you?' said Sidney bluntly. 'Come on, be honest. You just didn't like him.'

'Well, if you want me to be honest, Sidney,' Gerry said, turning to face him, 'no, I can't say I did. There was something about Mr Carter which didn't quite ring true. I can't put my finger on it, but I don't think he is all that he seems.'

'Methinks you worry unnecessarily, Geraldine, my dear,' said Sidney, looking at his watch and standing to go. 'I think you will find Simon Carter will be an excellent successor to Harold, and we will get on with him like a house on fire.'

Prophetic words as it turned out.

CHAPTER ELEVEN

'Do the mandarins at the Ministry of Education, in their sublime wisdom,' began the headteacher, 'appreciate the volume of reports, recommendations, national guidelines, statutory orders, assessment procedures, statistical analyses, comparative data, projects and initiatives and I don't know what else, which appear like the plagues of Egypt on the average headteacher's desk every week? Does anyone down there in London ever consider sitting down and attempting to co-ordinate this little lot?' She paused to indicate, with a sweep of her hand, the tower of thick files, fat brown envelopes and bulging folders before her on the desk. 'If I had to wade my way through this morass of unwieldy reports and glossy documents each week, I should

211

spend my entire time reading and paper-shuffling to the detriment of educating the young people which is my main concern. I really think it is quite ridiculous the amount of paper that headteachers and teachers are expected to deal with.'

I was sitting somewhat subdued before Mrs Rose, headteacher of Crompton Secondary School which was one of the most 'challenging' schools in the county. I felt it politic to listen. 'Now, as you well know, Mr Phinn,' she continued, 'we have in this school some of the most difficult, demanding and disruptive young people of any school and I honestly believe that we are trying our level best to educate them, teach them to co-operate, be good citizens, appreciate the value of working hard and achieving their potential, no matter what level that is. But it is an uphill battle.' She paused for a moment and looked down again at the desk piled high with papers. 'And now we have another major national initiative, which I am sure is well intentioned but is something which will add to the pressures and demands of an already very exhausting and stressful job. I just wish all these administrators, consultants, advisers and inspectors, present company excepted, would let us get on with the job which is about teaching.'

When I had arrived at the school earlier that morning the last thing I had expected or indeed needed after the week I had just had, was a long diatribe about the pressures and stresses of teaching. I had pressures and stresses of my own without listening to others' moans. And as for the plagues of Egypt, I thought to myself, I felt like the Egyptian messenger in the production of *Antony and Cleopatra* which Christine and I had seen some months back. As the messenger is beaten viciously about the head by the furious queen, after he informs her of her lover's marriage to Octavia, the poor man attempts to tell her: 'Gracious madam, I that do bring the news made not the match.' In other words—don't shoot the messenger. I felt like repeating the lines to Mrs Rose who sat regally at her desk with all the authority and bearing of the formidable Egyptian queen herself. I too could have well done without this particular 'little job' on top of everything I had on at the moment.

Someone in the Ministry of Education undoubtedly had enjoyed himself dreaming up the 'Language and Literacy for Learning' initiative which Dr Gore had dumped at my door. English inspectors from selected authorities were charged with observing a range of lessons and evaluating how effective teachers were in using questions, developing reading competence, organising group work, encouraging discussion and teaching writing skills such as summary and note-taking. We were also instructed to examine how teachers evaluated pupils' work. When I flicked through the lengthy commentary about the initiative from the Ministry and read the accompanying letter from Miss de la Mare, HMI, explaining the process, I knew it was not going to be a 'little job' at all but more like half a term's work. All the information had come in one of those beautifully-produced glossy folders to which Mrs Rose had referred so scathingly. On the cover was a group of smiling students dressed in smart blazers, pristine white shirts or blouses and school ties, all in animated conversation with each other in what appeared to me to be the best-equipped library in the country. Behind them posed a beaming young teacher who looked as if she were moonlighting from her day job as a fashion model. So while I could readily sympathise with Mrs Rose when she launched into her tirade about this particular initiative, I was in no mood to listen.

'Well, Mrs Rose,' I said irritably, cutting her off and starting to put the folders and the papers in my briefcase, 'perhaps this is not the best time to discuss the initiative.'

'There is never a best time, Mr Phinn,' she told me. 'We are up to our eyes all the time.' I got up to go. I was not intending to waste any more time convincing the headteacher of the efficacy of the project. 'Look,' she said, her voice now softening a little, 'I am the very last person to dismiss something out of hand before I have given it a chance, particularly if, in the long run, it might be to the benefit of the students. We need all the support and advice here and this project might have a spin off. You'd better sit down and tell me more about it and I will certainly consider it.'

So I explained the initiative and how the Ministry had asked that the sample should be taken across the board—high-achieving schools, ones where the results were low, large and small, urban and rural, grammar, secondary modern, comprehensive and special schools. The headteacher listened attentively as I tried to describe the scheme, stressing the advantages of taking part, especially the extra funding. 'So there it is,' I said at last.

'Tell me, Mr Phinn,' asked the headteacher, 'why have you asked me—this school—to take part in this enterprise?'

'Well, Mrs Rose,' I replied, smiling wryly, 'it's

because you are flexible in your thinking, dedicated, a very good manager and always willing to take on a challenge. You are—'

'Please don't continue, Mr Phinn,' she interrupted, holding up her hand as if stopping traffic, 'or I might break out into hysterical laughter. You know, you ought to try your hand at selling time-shares in Spain or second-hand cars. Now, let me get this straight. You will spend a day in the school examining the written work of the students in a range of subjects and a further day looking at the way the teachers use language in their lessons?'

'Yes, and I will also be interested in the kind of language the students use,' I added.

'Well, you will find, Mr Phinn,' replied Mrs Rose, 'that a good number of our students have a very colourful, if somewhat limited command of the English language.'

'Not that kind of language,' I told her, smiling.

'And you are going to focus on just one student, are you?'

'That's right. I would like to join a boy or a girl for the day in each of the various subjects he or she is studying and observe the teaching. It's called pupil pursuit.'

'Pupil pursuit,' repeated the headteacher, shaking her head. 'Well, there's a thing.'

'It's the term the Ministry of Education uses.'

'Why is it, do you think, that the Ministry is so very fond of custodial words, phrases and metaphors? Education is full of such terms, isn't it? We've got governors, inspectors, officers, detention, exclusion, suspension, discipline, terms, authority and, of course, those at the Ministry, judging from the letters I receive, are very adept at

215

using long sentences. As you can tell, Mr Phinn,' concluded Mrs Rose, smiling for the first time that morning, 'I do still have a sense of humour.' She tapped the folder on her desk and thought for a moment. 'All right, then, we'll give it a go.'

*   *   *

The following Friday I arrived at the school to undertake the pupil pursuit. Crompton Secondary School, a sprawling, flat-roofed, grey-coloured building built in the 1950s was situated in the very centre of a large run-down estate of red-brick, terraced housing. It was in a deeply depressing part of the town and surrounded by tall, blackened chimneys, deserted factories with every window smashed, overgrown areas of wasteland and decaying warehouses. Nearby was a small litter-strewn shopping precinct where each premise had a grill on the window. Crompton was not a happy place.

Mrs Rose had telephoned the previous afternoon to tell me which pupil she had selected to be 'pursued'. 'I couldn't decide between Bianca and Dean,' she had said. 'Their attitude to life is not dissimilar, but Dean can be more disruptive so I've chosen Bianca. In fact, she and Dean are friends, so I expect you will be seeing a fair bit of Dean anyway.'

Mrs Rose had asked me to meet Bianca in the library before the start of school. She was fifteen, a tall, morose-looking girl with lank hair and a long, pale, unhealthy-looking face and was dressed in an exceptionally tight blouse, very short skirt and huge platform shoes. She looked very different from the

216

students on the front of the glossy folder which I held in my hand.

'So whatcha gunna be doin', then?' she asked in a weary, apathetic tone of voice which she had clearly cultivated over the years for use when talking to adults in authority.

'I am going to be joining you for all today's lessons,' I explained.

'Eh?'

'I said, I am going to be joining you for all today's lessons. I shall observe the teaching and also be talking to the students.'

'Wha' for?'

'Because that's my job.'

'Who are you, then?'

'I'm a school inspector.'

'A wha'?'

'A school inspector,' I repeated.

'And you just watch teachers?'

'That's right.'

'And sit in classrooms an' that?'

'Yes.'

'Don't you have a proper job then?'

I decided not to answer that. 'I am here to see how well the students are doing in their lessons.'

'Well, it's dead boring,' she told me bluntly, scrutinising a broken nail.

'I'm sure it's not,' I replied.

'Oh yeah, it is. It's like watching those really really boring television programmes that you can't turn off. I don't understand what t'teachers are on about most of t'time.' She turned her attention to another broken nail. 'So watcha want to watch t'lessons for?'

'As I said, I am here to see how well the students

217

are doing in their lessons. I'm going to be listening to the language in the classroom.'

'You'll 'ear a lot. Some of t'lads have mouths like sewers.'

'No, not that sort of language,' I told her.

At this point, the most aggressive-looking adolescent I had ever seen in my life came into the library. He resembled a younger version of Magwitch, the convict in the Dickens' novel *Great Expectations* who terrifies poor Pip in the graveyard. The youth had a bullet-shaped, closely-shaven head, several large metal studs in his ear and an expression which would stop a clock. When he came closer, I saw that he was decorated with a selection of unusual tattoos. On his knuckles *LOVE* and *HATE* were spelled out in large blue letters, on his cheeks small tattooed tears descended from an eye like those on the face of a circus clown and stretching from ear to ear across the full width of his neck was a series of dots, between small tattooed scissors. In the middle just above his Adam's apple were the words *CUT HERE*. I learned later that one of his friends had decided to try and emulate this artistry himself with a needle and some Indian ink and using a mirror. He was now destined to go through life with the word *TUC* emblazoned across his throat.

'Who's 'e, then?' the youth asked Bianca in a deep, threatening tone of voice.

'Eh?' she grunted, chewing at the remains of the broken nail.

'Him, who is 'e?'

'Inspector,' said the girl.

'Copper?'

'Naw, school inspector.'

218

'What's 'e 'ere fer?'

'Eh?'

'I said, what's 'e 'ere fer?'

'He's following me around for t'day.'

'Tha wants to tell somebody.'

'Naw, he's watching what gus off in t'lessons.'

'What fer?'

'I dunno, ask him.'

'Well he's not watching me!'

I was being discussed as if I were not there. 'Excuse me,' I said to the boy. 'You can speak to me directly, you know. I'm not invisible.'

'Eh?'

'You can ask me yourself what I am doing today.'

'I know what tha doing. She's just told me and I'm telling thee, tha not watching me!'

'No, I don't intend to,' I replied.

'And don't thee eyeball me, neither,' he said, glaring.

Just what was I in for, I thought to myself, and just how do the teachers cope with the likes of this lad?

'His name's Dean,' Bianca told me, as he shuffled off, hands deep in his pockets, 'and he fancies me.'

Struth! I thought.

The first lesson was mathematics. The teacher, Mr McNab, a bear of a man with a thick red beard, lined the class up outside his door, before explaining that he believed in firm discipline and what a retrograde step it was when the poor misguided powers abolished corporal punishment. He went on to tell me that if he had his way he would bring in capital punishment for some of the pupils, never mind corporal punishment.

219

'When I taught in Glasgow, Mr Phinn, we were gi'en a thick leather strap called a taws when we started teaching and they didna mess aroond after getting a dose o' that across their backsides, I can tell ye.'

On each desk, which were in rows facing the front, had been placed a pencil, the end of which had been sliced away and a number written on the exposed wood, a square of paper, a rubber (also numbered) and a text book open at the appropriate page.

'I keep their noses to the grindstone here, Mr Phinn. Keep 'em busy, I do. Gi' this lot an inch and they'll tek a mile. I don't encourage any talking in my class because once started, they willna stop. I number everything in the room which makes it easier to check on things which go missing. It's the only way I can make sure I get ma pencils and ma rubbers back. This lot live by the code of "If it moves, nick it, if it doesnae, kick it." You see, they come from inadequate homes where they are allowed to get awa' wi' murder. They're left to roam the streets, watch television till all hoors, play truant, get up tae all sorts of mischief and mayhem. What a lot of these lads need is security. That's what they want—security.'

'Yes,' I agreed. 'Children tend to prosper from a caring and secure background.'

Mr McNab threw back his head and snorted. 'Waay, not that sort of security, man,' he blustered. 'I mean maximum security. I'd lock the buggers up!'

The lesson was largely a silent one. The students worked their way through the exercise in the text book with the teacher patrolling the desks, peering

220

over shoulders and fixing anyone who looked up with a rattlesnake glare. At the end of the lesson I accompanied Mr McNab, who was on yard duty, into the playground where he continued to enlighten me about his educational philosophy.

'Of course, I've tried group work, paired work, discussion, this interactive learning carry-on but it just doesnae work with this sort of pupil. They know every trick in the book. And they know all their rights as well. Canna lay so much as a little finger on 'em these days.'

When the bell rang for the end of break Mr McNab lined the pupils up and they filed into school. A large boy continued to sit on the wall, making no attempt to go in; he just sat there, chomping away on a large chocolate bar.

'You boy!' shouted the teacher.

'What?' the boy shouted back, spluttering bits of crumb and chocolate in the process.

Mr McNab clamped his mouth together and his eyes became hard and angry. He strode over to the wall and his loud voice rang over the school yard. 'When ye talk to a teacher, laddie, ya say "sir"!'

'What . . . sir?'

'Are ya deaf?'

'No.'

'Sir!' roared the teacher.

'No . . . sir.'

'Didna you hear the bell?'

'Yeah . . . sir.'

'What's yer name, laddie?'

'Sean.'

'Sean what?'

'Sir.'

'No! No! Your second name, yer great pudding!'

221

'Andrew . . . sir.'

'No! No! Yer other name.'

'Colin . . . sir.'

The veins in Mr McNab's forehead were now throbbing and his voice had increased several decibels. 'Yer last name! Yer surname!'

'Smith . . . sir.'

'Well, what are ye doing sitting on the wall when the bell has gone, Smith?'

'Having a rest . . . sir.'

Mr McNab's voice suddenly became low and threatening. He was as tense as an over-wound clock. 'I dinna like your attitude at all, Smith. Now, ye get up off that wall, dispose of that chocolate bar, tidy yerself up, move yer body smartly and get yerself to yer next lesson and I'll see you after school for a detention.'

'I can't, sir.'

'And why, pray, canna ya?' demanded the teacher, his eyes nearly popping from their sockets and his face as red as his hair.

'I don't go to this school any more,' replied the boy. 'I left last year. I work at the garage across the road, sir. I only came over to give my brother a message from our ma.'

I avoided meeting Mr McNab's eye as we made our way back into school.

The next lesson I observed was chemistry. 'Equipment!' the teacher repeated with a hollow laugh, when I asked about the various resources and materials the students would be using. 'You mean Bunsen burners, bottles of acid, glass beakers? I don't give this lot rulers, Mr Phinn, never mind equipment.'

During the very noisy lesson, while the tired-

222

looking woman in a white coat was attempting to explain about osmosis, a topic way beyond the pupils' understanding and of no interest to them whatsoever, Dean, the heavily tattooed individual, leaned back on his seat casually so his face was level with my own and commented in a voice loud enough to carry, 'She's not up to much, is she?'

'I suggest you keep your clever comments to yourself,' I retorted. 'Listen to the teacher and be quiet!'

He scowled and continued to rock on two legs of the chair.

The first lesson of the afternoon was geography. Dean was the centre of attention for the whole hour, talking loudly, poking the boy in front, flicking paper, making fatuous comments and generally being a nuisance. Bianca was calm in comparison; she just sat there with a bored look on her face. The teacher, a man with a long, wrinkled face of tragic potential, seemed to have become accustomed to the noise which was loud and penetrating, and appeared fully resigned to the poor behaviour of the pupils.

'The noise level in the room was deafening,' I told him after the lesson.

'Oh yes, I know, Mr Phinn,' he declared dolefully, 'but you only had to put up with it for an hour. I have this noise all the year round.'

'The lesson was terribly disorganised,' I continued.

'It was, wasn't it?' he agreed, nodding slowly.

'How do you feel about the criticism?' I asked him.

'How do I feel?' he repeated. His face seemed to express some amazement at the question. 'How do

223

I feel? Now, that's a question and a half, isn't it? I feel like a lion tamer without a whip, if you want me to be perfectly frank, or a swimmer in a pool of piranhas.'

I stared at him mutely for a moment. 'Is it always like this?'

'Mostly,' he replied, 'but I don't let it get to me. I've got high blood pressure, you see, so I can't get too excited. I'm on medication and a high fibre diet.' His face suddenly brightened. 'I've got a caravan on the coast, you know, and it's the only thing that keeps me sane. I finish at the end of next term.' He sighed happily. 'Then you won't see me for dust. I'm going to open a health food shop in Fettlesham and spend my days in peaceful retirement, selling dried fruit, branflakes and nuts. These pupils, as you have no doubt surmised, Mr Phinn, have very limited language skills. They find basic reading very difficult so when faced with some of the examination questions they just cannot make head nor tail of them. I mean, on last year's paper one of the questions was about Scottish lochs affording deep-water berthage. Well, I ask you, how many people could understand that? Then there was another question about an oil pipeline running across Alaska and they were asked why the oil wasn't flowing as quickly as it did in the Middle East. It was all to do with temperature but they had no idea that Alaska was cold and the Middle East hot. That's the extent of their general knowledge, you see.'

My response could not have been more forthright. 'Surely that is your job, to teach them?' I responded.

'Ooooh, easier said than done, Mr Phinn,' he

replied amiably and quite unperturbed, as if the criticism were some sort of commendation. 'I do try but I seem to get nowhere.'

'Have the students been on any geography field trips?' I asked, pretty sure what the answer would be.

'No, no. I did take a group once but it was more trouble than it was worth. I said after the disastrous trip to Whitby that I would never take a class on a trip to the coast again. They were up the cliffs, in the sea, on the abbey walls, dropping litter, throwing pebbles, chasing seagulls. Getting them on the coach was like rounding up a herd of wild horses. I was trying to count them when Francine, the big girl with the short hair, asked me if we could wait just another few minutes because she wanted to see Hipno. "Hippo, what hippo?" I asked. "Hip*no*, Hipno the rapist. He's just gone to get a cuppa, said he'd be back in five minutes," she said. "What rapist?" I asked her. "He's got a booth down there," she said and pointed to this big placard propped against the wall which announced in large, lurid lettering, HYPNOTHERAPIST. I ask you, Hypno the Rapist!'

At afternoon break Bianca told me that the final lesson of the day would be religious education with Mr Griffith. The idea of Dean and an RE class, the last thing on a Friday afternoon, did not bear thinking about.

'It's a right laugh,' added the girl, examining yet another chewed finger nail, before asking me. 'You 'aven't got a nail file on you, 'ave you?'

That phrase, 'it's a right laugh', I thought to myself, could mean one of two things. It could mean that the lesson would be generally entertaining and amusing or, on the other hand, complete and utter chaos. Having seen Dean and the class in action all day, I predicted that it would be the latter.

When Bianca and I arrived at the classroom, the students were, to my great surprise, lining up in an orderly fashion. There was no pushing or jostling, there was no shouting or arguing: in fact, the noise level for the first time that day was unusually low. Dean, who leaned quietly against the wall, seemed to have undergone a miraculous transformation. He just nodded at Bianca when she slipped in beside him. I joined the end of the line awaiting the arrival of Mr Griffith. I imagined that at any moment a great hairy mountain of a man with shoulders as broad as a barn door, the sort who looked as if he played prop forward for Wales, would emerge from around the corner. I was entirely mistaken, for a minute later a diminutive man dressed in a bright and baggy orange track-suit, circa 1950, the crackly nylon variety, appeared at the end of the corridor. He was carrying a large multi-coloured mug. Mr Griffith looked as if he had survived the electric chair for his wild hair, which was the colour and texture of wire wool, stuck up fantastically.

'Who is that at the back? Come out!' he roared. I stepped forward. 'Oh! I'm very sorry. It's a school inspector. I thought for moment it was the new boy.' He made a sort of flourish with his hand. 'We are greatly honoured this afternoon, five set nine, to have with us such an eminent visitor. Mr Flynn, is it?'

'Phinn,' I told him.

'Ah yes, Phinn, as in the shark.'

226

'Yes, that's right, Mr Griffith,' I replied, thinking of the ordeal ahead of me.

'And you are with us for this lesson?'

'I am.'

'Well, you are in, Mr Phinn, for a rare treat this afternoon, a rare treat. What's he in for, five set nine?'

'A rare treat!' the class chorused.

'Stand up straight there, Dean,' said the teacher, 'nice and smart. Look tidy boy, look tidy.'

Dean immediately did as he was told.

As soon as I had seen at close quarters the multi-coloured mug that the teacher held, I knew I was in for a rather different experience compared with the other lessons of the day, for emblazoned on the side were the words, 'Sticks and stones may break my bones, but whips and chains excite me.'

'This is my very favourite class, you know, Mr Phinn,' the teacher told me. 'They are a grand lot. What are you, five set nine?'

'A grand lot,' the pupils chorused.

'Of course,' Mr Griffith told me, whispering in my ear, 'as the head of religious education, I have an easy time, compared with my colleagues in other subjects, you know.'

'An easy time?' I repeated in disbelief.

'Yes, indeed. You see, unlike the head of the English department, I only have the one set book. Now, you come along in, Mr Phinn, but don't talk too fast otherwise they'll be up and dancing. Now, you are with Bianca, aren't you? Well, sit at the back next to her.' My heart sank. That would put me between her and Desperate Dean.

When the pupils had settled down in their seats the teacher began the lesson. He took centre stage,

227

fixed the class with a dramatic stare and began. 'Now, we got up to the part last week where Pontius Pilate had washed his hands of Jesus. Washed his hands! Do you know what they did then?'

'No, sir,' chorused the class.

'Great big whip!' Mr Griffith estimated the size of the whip by pulling his hands slowly apart to the length of about three feet. 'That big, Francine.'

'Ooooo!' whimpered a large girl on the front desk. Her eyes were wide in amazement.

'And they scourged Him with it.' The teacher provided us all with a most impressive and realistic mime of the whipping. 'Good word that, "scourge". I'll write it on the blackboard.' The teacher looked in my direction. 'Pity we can't do a bit of scourging in schools, Mr Phinn. A touch of the old scourging would do Dean a power of good, wouldn't it, Dean?'

'Yes, sir,' the boy replied with good humour.

'Now, after they had whipped Him and hit Him and spat at Him and kicked Him and called Him names, do you know what they did next?'

'No, sir,' chorused the class a second time.

'Great big piece of purple rag!' Again the teacher demonstrated the width. 'And they wrapped it around Him and laughed and jeered and scoffed and sneered and called Him "King of the Jews".'

'Aaaah!' whimpered the large girl at the front.

'Now, after they had whipped Him and hit Him and spat at Him and kicked Him and called Him names and wrapped Him in this piece of purple rag, do you know what they did next?'

'No, sir,' chorused the class a third time.

228

'Great big cross!' Mr Griffith estimated the size of the cross by stretching his hands heavenwards. 'That big, Francine.'

'Ooooo!' murmured the girl, her hand to her mouth.

'And they made Him drag it through the streets, all the while mocking and cursing and jeering Him. Simon of Cyrene came out of an alleyway to help Him with the cross, as you would, but he was pushed back by the Roman soldiers who made Jesus drag the instrument of His death to the Hill of Skulls.' Mr Griffith paused for effect. 'Now, I'm talking here about the Son of God. The Son of God! He could have clicked His fingers and they would have all been dust under His sandals. He had the power in His finger to devastate—to DEVASTATE—the whole world but He didn't, see. He let them do it. He let them hurt Him and humiliate Him and He never raised a finger against them. Now I bet you that if someone did that to you, Dean, and you had that power just by raising a finger to kill the lot of them, you wouldn't just stand there and take it, would you?'

'No, sir, I'd have killed the whole lot of 'em,' replied the boy forcefully.

'Then why didn't Jesus? Why did He let them do all that to Him? What was the point of all that suffering? Just think about it for a moment.' A silence descended on the class. 'You see,' continued the teacher after a minute, 'not only was Jesus the gentlest, most loving and completely harmless man in the world, He was also the most courageous to undergo that suffering. Do you know what they did then?'

'No, sir,' chorused the class.

229

I prepared myself for the gruesome account which would inevitably follow.

'They crucified Him. They nailed Him to that cross and He died. And the soldiers gambled over the only things He owned—the few clothes from His back—and His mother watched Him die a slow and painful death and His friends deserted him. His best friend, Peter, denied he even knew Him. Three times he said, "I do not know this man." And there hung the Son of God who had harmed no one.'

I had heard the story of the crucifixion a thousand times but, on this occasion, when that awesome silence fell on the class, I felt my heart begin to thump in my chest and tears pricking my eyes. I glanced across at Dean. He sat, mouth open like a netted fish, with real tears above the tattooed tears, totally captivated and moved by the saddest story of all time.

'But do you know what they did before they did that?' roared the teacher, making the whole class, myself included, jump in our seats.

'No, sir,' I heard myself saying.

'They took a crown of thorns—a crown of thorns—and they rammed it, yes, they rammed it on His head.'

In the deathly silence which greeted this, Dean turned to me and said with a curl of the top lip, 'The bastards!'

At the end of the lesson, when the pupils had set off home, Mr Griffith, whistling merrily to himself, packed away his books, straightened the classroom and walked with me to the staff room.

'How did I get on then, Mr Phinn?' he asked.

I looked down at the blank page in my notebook.

'I've not written a thing,' I replied. 'Not a thing.'

'My father was a great Baptist preacher in Wales, you know. After chapel, he valued education above all else. Of course, that's a Welsh characteristic, you know. Lloyd George once said: "The Welsh have a passion for education and the English have no particular objection to it." Well, my father brought the Bible to life, see. He lifted the sacred text off the page.' Mr Griffith stopped and gripped my arm. 'Now, if you think this afternoon was good, well, why don't you come back at Christmas—I do a lovely Herod!'

CHAPTER TWELVE

'Are you getting all nervous, then?' Julie asked, placing a cup of coffee on my desk. I was sorting though my early morning mail in the office prior to setting off for my last official school visit of the spring term.

'I am a bit, Julie,' I admitted. 'It's a big step, marriage.'

'Particularly if you've been living on your own for so long and used to a certain routine.'

'Well, it's a matter of give and take, isn't it?' I replied.

'In my experience, it's the woman who gives and the man who takes.'

'That is a typical cliché, and not all men are like that, Julie,' I said. 'Anyway, when you get married you have to get used to all your partner's little foibles, I realise that.'

'Little foibles!' exclaimed Julie. 'You mean dirty

habits and peculiar obsessions.'

'And what would a young woman like you know about dirty habits and peculiar obsessions?' I asked, laughing.

'Because I've lived with my parents for as long as I can remember and I have two sisters and two brothers.' Julie sat on the corner of my desk. 'My sisters, Karen and Anne, were love's young dreams until their new husbands started dropping their dirty underpants all over the place, coming in stinking of beer, watching football on the television into the early hours with their noisy mates, wearing their socks three days running, leaving the top off the toothpaste and the toilet seat up, snoring like bronchial hippopotamuses every night—just like my two brothers and my dad have done all their lives. Love soon flies out of the window when you have to put up with that.'

'I can't really imagine Christine dropping dirty underwear all over the place, coming in stinking of beer and snoring like a bronchial hippopotamus,' I told her mischievously.

'I'm not talking about Christine,' Julie said. 'I'm talking about you. Men are different from women.'

'Now there's an original observation,' I remarked. *'Vive la difference!'*

'You know what I mean. Men think differently and behave differently. For a start they are more untidy and unhygienic. They are more inconsiderate and irritating. Now take Mr Clamp as a prime example. Can you imagine anything worse than being married to him? He'd drive anyone to drink.'

'Not at all, Julie,' I told her. 'Sidney is a happily married man, his wife loves him dearly and I

232

believe he is very attractive to the opposite sex. Women want to mother him.'

'Smother him, more like. Mr Clamp is every woman's nightmare.'

At that very moment, the subject of our conversation breezed in through the office door. He was dressed in a light cotton suit, pale yellow silk tie and sported a wide-brimmed straw hat. He looked every inch the gentleman about town. 'Almost last day of term for us, Julie,' he exclaimed. 'And last week of freedom for you, Gervase.'

'Don't you start as well,' I told him. 'You two should be wishing me well, not trying to put me off.'

'Of course we wish you well, dear boy,' cried Sidney, putting his arm around my shoulder. 'I am certain beyond doubt that the wedding will go beautifully, the reception swimmingly—you might even make a passable speech—the honeymoon blissfully and your life with the Aphrodite of Winnery Nook, the drop-dead gorgeous Miss Bentley in your little love nest—' He stopped abruptly. 'By the way, did you get your cottage?'

*   *   *

Sidney's assessment of Peewit Cottage had been remarkably accurate. The 'beautiful listed cottage in a delightful position overlooking a watercolour landscape near the picture-postcard Dales village of Hawksrill' needed a great deal of work. The surveyor's report had arrived a week before the auction. Unlike the estate agent's description, it had been far from rosy; in fact, it made the property sound as though it were on the verge of

233

collapse. There were 'extensive timber infestations observed throughout the property, evidence of rising and penetrating damp, significant deflections to the roof pitches, serious weathering to the stonework due to the exposed condition and age, defective guttering, lack of lateral bracing between front and rear walls'—whatever that meant—and 'numerous other urgent repairs' which required immediate attention.

Christine and I were sitting in the front room of my flat above the Rumbling Tum Café with the greasy aroma drifting up the stairs and the noise of traffic in the High Street outside, and were reading through page after page of problems. Finally I threw the surveyor's bulky report onto the table and sat back. I put my arm around Christine who looked devastated.

'I knew it needed work doing to it,' I said. 'I mean, it's old and hasn't been lived in for ages, but I didn't reckon on all that amount.'

'Me neither,' she replied sadly.

We didn't say anything for a while. We just sat there in our silent disappointment.

'Well,' I said at last, 'I suppose we had better look for something else—and quickly or we will find ourselves living in this dump for months to come.'

'I suppose so,' Christine replied. There were tears in her eyes.

'It is so sad. It's such a lovely cottage.'

'It is,' she murmured. 'I love it from the name onwards. Peewit Cottage—it has such a sonorous ring to it.'

'And a beautiful setting.'

'Yes.'

'Just the right size.'

'Mmm.'

'And those magnificent views. We'll never find a view like that again.'

'Oh, don't go on, Gervase, you're making it worse. I need you to tell me it's a dump and it wants pulling down. Tell me that the people who buy it will have bought a millstone which will be around their necks for the rest of their lives. Just don't tell me how beautiful it is.' And she began to cry.

'Come on, Chris,' I said, holding her close and wiping away her tears. 'We'll find somewhere else. I promise.'

'Like one of those smart but oh so predictable apartments or town houses in Fettlesham which Sidney suggested? I had my heart set on that cottage. I fell in love with it as soon as I saw it.'

'But just think of all the work needed.'

'I know,' she said, snuggling closer. 'I know.'

'We'd be spending all our lives renovating it and—'

'You needn't go on, darling,' she told me. 'I know it's impossible. I know we'll never have it now.'

Later that evening, after a subdued supper, most of which we left, Christine said quietly, 'Do you remember what brought us together in the first place?'

'Your blue eyes,' I said immediately. 'I was captivated by your blue eyes.'

'Yes, well, I was in fact thinking of something else. Something else blue.'

'Blue?' I said. 'Blue what?'

'How about a certain blue-and-white plate?'

'Ah, if you'd said "blue-and-white",' I laughed, 'I'd have known exactly what you meant. But why bring that up now?'

'Well, it occurred to me that that plate brought us together—we were in Roper's Saleroom in Collington at an auction. And look where it led? We could go to next Saturday's auction—we've nothing on—if only to see what the cottage goes for. I mean, we wouldn't bid or anything. Just go out of interest.'

'I suppose we could,' I replied.

'I mean, it's sure to be out of our price range anyway.'

'That's true,' I said and, remembering the occasion when Christine left me to bid for the blue-and-white plate on her behalf, added, 'We could go, for old times' sake.'

'It can't do any harm seeing what it fetches.'

So at twelve noon the following Saturday, Christine and I sat nervously on hard stackable chairs in the back row in Hawksrill Village Hall for the auction of Peewit Cottage.

The estate agent, a round, jovial man with a shock of silver-white hair, a paunch of mountainous proportions and a nose like a hatchet, consulted his heavy silver pocket watch and banged his gavel on the table.

'Good day, all,' he said. 'My name is Wesley Harper of Harper, Read and Harper, Auctioneers, Valuers and Estate Agents of Fettlesham. On my right is the vendor's solicitor, Mrs Sonia Stackpole.' He gestured in the direction of an elegant young woman in a dark suit sitting on his right. 'We are here for the public auction of the freehold property known as Peewit Cottage, Hawksrill, in the county

236

of Yorkshire. The particulars of the sale, setting out the conditions, are here'—he stabbed a large official-looking folder before him on the table—'should anyone who has not received a copy wish to view them before the sale commences. Peewit Cottage is sold with vacant possession on completion of the contract. I would like to remind the successful bidder that ten per cent deposit is payable today and that, in addition to the purchase price, there will be, of course, stamp duty, land registry fee and solicitor's charges.' He smiled and scratched his hatchet nose. 'So, is there anyone wishing to view the particulars of sale?' He scanned the faces before him. 'No? Has anyone anything to say before we begin with the auction?' He glanced around the room. 'Good. So, will anyone start the bidding. Shall we say . . .'

*   *   *

Christine and I sat outside the Golden Ball pub in Hawksrill, staring in silence at the wonderful view before us. The auction had finished over an hour before.

'Well,' I said, breathing out heavily.

'Are you worried?' Christine asked.

'Very, and still a bit shell-shocked.'

'You don't regret it now, do you?'

'Of course not.'

'I never realised you were so impulsive. I couldn't believe it when you started bidding.'

'I didn't notice your stopping me,' I replied, looking into her beautiful blue eyes. 'I knew you had your heart set on it. I did too. I just couldn't stop myself, once I'd started. Just like the blue-and-

237

white plate—it was something you really wanted.'

'Come here,' Christine said and gave me a great hug and a kiss. 'Oh Gervase, think of the views and the beams and the quarry-tiled floors and the old fireplaces and the little garden.'

'And all the work.'

'We'll manage that even if we have to sleep on the floor for a few years and put up with the damp and woodworm and collapsing gutters and crumbling walls. I can't believe it. It's ours, that lovely cottage. It's ours.'

Although the village hall had been packed to the walls there had only been three people interested in buying: a local builder, an architect from Leeds and myself. The others who crowded into the musty room were, no doubt, the villagers who were interested in what the cottage would fetch and who the new owners were.

The bidding had started low but increased quickly past the guide price. Apart from the serendipitous visit to Roper's Saleroom in Collington, I had only been to a few auctions and then to buy books, so I was not at all experienced. However, when the builder waved his paper ostentatiously and the architect nodded confidently, I had entered the fray, and like a bulldog with a bone, hung on until Mr Harper of Harper, Read and Harper, Auctioneers, Valuers and Estate Agents had banged his gavel loud enough to wake the dead and shouted: 'Sold to the young gentleman at the back.'

People in front of us swivelled in their seats to see who this 'young gentleman' was. 'Young, mad gentleman' would have been more apt, I thought, my heart hammering so loudly that I thought

238

everyone could hear it.

Before going for our celebratory drink at the Golden Ball, we had walked out of the village and into the open country beyond, in order to turn back and look at the property we had just bought. The cottage looked small and rather sad in the early afternoon sunshine. The roof, covered in cracked orange tiles, sagged in the middle and the chimney leaned to one side. Tiny windows were set in the old red sandstone walls and the paint was flaking from the wooden shutters. A thick stem of ivy writhed like a snake over the porch and grass sprouted like tufts of green hair from the broken guttering. The small garden was—well, no one could call it a garden: it was a jungle of weeds and thistles, choking brambles and wild bushes which might once have been called shrubs.

Christine wrapped her arms around me and hugged me tightly. 'Isn't it just idyllic?' she sighed.

I could have provided a more appropriate adjective but bit my tongue and thought of all the hard graft ahead. The thought uppermost in my mind was thank heavens I had not got the Senior Inspector's post after all because I would be spending every spare moment trying to get Peewit Cottage habitable.

'Happy?' I asked.

'What do you think?' she replied and her eyes shone.

*   *   *

That afternoon I had agreed to speak about children's books on the local radio. The usual contributor, a librarian with the county library

239

service, was on holiday and I had agreed to step in. I had not spoken on radio before and, although I was in a buoyant mood thinking about the cottage, I also felt more than a twinge of nerves as I sat in the small studio, headphones on waiting to be introduced.

The radio presenter, Lenny Walters, was a loud young black man with a completely bald head and an assortment of gold rings in one ear and on his fingers. He told me that each week there was this slot—not too long—when the librarian recommended a few books for children. 'All very laid back and chatty, nothing too heavy,' he explained. I gulped and looked down at my notes.

The music that was playing came to an end, and Lenny leant towards the microphone. 'For those of you who have just tuned in,' he said, 'this is the "Listen in with Lenny" show and I am Lenny Walters and I will be with you for the next hour with all the news, views, reviews, record requests and lots and lots of old-time favourites and popular hits. If you have a point of view, if you have something you want to say, if you have anything you want to get off your chest or if you just want a record playing for someone special, then pick up the phone and dial Lenny on Fettlesham 820340. Now,' and he picked an index card from the top of the pile in front of him, 'the next record is for Mrs Doreen Roberts of Victoria Terrace, Fettlesham who wants me to play "Come back to Sorrento" sung by the late, great Josef Locke. Doreen tells me she's never been to Sorrento—she's a Skegness person herself—but the record will bring back very happy memories of the Italian prisoner-of-war she met when she was a Land Girl.'

Lenny pressed a button on the huge deck before him and Josef Locke began his very emotional rendering of "Come back to Sorrento" for lucky Mrs Doreen Roberts of Victoria Terrace, Fettlesham, then he swivelled around in his chair to face me.

'So, what's it like being a school inspector then?' he asked, tilting back and reaching for a plastic cup of coffee. Before I could respond he rattled on: 'I bet you put the fear of God into teachers, don't you, when you arrive at their classroom door? It's the sort of job I reckon you never admit to doing, is it? School inspector? Like a traffic warden or a tax inspector. If I were you, I wouldn't mention being a school inspector when I put you on. I'll just tell the listeners you're filling in this week for June. We don't want a load of angry teachers shouting down the line, do we?'

'OK,' I replied.

Josef Locke faded, Lenny prodded another button on his deck and announced: 'And now for our weekly look at books. This week, we have a new face in the studio. Jarvis Phipps, who's standing in for our lovely June, is with me this afternoon. June's on holiday this week, sunning herself on a beach in Tunisia, lucky June, so we have another bookworm here—if I may call you that, Jarvis—to tell us what books are in the shops and what you might enjoy reading over Easter.'

I talked a little about some popular books for five minutes or so and then Lenny came back in. 'Thanks, Jarvis. Stay with us because there might be some listeners out there who want to phone in.' He picked up the next card off the pile on the console in front of him. 'The next record is for

241

Rosemary Mulligan of Broom Valley Road, Kirby Ruston. Rosemary wants a record for her dear grandfather, Patrick—known as Paddy—Mulligan who lives at Holly House Residential Home, Fettlesham, and is one hundred and eleven years old. Wow! That's a fair old age, Paddy, and no mistake. One hundred and eleven and not out! Did you know that score in cricket is called a Nelson and is considered bad luck? I hope it doesn't bring you bad luck, Paddy. David Sheppard, the England cricket umpire, always stands on one leg when that score is reached. Perhaps Paddy should stand on one leg all year! Anyway, Rosemary wants Tina Turner singing, "When the Heartache is Over".' Lenny tried to suppress his laughter. 'I'll tell you what, Paddy, if I reach a hundred and eleven and still like listening to the likes of Tina Turner, I'll be happy man. And I can see Jarvis nodding away in the studio. So here's Tina Turner singing "When the Heartache is Over" for the remarkable one-hundred-and-eleven-year-old Patrick "call me Paddy" Mulligan.'

'Actually, it's Gervase,' I told Lenny while Tina was belting out her song.

'What is?'

'My name, it's not Jarvis, it's Gervase.'

Lenny's mind was clearly on other things. He was flicking switches and pressing buttons on his consul. 'Right,' he said. 'Hey, it's amazing, isn't it? This old bloke. One hundred and eleven!'

'He must be the oldest man in England,' I said.

'Yeah, I suppose he is,' replied Lenny.

When Tina Turner had finished singing, he stabbed the consul before him. 'Jarvis and me have been having a little discussion here in the studio,'

Lenny told his listeners, 'and we reckon Paddy Mulligan of Holly House Residential Home is the oldest man in England. I've heard of a woman in France who's one hundred and fifteen and she's the oldest person in Europe, and there's a man in India, I think, who's older, but I reckon Paddy Mulligan at one hundred and eleven must be the oldest man in England. Now, this is what I'm going to do. I'm going to invite Paddy to come into the studio and tell the listeners about his wonderful long life. He must have seen some things in his one hundred and eleven years. I'll arrange a car to collect you, Paddy, and your lovely granddaughter, Rosemary, of course, and we'll get you into the studio next week. And there'll be a bottle of champagne waiting for you to celebrate your long life. How about that? I'm sure the listeners would love to hear from you. Give us a ring, Rosemary, and tell us if you're willing. Now I'm gong to play the next track for Paddy, and it's another Tina Turner number, "Simply the Best" because that's what you are, Paddy, simply the best.'

During the next record the consul before Lenny began flashing madly. He prodded a button and spoke to some disembodied voice. 'Yeah, yeah, I see. What did she say? Really?' He stroked his bald head. 'Oh, no! Is he? OK, OK. Yeah, I'll sort it. I said, I'll sort it.' He looked at me shrugged and shook his head. 'We've got a problem,' he mouthed.

My immediate thought was that poor old Paddy had finally gone to meet his maker.

'That was Tina Turner singing "Simply the Best",' announced Lenny into the microphone in a rather more subdued voice. 'Now, we've just

243

received a telephone call from a rather distressed Rosemary Mulligan of Broom Valley Road, Kirby Ruston. Her grandfather, Patrick, is not, as I stated earlier, a hundred and eleven years old.' He paused, looking at the index card he held in front of him. 'He's ill.'

*   *   *

That evening, Christine and I were curled up on the sofa together in my flat. We had enjoyed a splendid supper and a bottle of good wine. It had been memorable day. We were so happy.

'It frightens me sometimes,' I told her.

'What does?'

'Just how lucky I am. To have you for the rest of my life in our dream cottage. It sometimes feels just too good to be true.'

'I'm lucky, too,' Christine said, giving me a kiss.

'On the radio programme today,' I told her, 'the presenter played this record, "Simply the Best", and I thought of you. That's what you are, Chris, simply the best thing that's happened to me. I'm the luckiest man alive.'

'I love you too,' she replied, snuggling close to me and then, after a pause, murmured, 'Gervase?'

'Yes, what is it, darling?'

'You will always be honest with me, won't you? Tell me if there is anything that's on your mind, anything which I do which upsets you?'

'Of course, and you'll be honest with me as well, won't you?'

'Yes, of course I will. In fact, on that subject, I hope you won't mind my mentioning this but when we are married you won't leave your dirty clothes

244

on the floor, will you, and . . . er . . . about your socks . . . '

CHAPTER THIRTEEN

Christine and I were married on 15 April at St Walburga's Church. I wore a charcoal-grey morning coat and Christine a simple white dress and veil. She needed no elaborate silk wedding gown, embellished with intricate embroidery and studded with pearls, she needed no long lace train held by page boys in velvet, no fancy necklace or diamond tiara to look stunning. She would have looked the same to me in a threadbare army greatcoat. On that bright spring morning with the sun shining through the stained glass and bathing her in a pale golden light, Christine looked a vision as she walked down the aisle on her father's arm. In her hands she held a delicate posy of muscari and freesia in the centre of which was a small, but very special sprig of broom.

*　　　*　　　*

The last day of term had been an emotional occasion. I had been invited to Winnery Nook Nursery and Infants School to be introduced to the children not as the school inspector but as Miss Bentley's future husband and for a presentation from the governors, staff and children. One small boy in particular had touched our hearts.

Barry was six and it was clear to everyone who met him that he was a neglected child who desperately sought affection. His shirt was invariably dirty, his trousers frayed, his jumper spattered with stains and he had that unpleasant, unwashed smell about him.

'He's from a large one-parent family,' Christine had told me, when I had met the little boy on a previous visit to the school. 'I don't suppose he gets much attention at home. His mother is a sharp-tongued, miserable woman and, from what I gather, finds it difficult to cope. Demanding young children, too little money, mounting debts, absentee father—or, more likely, fathers—a string of violent boyfriends. It's perhaps no surprise that she looks permanently exhausted and that she flies off the handle at every opportunity. But Barry deserves better. She seems to have no interest in him at all.'

'What a life!' I had said.

Despite his background, Barry was a remarkably cheerful little boy who never complained and always tried his limited best at his school work. 'Hello, Miss Bentley,' he would shout brightly each morning as he waited for her at the entrance to the school. 'Any jobs, miss?' He loved nothing better than straightening the chairs, giving out the paper and pencils, collecting the books, tidying up the classroom and picking up litter and he took on all these tasks cheerfully, whistling away as if he had not a care in the world.

It was just after the assembly on this final morning, where we had been presented with a large box wrapped in pale flowery wedding paper and festooned with ribbons and silver horseshoes, that Barry had appeared. Some of the children had brought individual presents and cards, others had

246

arrived at school with great bunches of daffodils, tulips and other spring flowers. Soon we had been surrounded by a chattering, excited throng of children, all eager to wish us well. Barry had held back until Christine and I had begun to make our way to her room.

'Hello, Barry,' Christine had said, having caught sight of him lingering in the corridor. 'Come along and meet my fiancé. Do you remember Mr Phinn?'

The little boy had surveyed me seriously. He was carrying two small branches of faded broom which had seen better days and a couple of forlorn irises, wrapped in a piece of colourful paper which I realised was a page torn out of a magazine.

'Are you really getting married then, miss?' he had asked sadly.

'Yes, I am,' Christine had replied, crouching down so she had been on his level. She had taken his grubby little hand in hers. 'Aren't you going to say "hello" to my husband-to-be?'

'Hello,' the little boy had mumbled disconsolately.

'Hello, Barry,' I had replied.

'And next term I'll be Mrs Phinn,' Christine had told him. 'Isn't it exciting?'

'I like you as Miss Bentley,' he had said unhappily. 'I don't want you getting married. I don't want you to. I don't, I don't!' And he had burst into tears.

'I'll still be the same person, Barry. I won't be any different.'

'You will! You will!' he had wailed piteously. 'I know you will.' Then he had looked up at Christine, sniffing and sobbing and rubbing his eyes. 'I wanted to marry you.'

Christine had wrapped her arms around his small shaking body. 'And are these lovely flowers for me?' she had asked in a trembling voice. I knew she was as affected by this pathetic little scene as I was. He had nodded and sniffed. 'They're beautiful, and I shall put them in water and have them on my desk. These shall be my very special flowers.'

She had taken his hand, led him into the staff room, with me following, and found the most colourful vase from under the sink. The flowers had been arranged and we had followed Christine back to her room where she had put the vase in pride of place on her desk. She had then given the little boy a hug. 'These are my very special flowers, Barry. Thank you so much. I like them better than any other flowers I have been given.'

Chris told me later that, at the end of the day, the little boy had appeared at her door.

'Hello, Barry,' Christine had said brightly. 'Have you come to wish me all the best for my wedding next week?'

'I've come for my flowers, miss,' he had said bluntly.

'Your flowers? Oh, I thought they were for me.'

'They're very special,' the child had said solemnly. 'You said they were very special.'

'And they are,' Christine had told him. 'I think they are beautiful but I thought you brought them for me.'

'They're very special,' Barry had repeated, 'and I want to give them to my mam.'

Christine had smiled. 'Of course, you do.' She had removed the broom, virtually bare of its yellow blossom, and the two wilting irises from the vase and had wrapped them in some bright red tissue paper. Then, taking a ribbon from one of the wedding presents, she had tied them in a bunch. 'They look really nice now, don't they?' she had said. 'What a lovely surprise for your mummy.' Christine had placed the flowers in the child's hands. 'Do you think I might have just a little sprig of broom for good luck? I'll put it with my bouquet when I get married.' The child had nodded and snapped a sprig from a branch.

Christine had watched Barry scurry down the school path to be met at the gates by a stocky, unkempt woman with short bleached hair and a cigarette dangling from her mouth. Two screaming toddlers were writhing and wriggling in the push-chair beside her. On seeing her son, she had stabbed the air with a finger and had begun shouting at him. Reaching her, the little boy had held up his bouquet like a priest at the altar making an offering. The flowers had been promptly plucked from his hand and deposited in the nearest bin.

'What a life,' I had said to Christine when she told me this. 'What a life!'

∗ ∗ ∗

The day of our wedding went like clockwork. For a start, the weather was perfect: it was one of those bright spring days when there was even a little warmth in the sun and the air was alive with bird song. The reception was held at the Bankfield Hotel, a grey, turreted building covered in thick ivy and surrounded by long lawns which were carpeted with great swathes of daffodils. We left the church and village square in a smart pony and trap and, as we approached the hotel, the building seemed to rise like a castle from a sea of green and gold.

All the speeches had been well received, particularly 'Legs' Bentley's, Christine's father. At one moment he had us all roaring with laughter as he described her childhood antics and the next he moved us to tears describing how much he loved this gentle, compassionate woman who had brought such joy into his life. Sidney threatened to make a speech about me, but I think he was only joking and was, for once, quiet when Geraldine playfully put her hand across his mouth. We were overwhelmed with presents and good wishes, and we even received a card from Simon Carter, wishing us all the very best and saying how much he was looking forward to working with me. So, my lovely bride and I could not have hoped for a better start to our married life. The honeymoon, however, was not without incident.

Christine and I drove to the Lake District in her Morris Traveller, talking non-stop. Most of the conversation was about Peewit Cottage—what we intended to do with the overgrown garden (typical of us to worry about the least important first), the improvements we envisaged to the completely out-dated kitchen, our plans for the cold damp bedrooms and the essential changes needed to the plumbing. We chatted about colour schemes and furniture, curtains and carpets, wallpaper and widow-boxes all the way to the Salutation Hotel in Ambleside.

On that first evening I was waiting for Christine to join me in the bar before dinner when I became aware of a familiar perfume, a perfume which

250

brought back many memories. Turning, I came face-to-face with someone I had not seen for years.

'Susan!' I exclaimed, nearly dropping my drink. 'Whatever are you doing here?'

'Hello, Gervase,' she said calmly. 'I thought in this situation, when one hasn't seen someone for a long time, that the line is usually: "How lovely to see you again."'

I had met Susan at the Charlotte Mason College in Ambleside six or seven years before. I was still a teacher at the time and was attending a weekend course at the college where I met this stunningly attractive woman with long auburn hair and eyes the colour of polished jade. She was teaching in a large comprehensive school in Birmingham and I had been well and truly smitten. Susan was a lively, intelligent and amusing person and, when we had both returned home, I had plucked up the courage, telephoned her and asked her out. We had spent most weekends for the next year together. We went to the theatre and concerts, and spent many hours walking in Derbyshire which was about the halfway point between our two homes. Occasionally, we went further afield, liking especially to walk on the beach at Whitby. For me, the relationship soon began to become more and more serious. It was not quite the same for Susan. She was so consumed by her work that I suddenly realised she did not want the relationship to develop into anything permanent. There had been no mention of our settling down together, or engagement or marriage. Then one evening, after a quiet and unusually strained conversation over dinner, she had told me that she had decided to accept a senior position teaching in an army school in Germany. So we had parted on amicable terms to go our separate ways. Now here she was, with the same long auburn hair and eyes the colour of polished jade.

'I'm sorry, Susan,' I stuttered now, 'it's . . . it's . . . just that it's such a shock seeing you here.'

'Yes, it's a bit of a surprise for me, too,' she said. 'I couldn't believe my eyes when I saw you propping up the bar.'

'I just can't believe it's you.'

'You really do look as if you've seen a ghost,' she said. 'I don't look all that dire, do I?'

'No, no, of course you don't . . . well . . . you look . . . er . . . wonderful. You haven't changed a bit.'

'Neither have you.'

'It's just such a surprise finding you here of all places. I'm sorry, I . . .'

'I do wish you would stop apologising,' she said.

'I'm sorry, it's just such a shock. So, you're back from Germany?'

'Yes, about a year. I'm a deputy headteacher now, in Buxton, but it has the rather quaint title of Senior Mistress.'

'Congratulations. I knew you were destined for the top. Headteacher next.'

'Hope so.'

'And are you still working too hard, putting in all those hours?'

'That's the nature of the job,' she replied, 'as you well know.'

'You look as if you are enjoying life, anyway.'

'Oh, I am. I love the work. I live in a house with fabulous views, and am always busy. All the ingredients, in fact, for a very happy and fulfilled life.' She did not sound all that happy and fulfilled, I thought to myself. It was as if she were trying to

252

convince herself.

'I just can't get over seeing you. And what are you doing here in the Salutation?'

'I'm attending a management and leadership course at the college. Lots of long lectures and discussion groups. We have a free evening tonight, though, so we are letting our hair down a bit. You are very welcome to join us if you'd like to.' Before I could answer, she continued, 'I did try and get in touch, you know.'

'Really?'

'I did, yes, but you were out inspecting every time I called your office and your secretary wouldn't give me your home number.'

'No, Julie never gives out our personal numbers. If she did, we'd be inundated with calls from angry parents and teachers and governors and I don't know who else. Why didn't you leave a message?'

'Oh, I don't know,' she replied quietly.

'Why not?'

'Pride, I guess. I suppose I was a bit afraid that you wouldn't ring back. I was intending to try again but time moved on and I was busy and . . . oh . . . I don't know.'

'You don't know me very well, Susan,' I replied.

'How do you mean?'

'Of course I would have got back to you. You know how I felt about you.'

'Yes, I know,' she said. 'I think about our times together often enough. Anyway, that's water under the bridge now, isn't it?' When I didn't answer, she continued trying to sound cheerful. 'And what about you? Do you like school inspecting?'

'Yes, I love it. Best move I ever made.'

'And are you the Chief Inspector yet?'

253

'No, I did try for a senior inspector's job, but wasn't even interviewed.'

'More fool them.'

'I'm really glad things have worked out for you,' I said. 'I was sure you'd get to the top.'

'Yes, I was always ambitious, perhaps a bit too much.' I did not know what to say. 'It was only when I had moved to Germany that I began to miss things. I missed the theatre trips and the walks, and our trips to Whitby and those ridiculously unhealthy fish and chips at The Magpies. Do you remember? And looking for pieces of jet on the beach. I even missed the school plays you dragged me along to.' She looked into my eyes. 'And I missed you, Gervase. I've thought about you a lot.'

'Susan . . .' I began. I could feel my face beginning to get hot with embarrassment. I was stuck for words again.

'I suppose it's one of life's most hackneyed phrases,' she continued. 'If only . . .'

'Ah, well . . .' I began again.

'To be truthful, if I had my time over again and had those choices to make and if . . .'

'Yes . . . well . . .'

'So, perhaps I should give you that ring?'

'Ring!' I gulped. 'W . . . what ring?'

'Give you that ring and arrange something, that's if you are still . . . well, you know, unattached.'

'Susan,' I said gently, 'I'm with someone tonight. A terrible cliché, perhaps, but true—I am with someone tonight . . .' My voice trailed off.

'Oh,' was all she said.

I knew I had to get the truth out. 'I met her just after I had started the inspector's job in Yorkshire. We've been going out now for two years. Her name's Christine.'

'I see,' she said again. There was an awkward silence. 'Is she beautiful?'

'Yes, she's very beautiful.'

'Silly question. Of course she's beautiful and probably very clever and charming and successful as well.'

'Susan,' I said, 'I'm married now. In fact, today. We are here on our honeymoon.' The words now came tumbling out.

She looked aghast. 'Oh dear. How embarrassing! This is the sort of terrible situation we all dread. I think I'm supposed to say, "Well, I hope you'll be very happy together."' She looked up and there were tears in her eyes. 'I've made a bit of a fool of myself, haven't I?'

'No, of course not,' I replied. 'You weren't to know.'

'I *do* hope you will be very happy together, Gervase, I really do. You deserve it.' She kissed me lightly on the cheek. 'I had better go, the others will be missing me.'

'Susan—' I began, but she quickly walked away and was gone before I could complete the sentence. I could feel my heart pounding in my chest.

'Could I have a whisky, please?' I asked the barman. 'And make it a double.'

*   *   *

'So who was that woman you were talking to at the bar?' asked Christine when we sat down for dinner.

I had hoped she hadn't noticed when she'd walked into the bar by one door just as Susan was leaving the bar by its second door. I had immediately cancelled my whisky and asked the barman to open the champagne I had ordered previously.

'She's a deputy headteacher, here on some sort of study course,' I replied, now reading the menu and attempting to sound casual and rather vague. 'I used to know her.'

'She's very attractive.'

'Yes, she is, isn't she, very attractive. What are you going to start with?'

'And beautifully dressed.'

'Yes, she was. I think I'll start with the scallops.'

'So how did you know her?'

'Oh, it was some years ago. I met her on a course. Here in Ambleside, as a matter of fact.'

'Gosh!' exclaimed Christine. 'You have a remarkably good memory for faces, pretty faces anyway.'

'Actually, I knew her very well.' I took rather a large gulp of champagne, and the bubbles fizzed in my nose. 'In fact, I knew her very well indeed. I went out with her for nearly a year. We were just catching up on old times.'

Christine took a sip of her champagne and smiled at me. 'You know one of these days, Gervase Phinn, someone will take you seriously.' She laughed, throwing back her head.

'Christine, it's true!'

She clearly still did not believe me and thought I was teasing her. 'Did you notice she was wearing an ankle bracelet?'

'No, I didn't. I don't go around, especially on my honeymoon, looking at attractive women's ankles.'

'Well, she was. She didn't look very much like a

deputy headteacher to me.'

'And what, pray, does a deputy headteacher look like?'

'Well, certainly not like the woman at the bar.'

'Christine—' I began.

'It would be something to tell your colleagues at work, wouldn't it,' she said, smiling again.

'What would?'

'That on your honeymoon you had met an old flame in the hotel. You have a wild and wonderful imagination, do you know that? Who *was* she really?'

'Oh, just someone I met at the bar,' I replied. 'Now, Mrs Phinn, have you decided what to have?'

*   *   *

We stayed for just a week in Ambleside, walking on some of the Lake District's beautiful fells. We spent the other week of the Easter holidays starting work on Peewit Cottage. An ancient great-aunt of Chris's had died at the beginning of the year, and had left her some furniture which had been stored temporarily in her parents' garage. To start with, we just took over a table and some chairs, ostensibly so we could eat in comfort the cold food we brought with us from the flat—but the end of a hard day's work often found us eating the excellent pies produced by the Golden Ball.

There was absolutely no point in bringing any more furniture, nor having carpets laid, until the verminous woodwork was treated, the damp dealt with in the bedrooms and the walls then replastered. Only then could we make a start on transforming the place into our dream cottage. We didn't want to spend a single night more than necessary in my small flat above the Rumbling Tum Café and aimed to move in during the school half-term holiday.

One afternoon, I abandoned the job of rubbing down the bathroom walls and came outside to have a breath of fresh air. I was sitting on the drystone wall which enclosed the small garden, staring abstractedly at the breathtaking panorama before me. I could not believe that we had this view from the bedroom window, that we would pull back the curtains every morning and gaze upon acres of green undulating fields studded with grey outcrops of rock and divided by thin white walls which rose like veins impossibly high to the craggy fellsides beyond. I suddenly became aware of a figure observing me from the gate. He was a grizzled old man with a wide-boned, pitted face the colour and texture of an unscrubbed potato, a long beak of a nose with flared nostrils and an impressive shock of white hair.

'How do, squire,' he said.

'Oh, good afternoon,' I replied, clambering down from the wall and joining him.

'Admirin' t'view, are tha?'

'Yes and having a bit of rest.'

'Hard work, then?' he asked, gesturing towards the cottage.

'Yes, and very dirty,' I replied, brushing a cloud of dust from my overalls.

'Tha must be t'new people 'ere, then?' he observed. 'T'wife said a young couple 'ad moved in.'

'That's right.'

'I'm Harry Cotton. Live up by t'beck. I'm tha
258

nearest neighbour.'

'I'm pleased to meet you, Mr Cotton,' I replied, shaking a large hand as rough as sandpaper. 'I'm Gervase Phinn.'

'Foreign then, are tha?'

'No, as Yorkshire as you are.'

'Oh aye?' He sucked in his breath, surveyed the cottage and then with slow deliberation announced, 'I reckon there's a fair bit for tha to do theer, Mester Phinn.'

'There is indeed,' I agreed.

'I wun't like to tek it on, I'll tell thee that. Been empty for a fair owld time, that cottage, tha knaas. Old Mrs Olleranshaw, 'er who 'ad it afore thee and lived theer all 'er life, must 'ave been deead near on two year now. Her nephew, who inherited it, couldna make up his mind whether to live in it 'imself. That's why it's bin empty so long. Aye, I reckon there's a fair bit to do.'

'Oh, I'm sure we'll get there,' I replied, attempting to sound cheerful.

My rustic companion rubbed his chin, twisted his mouth and cocked his head in the direction of the cottage. 'Damp,' the old man announced.

'I beg your pardon?'

'Fair bit of damp, is there?' he enquired grimly.

'Yes, there's damp all right.'

'I thowt so. And woodworm, I reckon?'

'Yes, we have woodworm as well.'

'And tha chimney needs pointin' by looks on it.'

'Yes, it does.'

'Bit of subsidence at t'front an' all.'

'Well, I suppose you have to expect that sort of thing in a cottage this old.'

'Oh, it's old all reight. One o' oldest in t'village,

259

they reckon. Prob'ly a few ghooasts knockin' abaat. Tha wants to get t'vicar in to do bit o' exorcisin'.'

'I think not,' I replied, smiling.

'At least tha dunt 'ave a reight big garden to keep on t' top of, any rooad.'

'No, it's very small and, once I've tamed it, should be quite manageable,' I replied, looking with some foreboding at the tangle of bushes and shrubs.

'Mrs Olleranshaw owned all that little lot what's next to thee.' He gestured with his hand towards a large area of overgrown land. 'Sold separate, I believe, by 'er nephew few months back. I reckon they'll be buildin' some o' them swanky, gret 'ouses theer afore too long.'

'I doubt they'd be allowed to,' I replied.

'Aye, well, they do all sorts of things, these planners and architects an' surveyors. Wouldn't trust 'em as far as I could throw 'em. Estate agents an all. They're all t'same. Only out to mek a bob or two.' The grizzled old man rubbed his stubble and nodded knowingly. 'You mark my words, they'll have a whole lot o'new houses theer afore year's out, blockin' tha view.'

'I certainly hope not!' I exclaimed.

'Any rooad, you won't 'ave a big garden to deal with.'

'Actually, I wouldn't have minded a bit more land,' I admitted. 'To grow a few vegetables—that sort of thing. Not enough room here.'

'Well, tha can allus get thissen an allotment. There's one goin' just down from me. Ted Poskitt give it up a couple o' years back. Too much for 'im what wi' accident an' all. Tha wants to talk to George on t'parish council, and ask abaat it. Nice little plot reight in corner, it is, sheltered. I'd tek it on missen but I've got enough on wi' mi own. Mind you, it'd tek a fair bit of graftin' to clear it and dig it ovver. Ted Poskitt let it go, tha sees, after 'is accident. He was nivver same. Any rooad, tha wants to think abaat it. Tha go an' talk to George Hemmings on t'parish council, he'll see you reight.'

'I'll do that,' I said, thinking that it would be rather nice to have an allotment to provide endless supplies of fresh vegetables. 'Thank you for mentioning it.'

'Dry rot,' the old man announced suddenly.

'I beg your pardon?'

'I reckon thas got a bit o' dry rot in that cottage, an' all.'

'I should imagine we have,' I sighed.

'Well, I hope tha fettles it,' he said, staring up at the grey clouds oozing over the felltops. 'I reckon we're in for a bit o' rain. My owld dad used to say when t'blackthorn blossoms come out in early March and when t'sheep is behind walls at midday and when you see worms crawlin' on t'rooad, it's a sure sign of a wet month ahead. Aye, we get a fair bit o' rain up 'ere. Thy shall 'ave to get used to a bit o' wet. I reckon yer roof leaks, an' all. Well, I'll be off.' He raised his hand in greeting before going on his way. The prophet of doom, I thought wryly, and went back into the cottage to do battle with the bathroom walls again.

*   *   *

Over the next few weekends, I worked not in the cottage but on my allotment. Chris had discovered that I wasn't particularly handy when it came to

261

painting. 'I'd rather do it myself in the first place than spend precious time re-doing your botched attempts. Go and dig,' she'd said, giving me a hug.

I had tracked down George Hemmings the day after Harry Cotton had spoken to me about the spare allotment, paid the enormous rent of £5 for the year and was officially given the lease to cultivate plot 4. Each Saturday morning, I got dressed in my oldest pair of trousers and a shirt frayed at the neck. Once I had seen that Christine was happy with her paintbrush, I would walk at a brisk pace to the other side of the little village where the allotments were. I was like a child with a new toy. Here I set to and tackled the jungle. It was a back-breaking business. All the allotments, save mine and another at the far side, were lovingly tended and surrounded by either low, neatly-pruned hedges or wooden fencing. Some had brightly-painted sheds, one with a small wooden figure on top which moved in a digging motion in the wind. There was little growing at this time of year save for the fat shoots of early rhubarb pushing their way though the soil and tiny tongues of green where the onions and shallots were poking out. One allotment had a short row of cabbages, and one with the last of the leeks, standing erect like a line of soldiers.

My allotment was quite different. It was thick with twisting brambles and sharp-stemmed briars, a crop of dandelions to have pleased a thousand rabbits, frothy white cow parsley, clumps of young and very painful stinging nettles and a mass of other weeds I didn't know the names of. I set to work with a scythe, hacking, slashing, cutting and chopping, and eventually managed to clear the

262

whole area. I carefully lifted the maverick daffodil and bluebell bulbs to the side; they could be replanted in the cottage's garden. The worst job was clearing the tangle of deep-rooted prickly bushes which seemed to cover half the plot.

Then, one memorable Saturday afternoon, I lit a huge bonfire and watched with great satisfaction as the whole mountain of weeds and branches, bushes and briars went up in smoke.

'Tha's made a good job of that, and no mistake.'

I turned to find my neighbour, Mr Cotton, watching over the wall.

'Thank you,' I said, feeling pretty proud of my handiwork.

'Aye, tha 'as that. Cleared the lot.'

'I'm glad I've finished,' I told him, wiping my brow. 'It was a big job.'

'It would be,' he commented.

'Those prickly bushes were the worst. The roots seemed to go down for ever.'

'Aye, they do an' all,' agreed my companion.

'Anyhow, it's all cleared now and ready for planting.'

'I nivver knew that owld Albert Tattersall had given up his allotment,' my companion observed.

'Who?' I asked.

'Albert Tattersall. He had this plot. He's 'ad it for near on fifteen year. I nivver knew he'd given it up. I was only in t'pub wi' him past week and 'e never mentioned owt abaat givin' his allotment up.'

'Well, I guess he must have done,' I said. 'George Hemmings confirmed that plot 4 was free for me to take on.'

'Plot 4,' he repeated.

'That's right,' I said, 'I've leased plot 4.'

263

'Aye, well, that one you've just dug up is plot 7.'

'*What!*' I exclaimed.

'Albert Tattersall's, plot 7. Plot 4 is at t'other side of allotment.' He waved a hand towards the jungle by the far wall. 'It's reight ovver theer. Tha's gone an' dug wrong plot, sithee.'

'It can't be,' I said feebly. I pointed to the neighbouring plots. There were little white squares fixed in the earth with the plot number on. 'Look, that's plot 3 and there's plot 5 so this one in the middle must be plot 4.'

'It should be by rights, but it's not,' the old man told me. 'This is Yorkshire, lad. Things are a bit different 'ere. We're one on us own. Tha sees it goes alternate like. It sort o' runs contrary like a lot o' things around 'ere.'

'You mean, I've gone and cleared the wrong plot?' I asked.

'Aye, that's the truth on it,' replied Mr Cotton, nodding sagely.

'But it was all overgrown. Nobody has done anything to it for years and years.'

'Aye, tha's reight theer. Others who 'ad an allotment were allus gerrin on to owld Albert to do summat wi' it. I mean, all them weeds spread. Seeds blow ovver onto other people's land. They were allus on at 'im.'

'But why did Mr Tattersall keep an allotment that he never cultivated and never intended to cultivate?' I asked, still unwilling to believe what I had been told.

'Gooseberries.'

'Gooseberries?' I repeated.

'You see, owld Albert kept it on for t'gooseberries and then, of course, there's the blackcurrants?'

'Gooseberries? Blackcurrants?' I cried. 'What gooseberries and blackcurrants?'

'Them what would have been growin' on them bushes which you dug up and are now burnin' on tha bonfire.'

'I don't believe it,' I whispered. 'I don't believe it.'

'His wife wins prizes with her gooseberry and blackcurrant jams. Then there's the briars and the parsley and the dandelions. Owld Albert makes a powerful wine, specially his dandelion wine—or used to, more like.'

'And I've dug them all up?'

The old man rubbed his chin and chuckled. 'Every one.' He looked up at the sky. 'Aye well, I shall 'ave to be off. Happen tha'll mek it reight wi' owld Albert,' he remarked.

CHAPTER FOURTEEN

It was the first day back after the Easter holidays and the full team was in the office, awaiting the arrival of the Senior Inspector designate who had asked to meet with us.

'So how does it feel to be a married man?' Gerry asked me.

'Wonderful!' I replied. 'Marvellous!'

'Let's hope it stays that way,' remarked Sidney, placing his hands behind his head and leaning back dangerously in his chair, 'and that you feel the same way after twenty-five years of it. Marriage is not a bed of roses, you know, particularly for those like you, Gervase, who are dragged to the nuptial altar rather late in life.'

'I was not *dragged* to the altar, Sidney,' I replied, 'and I am not yet in my dotage.'

'I know you are not, old chap, but you have been used to only considering yourself, and no doubt are somewhat set in your ways. You will find that having to live with another person, cheek by jowl, day after day, sharing the toothpaste, waiting for the bathroom to be free, discovering damp bras draped over radiators, finding your favourite records scratched, means you have to make certain changes and concessions—some of which you will not like.'

'I'm sure I'll manage,' I said. 'Millions do.'

'And, of course, millions do not,' continued Sidney, unabashed. 'One in three marriages ends in divorce or separation, you know. A sad fact but very true.'

'Cynic,' mumbled David who, until this point, had remained uncharacteristically silent.

'No,' continued Sidney, ignoring him, 'marriage is not all it's cracked up to be.'

'You will be getting a crack in a minute,' David told him, 'if you don't shut up.'

'I don't know how his wife puts up with him,' said Julie, having overheard Sidney's doom-laden speech as she brought in the coffee. 'His wife must be a martyr.'

'Martyrs tend to be dead, Julie,' Sidney told her, smiling.

'A saint then.'

'Those as well.'

'His wife deserves a medal for bravery, having to put up with him.'

'Oh, I wouldn't go that far,' said Sidney. 'Gervase is a decent enough sort of fellow and I am sure the delectable Miss Bentley, or I should say the delectable Mrs Phinn, will learn to put up with him in time.'

'I was talking about you!' snapped Julie, placing down the tray noisily on the nearest desk. 'And you know very well I was.'

'My dear wife, Lila,' announced Sidney, putting on an angelic expression, 'far from considering herself a saint and martyr, thanks her lucky stars she is married to such a creative genius as myself and she is prepared to take the rough with the smooth, the highs with the lows, the ups with the downs. It's all a matter of give and take. Lila knows how to deal with my little mood swings, foibles and minor peccadilloes.'

'I know how I'd deal with your little mood swings, foibles and minor peccadilloes,' said Julie, placing a mug of steaming coffee before him. 'Poison!'

'Do you know, Julie,' said Sidney, sitting up and pushing the coffee away from him in a very theatrical manner, 'I think I will forgo the morning libation.'

'If I had wanted to poison you, Mr Clamp,' Julie retorted, heading for the door, 'I could have done it long ago.'

'And I suppose you will be the next one, Geraldine,' Sidney casually remarked, picking up the mug and taking a gulp.

'The next what?' she asked. 'The next one to poison you?'

'To tie the old knot.'

'Sidney,' sighed Gerry, 'you sometimes can be

really tiresome. I am certainly not going to discuss my private life with you.' She then pointedly changed the subject. 'And how's the cottage coming on, Gervase? Are you settled in at Hawksrill?'

'Settled? You must be joking! You should see the state of it. We've managed to get a bit done. There's a great deal more to do before we can move in but we are aiming for half term.'

'I did warn you, dear boy,' said Sidney smugly. 'It will take an age to put the place right, by the sound of it.'

There was certainly much to do but I was not going to fuel Sidney's barrage of grim predictions by telling him about the leaking roof, the faulty guttering, the damp patches upstairs, the woodworm and the mass of other things which required attention.

'We are really pleased with it,' I told Sidney. 'The cottage is well built, cosy, has magnificent views across the dale and we know we will be very happy there.'

'Where is he, then?' Sidney suddenly asked, glancing at his watch.

'Who?'

'Mr Carter. Simon. I thought we were here to meet our new leader early this morning?'

'He said nine,' I told him. 'It's only ten minutes to.'

The Senior Inspector designate had called a meeting for us to get to know something about his educational philosophy, as he put it, and for him to consult with us well in advance about his plans for the future. We were all looking forward to meeting him but, understandably, were a little apprehensive.

'Is Harold not coming, then?' asked Gerry.

'No,' I replied. 'I think he felt it politic to let Mr Carter meet us himself. He thought he might inhibit him.'

'Not much chance of that,' murmured Gerry, picking up her mug of coffee. 'I think it might have been courteous for Mr Carter to have asked Harold.'

'Harold didn't want to come,' said Sidney. 'I can see he would have found it rather difficult. Mind you, *Mister* Carter is certainly very keen. Making his presence felt. After all, he doesn't start until September.'

'I suppose he wants to meet us, get to know a bit about us before he starts and discuss the future of the service as he sees it,' said David. 'I expect he will want to make some changes and wants to talk to us about them. It seems a very sensible idea to me.'

'Well, I sincerely hope there won't be too many changes,' said Sidney.

At the very moment the clock on the County Hall tower struck nine, the door opened and the man himself entered. Mr Simon Carter was a lean, middle-aged man, impeccably groomed in an expensive light-grey designer suit, pristine white shirt and discretely patterned silk tie. His pale face was long and angular; his hair, combed back in rippling waves, was coal-black and shiny, and his eyes were dark and narrow. He looked at the four of us staring up at him with an expression of impassive curiosity. Then the thin bloodless lips parted and he gave us the fullest and most charming of smiles.

'Good morning,' he intoned like a vicar about to start the morning service.

269

As one, we four inspectors got to our feet. 'Good morning, Mr Carter,' we chorused—just like a class might welcome a school inspector into their midst.

Simon Carter wasted no time. 'Let us commence our discussion,' he said, placing a large black briefcase on Sidney's desk and pulling out a chair.

The meeting started well with the Senior Inspector designate telling us how pleased he was to have the opportunity of meeting us, that he hoped we would all work together as a team, supporting one another and pulling in the same direction to raise standards of achievement in the county's schools.

We had had about an hour of what I reckoned to be fairly constructive discussion when he placed his folded hands carefully in front of him, like a priest about to hear confession, and said, 'I have to say, colleagues, that there seems a great deal to be done. I have been appointed, as you are aware, to take the service forward, to breathe some fresh air into the department and thus changes will be necessary. It is often the case, I have found, that in large education authorities, such as this, which have been relatively successful in retaining high standards and which have rebuffed the pressures to jump on every educational band-wagon that happens to roll up, that a certain complacency develops. There is a general feeling that everything is working well—so why change things? This complacency very often extends from the senior officers right down to the humble cleaner of the Staff Development Centre.' I could not resist a smile and he pounced on it at once. 'Is there something which amuses you, Gervase?' asked Mr Carter, like a teacher talking to a recalcitrant child.

'Yes, there is actually,' I replied. 'You have obviously not yet met Connie.'

'Connie?' he repeated. 'Who is Connie?'

'She's the cleaner at the Staff Development Centre and of all the words one could use to describe her, I think "complacent" and "humble" would come near the very bottom of the list.'

'She's like Attila the Hun with a feather duster,' added Sidney.

'Ah, I rather think I have met her,' said Mr Carter without a trace of a smile. 'There was a woman in a pink overall and with a feather duster who was quite rude and abrupt with me at the interviews. I apparently did something which displeased her—ah, yes, I failed to return my cup to the hatch.'

'That's Connie,' said Sidney, nodding.

'Anyway, that is by the by. What I was endeavouring to say,' he continued, rather thrown by the interruption but not wishing to deviate from his prepared speech, 'is that there is a tendency for large institutions which have plodded on in the same easygoing manner for many years and failed to move with the times, to become moribund.'

'Moribund?' murmured David. I could see he was beginning to bristle with irritation.

'Yes, moribund,' said Mr Carter. 'Moribund. Rather set in its ways, unmoveable, lacking in vitality and verve.'

'I always thought "moribund" meant on the point of death,' observed Sidney.

'Well, I'm certainly not saying that the department is at death's door,' stated Mr Carter, sounding more conciliatory. 'It is just that some people, from what I have seen so far, cannot think

271

outside the box, see the big picture, go that extra mile. Now, to be perfectly honest, I am not the sort of person to carry passengers. I want to empower people and put us at the cutting edge. I want a proactive not a reactive team.'

'Don't you think, Mr Carter,' said David, 'that it would be better to wait and see what you find before jumping to conclusions about the department and making changes. The county has outstanding academic results, excellent schools, a teaching force second to none, superb initiatives, a whole range of projects. Now, if that is moribund—'

'Mr Pritchard, David,' interrupted Mr Carter, 'of course I appreciate all the hard work and have been most impressed by the splendid activities which have taken place and I would be the last person to denigrate the inspectors' efforts, but I have read the county documents, guidelines and the school reports emanating from this office, and from other departments at County Hall and there is, to be frank, room for improvement. We must all work from the premise that we can make things better.'

'I'm not saying that everything is perfect,' started David. 'What I am saying—'

'What's wrong with the reports?' snapped Sidney.

'To be frank,' said Mr Carter, quietly but firmly, 'I found the inspectors' reports on schools certainly informative and, to some extent, useful but they were too wordy, largely lacking in focus and with a tendency to be far too anecdotal. I would like to see them sharper, more incisive. That is one of the reasons why I wished to consult with you before the start of the new term, to try and agree on a better system of reporting on schools.'

'And what form will this take, or rather what form do you feel it should take?' asked Gerry.

'Well, let me explain, Geraldine,' he said, becoming genuinely enthusiastic for the first time that morning. 'In addition to your school-visit reports, in which you will continue to outline the school's strengths and weaknesses and issues for action, I would like more reliable objective data recorded. I would like to set up some benchmarks. The work that Mrs Savage does for you—all those questionnaires and surveys—are of little practical use.' Sidney gave David a knowing look. I could tell what he was thinking. 'What I want to introduce is a teacher-effectiveness inventory, a pupil-attitude questionnaire, a classroom-climate assessment and a resources and materials audit. That sort of thing. These are the objective tools which will help us create an extensive database of information and assist the schools in improving their performance. From this information a league table can then be devised—'

'Sounds like the football pools to me,' said David. 'Will we have premier schools, first division schools, second division schools? Will schools be relegated? Will schools be able to buy teachers as a football team buys players? Can headteachers be sacked like football managers?'

'No, no, don't be facile,' said Mr Carter, 'but there will be an educational league table to encourage schools which are failing to try that bit harder, to go that extra mile. If they are compared with more successful schools, placed in competition, so to speak, with others, the poor schools will strive to improve their performance,

273

don't you think?'

'No, not really,' replied David. 'I think it is more likely to be divisive. It seems to me pretty self-evident that Sir Cosmo's Grammar will always come near the top of the league and Crompton Secondary School will always be lingering near the bottom. The pupils are of very differing abilities. It doesn't mean that one school is better than the other. They are just different.'

'I think you are rather missing the point,' said Mr Carter irritably. 'What I was endeavouring to explain—'

'Mr Carter, Simon,' said Sidney, interrupting, 'we are, in addition to being inspectors, also advisers, counsellors, critical friends, course providers, curriculum developers and many more things. Don't you think that doing all these objective tests and assessments will take us away from one of our main tasks—that of *helping* and *supporting* teachers? Are we not in danger of spending too much time weighing the pig and not enough time feeding it?'

Mr Carter sighed. 'It is early days, Sidney. I am sure that when I am in post and in a position to explain my vision more clearly, you will become convinced of the value of these changes.' He glanced at his watch. 'Well, I think this has been a most productive meeting, don't you, but I must be on my way. I have a session with Mrs Savage in a moment.' A number of eyebrows were raised at this declaration. 'I'm going to touch base with her and talk through my game plan.'

'That should prove very interesting,' muttered David, undoubtedly still smarting at being told he was 'facile'.

And that was that. Mr Carter told us how much he was looking forward to working with us, wished us goodbye and departed.

When Julie entered the office a moment later she found the four of us sitting at our desks, stunned into silence.

'Is everything all right?' she asked.

'Please don't say anything, Geraldine,' said Sidney as his colleague opened her mouth to speak. 'Just don't say a word.'

*   *   *

Towards the end of that afternoon, I had a meeting with Miss de la Mare, HMI, at the Staff Development Centre to discuss the 'Language and Literacy for Learning' initiative. She was wearing a bright crimson silk shirt and looked terrific. To think how nervous we had all been when she first took on our area for the Ministry. We sat now in the small staff room and she took me through my report, staring fixedly at the page on one point, occasionally grunting with approval or nodding vigorously at other times.

'Very thorough, Gervase,' she said at last, closing the file. 'A very thorough and well-written document which will be extremely useful when we put together the national framework. Thank you so much for taking all this trouble and spending so much time.' So much for Mr Carter's comments about our reports being 'too wordy and largely lacking in focus'. I was beginning to feel better already.

'Actually I found it very useful and interesting,' I said. 'I don't usually have the opportunity of observing science and maths lessons. It was really instructive and, do you know, some of the very best oral work was in the art and technology lessons and some of the best written material was in history and geography. It doesn't always take place in English which was quite a surprise.'

'Well, I hope we will be able to use a couple of these reports as case studies. What I really like is the examples you quote and the enthusiasm for the really good lessons. It makes an otherwise rather serious and detailed text that bit more readable and interesting. The RE chappie sounds splendid.'

So much for Mr Carter's comments about our reports having 'a tendency to be far too anecdotal'.

'Mr Griffith?' I said. 'He was one in a million.'

'Well, I'll get working on this next week when the other reports come in and let you see the draft before we go to print. I think we'll be able to produce a very practical and helpful document.'

'Much as I enjoyed working on this,' I told Miss de la Mare, 'I could do without another of Dr Gore's "little jobs"—for the time being anyway.'

'Don't worry, Gervase,' she chuckled. 'I'll make certain nothing else comes your way. After all, you need to spend time with that new wife of yours. A little bird, in the form of Dr Yeats, told me you got married recently.'

'That's right.'

'To that delightful young headteacher of Winnery Nook, I believe. You are a lucky man.'

'Don't I know it!'

'Well, congratulations. I hope you'll be very happy together.'

'Thanks! There have been real changes in my life over the past few months and, of course, there are likely to be more with the retirement of Harold Yeats.'

'Ah yes, indeed,' said Miss de la Mare. 'He will be greatly missed. A true gentleman, Dr Yeats.'

'And we have Mr Simon Carter stepping into his shoes next term.'

'So I believe.'

'Do you know him?'

'Oh yes,' she replied, 'I know Mr Carter. Our paths have crossed on a number of occasions. Dr Yeats will be greatly missed.'

Miss de la Mare was obviously not going to elaborate about our new SI, for she began packing her papers away in her briefcase. She knows more, I thought, and decided to engage in a little subtle probing. 'I understand Mr Carter is very well qualified and experienced.'

'Yes, indeed,' replied Miss de la Mare. 'He has amassed a great many qualifications over the years and packed a lot in. His career had been very varied.'

'From what he said at our meeting with him this morning, I think he is intent on making a great many changes.'

'Oh, he is a great one for changes, is Mr Carter.' She thought for a moment. 'Change is all very well, Gervase, but change for change's sake can be very destructive.'

'How do you mean?'

'If something is working well, why change it? Sometimes it is best to leave well alone.'

'Has Mr Carter a reputation for changing things for the worse, then?' I asked.

'I've said too much already. What I will say to you is that Mr Simon Carter is a very different

277

kettle of fish from Dr Yeats. Well, I must be off, Gervase. Many thanks again for all your hard work.'

Having been buoyed up by Miss de la Mare's praise, I was now back in the doldrums. The scenario for the inspectors looked somewhat bleak. I stayed on for a while in the staff room and thought about the day. How one's life and career could change so dramatically, I thought. Everything had been so perfect: getting married to the most wonderful woman in the world, finding the cottage of our dreams, working with interesting and friendly colleagues in a job I really enjoyed—the future was filled with promise. Now, suddenly, the future looked distinctly wobbly. Having sat through the meeting that morning and listened to his plans for change, I knew that I wasn't going to get on with Simon Carter. I just knew it.

'Are you going to be long?' It was Connie standing at the door, brandishing the largest bottle of bleach I had ever seen. 'I've done my surfaces and just have the Gents to do, and then I want to get off. It's my bingo night tonight. I like everything to be ship-shape and Bristol fashion before I knock off.'

'I won't be long, Connie,' I said.

'I would have thought you would have been off long ago, you being newly married and all.'

'I was just thinking.'

'I try not to,' Connie said. 'It only causes you to worry and whittle, does thinking. I went through my father's papers last week and I couldn't stop thinking. I put all the papers in a box when we cleared his house and I just couldn't bear to touch them. Ted took all his clothes down to the Oxfam

278

shop and his bits and pieces have been shared between my sisters and myself. He didn't have much to show for all his years in the army and his time down the pit. Anyway, Ted said we ought to sort his papers out soon or we'd never do it. Looking through all the old photos and letters got me to thinking. Thinking about things I never said to him and wished I had, thinking about things I did say to him and wished I hadn't, thinking about the times we had when me and my sisters were little and Dad used to take us down the park or up the clough. And I remembered what he said to Ted when I brought him home for the first time. "There'll be no hanky panky," he told him. "She's a good lass is my Constance and she's been brought up proper." It did upset me, seeing all those photos and looking through all them letters and papers.' Connie put down the bottle of bleach, and wiped a tear away with a tissue brought out of the pocket of her pink nylon overall. 'We found this little orange wallet with the address of the War Office on the front. It was his sustificate for employment for when he came out of the army. He was wounded twice, was Dad, lost two fingers and was hospitalisationed for two months and he won medals. His colonel—Dad was in the Fourth Battalion, Duke of Wellington's West Riding Regiment—had to give a character reference and he'd written on it, "Lance Corporal Wood is sober and honest (as far as I know)". "As far as I know", I ask you! He deserved better than that, did Dad. I was crying half the night.'

'Well, Connie, you have many happy memories and a father to be proud of.'

'I do and I am.'

'Well, I'll leave you to finish off here, Connie,' I said. 'I hope you haven't missed your bingo.'

'I'm not sure I'll bother to go now. It's not that I ever win anything. Oh, before you go, I saw that nun last week at the bus stop and she asked to be remembered to you. That Sister Brenda.'

'Sister Brendan.'

'And do you know, she was dressed like a nun for once. All in black and white like a big magpie, she was. I didn't recognise her at first because every time she's been here for one of your courses or meetings, she's been in a suit like the ones that air hostesses wear. I mean, I never knew she was a nun until you said. Skirt was nearly up to her knees and she had nothing on her head save for a bit of a scarf. Anyway, she was there at the bus stop in full rig, with a big bunch of gladioli under her arm. We got chatting and she said she was off to St Walburga's to do the altar flowers. I used to do the flowers at our church, you know, but the new young vicar gets hay fever something terrible so it's all teasels and dried twigs now. What was I saying?'

'About the nun at the bus stop,' I prompted her.

'Oh yes. Well, while we was standing there at the bus stop this tramp comes up. He looked as if he'd been dragged through a hedge backwards and then thrown in the canal before being left to dry in the sun. And smell! He bypasses all the others in the queue and makes straight for the nun. So he asks Sister Brenda if she could spare a few old coppers for a poor gentleman of the road. She gave him short shift, I can tell you. Course, seeing a nun, I suppose he must have thought he was on to a soft touch and made a beeline for her. Anyhow, she tells him he was getting no old coppers from her because he would only spend it on the drink. Well, you would not believe the language that came out of his mouth and in front of a nun as well. "Standing there, holier than thou," he shouts, "dressed in yer so and so nun's habit with your so and so gladioli stuck under your so and so arm." It would have made a stevedore blush. It caused me to colour up, I can tell you, and I've heard some foul language in my time, specially when I was on the cashews when I worked at the roasted nut factory. Sister Brenda didn't blink an eyelid. She held on to her gladioli and just told him to be on his way and stop using profantities. Well, he started on again at her, cursing and swearing and heffing and blinding and telling her she ought to be ashamed of wearing a nun's habit, looking all innocent with those so and so gladioli stuck under her arm. She was supposed to be walking in the footsteps of Jesus, he tells her. "If you don't move on," she told him, "I'll be walking all the way down to the police station to get you arrested. If you want something to eat and a warm drink," she tells him, "you come down the convent, but you are not getting any money from me to spend on alcohol." Well, that stopped him. Just then the bus arrived and we thought we'd seen the back of him but when we climbed on, he was right there behind us. Well, I nearly died. He stands there at the end of the aisle and shouts the full length of the bus. "I can see you sitting there on yer holy so and so," he says to the nun and then he starts quoting scripture. "You came into this world naked, sister," he shouts, "and you'll go out of this world naked, but you'll still have them bloody gladioli tucked under your arm." I mean, we all had to laugh and

281

the loudest was Sister Brenda herself. I never knew that nuns had a sense of humour.'

*   *   *

That evening I snuggled up with Christine on the old sofa we had bought from Roper's Saleroom. We had spent an hour stripping faded and peeling wallpaper off the bedroom walls and were relaxing before returning to the flat in Fettlesham for supper. She rested her head on my chest.

'You're in a very pensive mood,' she said.

'Chris, what would you say if I said I wanted to look for another job?'

'I thought you had got over not being shortlisted for the Senior Inspector's post.'

'I have.'

'Well, what's brought all this on, then?'

'Oh, I don't know. I just feel with Harold going things are going to change.'

'Well, of course things are going to change. There's nothing wrong with change. You've changed into a happily-married man—I hope—and we're going to change this cottage. Things need to change. Things can't stay the same for ever.'

'Some things don't need to change, though. You wouldn't want the view from this window to change, for example, would you?'

'That's different.'

'Exactly. Some changes are for the good, but others are not. The thing is, I think work is going to change for the worse when Harold goes.'

'Why do you say that?'

'The new SI came in today and none of us really like him.'

282

'I thought you did?'

'We did at first but after the meeting today we changed our minds. He's single-minded and it's clear he wants his own way and everyone to agree with him. He's a systems man and, worst of all, he seems completely humourless.'

'Wow!' exclaimed Christine. 'You really don't like him, do you?'

'All he talks about is appraisal and assessment and tests and audits. He rarely mentions children. He's hell-bent on bringing in these dreadful form-filling procedures. It sounds a nightmare. It's not what I came into this job for. I want to work with teachers and children, not be pen-pushing morning, noon and night.'

'Give the poor man a chance. He hasn't even started yet.'

'That's what I said to Sidney, but then I got talking to Della Mare—you know, the HMI who has been working on the 'Language and Literacy' project—and she dropped a few none-too-subtle hints about him.'

'Such as?'

'Well, that he is big on change and then she said in a pointed way that some changes can be destructive. She said he is a very different kettle of fish from Harold.'

'Harold's pretty special, though, isn't he? You can't expect his successor to be a carbon copy of Harold.'

'I don't expect that. It's just that I know I'm not going to get on with Simon Carter. None of us will. I don't think he will be a good boss to work for.'

'There wouldn't be a few sour grapes here, would there?' asked Christine.

'Not at all. Hey, Chris, you're supposed to be sympathetic and understanding and—'

'Agree with everything you say? Look, love, I'm sorry you are feeling depressed about this but it's early days yet. If this ogre of a new Senior Inspector does turn out to be difficult and demanding and you begin to hate the job, then you can think about a move. But let's not rush into things. We've just got married and will be moving in here in a few weeks' time. I don't intend giving up work so it would be a bit silly, don't you think, to start looking for other jobs. Give the man a chance.' She looked up with those great blue eyes. 'OK?'

'I suppose so,' I replied.

'Now, I've got something really really important to ask you before we go back to Fettlesham?'

'What?'

'Did you remember to do the shopping, Mr Phinn? I think you said you would cook tonight.'

CHAPTER FIFTEEN

A few days before the half-term break, I was due at Pope Pius X Roman Catholic Primary School in the little market town of Ribsdyke. I was looking forward to the visit because I was going to be accompanied by a man I much admired, Lord Marrick, a man whom I had originally met in the strangest of circumstances.

A pheasant had just shattered my windscreen as I was driving along a narrow road on my way to visit a Dales' school, and the person who climbed over the drystone wall a moment later to claim his bird turned out to be Valentine Courtnay-Cunninghame, 9th Earl Marrick, Viscount Manston, Baron Brafferton, MC, DL.

One visit I had made with Lord Marrick was soon after he had been appointed the representative on the Governing Body of Pope Pius X Roman Catholic Primary School. That first visit had not been without incident for he had become apoplectic about the run-down condition of the premises. 'You inspectors are supposed to comment on the poor state of buildings and the effects upon the children's education,' he had told me sternly. 'The whole place wants pulling down and rebuilding.' Lord Marrick had then promised the headteacher that he would be contacting Dr Gore when he returned to the Education Department and would ensure that improvements would be put in hand. Lord Marrick had been true to his word.

I collected Lord Marrick now from the Small Committee Room of County Hall and we were soon heading for the rolling hills of the Dales, leaving behind the noise and bustle of Fettlesham. We were going to attend the opening of the new school building, a development which was largely the result of Lord Marrick's strenuous efforts on the school's behalf.

'Have you met the new Senior Inspector, then?' he asked, stroking his impressive walrus moustache.

'Yes, we had a meeting with him right at the beginning of this term,' I replied.

'Seems a decent sort of chap.'

'Yes,' I replied.

'He's a very clever man by all accounts.'

285

'Very clever.' A bit too clever by half, I thought to myself. I was still feeling rather apprehensive after that meeting but, as I had promised Christine, had not given any more thought to finding a new job.

'Well qualified, too. All these letters after his name, degrees in this, diplomas in that, member of this, fellow of that. I thought I'd met a kindred spirit when I saw one set of letters after his name. Thought he was a member of the Bull Breeders' Association, too. But then realised it was MBA not MBBA.' He chuckled.

I smiled, too, thinking of the intense-looking man with the piercing eyes and dressed immaculately in a designer suit trying to lead a frisky bull in from the field. 'MBA indicates a Master of Business Administration degree,' I informed Lord Marrick. 'It's a top qualification.'

'So I gather. Then he has those other letters—BAA. I told him that it sounded like a degree in sheep-shearing but I don't think he was amused.'

No, I thought, it wouldn't amuse our Mr Carter. I wondered what, if anything, *would* amuse him. 'I think that is yet another qualification in accounts and administration,' I said.

'Well, he seems to be very experienced in management and supervision.'

He'll get on well with Mrs Savage then, I thought waspishly. They talk the same language. 'Yes,' I remarked, hoping we could leave this particular topic of conversation. I was finding it hugely depressing.

'Gave a very impressive presentation and his interview was a *tour de force*. Never seen Councillor George Peterson stuck for words. He just sat and

286

stared like a Toby jug. Mr Carter was never stumped for an answer and seems to have done just about everything there is to do in the educational field.'

As much as I liked the jovial Lord Marrick, this chatter about Simon Carter was making me feel very despondent. 'Really,' I replied.

'Been a headmaster, adviser, lecturer, management consultant. One wonders what he wanted to become a school inspector in Yorkshire for. Must like the scenery.'

'Yes, indeed,' I said.

'You're very quiet this morning, Gervase. Cat must have got your tongue. Is it because you were not considered for the position?' Lord Marrick was nothing if not blunt. 'Is that what's getting you down? Dr Gore did mention that you had put in an application.'

Oh no, I thought. I hope he's not going to be another on the long list of people to tell me I hadn't had enough experience for such a senior position, that I should look on the bright side, that my time would come. 'I did apply, Lord Marrick, yes, that's true,' I replied. 'I was disappointed, of course, but—'

'You need a few more years under your belt yet, if you don't mind me saying.'

'No, of course not.'

'Hardly got your feet under the table. Takes that much longer in the Dales, you know, than in other parts of the country, for people to get to know you. It takes some time to get used to "off-comed-uns", as they say. My family are just about accepted by the locals and we've been here since the time of the Normans. Give it a few more years.'

287

'I will,' I replied. 'Thank you for the advice.'

'I hope it doesn't sound like advice. I was merely making an observation. I was always told by my father never to give unsolicited advice—the clever man doesn't need it and the foolish man never takes it.'

I continued to drive with my eyes firmly on the road, past grey-stone farmhouses and cottages, long hedgerows in bright new leaf, and the fields studded with hawthorn trees in luxuriant blossom. Despite all this beauty, which would normally lift my spirits sky-high, I just felt in the dumps.

'Yes, he has more degrees than a thermometer, has Mr Carter,' remarked Lord Marrick. 'A very clever man.'

'He sounds it,' I replied.

'Of course, I never pulled up any roots at school, you know,' Lord Marrick admitted, twisting the ends of his moustache. 'Sent away at nine, I was, mother crying her eyes out at the station, nanny having hysterics, sisters clinging on to me for dear life, father telling me to keep my chin up, stiff upper lip and all that. Pretty bleak those first couple of years, I don't mind telling you. Then I got into sport. Spent most of my time on the rugger or cricket pitch after that, and the hardest work I did was to ensure that I attended the minimum number of lessons. My grandson found my old school report a few weeks ago. One of the masters had written: "Now I have deciphered Courtnay-Cunninghame's spidery scribble, I have discovered that he is unable to spell." Not a lot of laughs when I was at school. I do think it's important to have a sense of humour. There's enough doom and gloom in the world. A good laugh does you good, that's what I always think.' He thought for a moment, then said, 'You know, this new chap, Carter, was a bit of a serious cove. I hope he's going to be all right.'

So do I, I thought to myself. So do I.

*   *   *

We soon arrived at the school and its new appearance came as quite a shock. I had not visited Pope Pius X Primary for a couple of years and, at that time, it was a featureless building which had been erected just after the war and, indeed, had had the appearance of an army barracks. It was a big surprise, therefore, to see such a transformation. There now stood a handsome red-brick building with long picture windows and an orange pantile roof. The area around the school had been landscaped and scrubby lawn and cracked paving had been replaced with a spacious play area with benches and picnic tables, surrounded by flowering shrubs and young newly-planted trees.

Lord Marrick clambered from the car, put his hands on his wide hips, surveyed the building with great satisfaction and growled, 'Not bloody bad, eh?'

The entrance hall to the school was very different as well. On my previous visit I had been reminded more of a hospital than a school. Now the area was brightly decorated and an eye-catching mural, depicting happy children, stretched the full length of the wall. There were modern tables and chairs, tall glass display panels, attractively framed prints and, in pride of place, a large portrait of Pope Pius X with arms outstretched and eyes looking heavenwards.

Mrs Callaghan, the headteacher, was an attractive woman with friendly eyes and light sandy hair tied back. She hurried across the hall to greet us.

'Lord Marrick, Mr Phinn,' she panted in an amiable voice. 'It's so nice to see you again.'

We followed her into her room and listened as she outlined the programme for the afternoon. First, we would attend assembly, then be given a tour of the school. At the end of the afternoon, when the governors and parents had arrived, everyone would gather in the school hall and Lord Marrick would undertake the official opening of the new building. I was representing Dr Gore and had nothing to do but mingle and be pleasant. I was still not, however, feeling in a very pleasant frame of mind.

Lord Marrick and I chose to sit at the back of the new school hall and watched the children enter—smart, cheerful and well behaved—to the taped strains of some lively martial music. I have spent many an hour observing school assemblies and have heard countless homilies from headteachers. Some have been tedious affairs with rows of wriggling, inattentive children and bored teachers having to endure a rambling headteacher who frequently finishes by launching into a good telling-off about some infringement to the school rules. Other assemblies have been inspirational and thought-provoking, capturing the children's interests and imaginations. The assembly I watched that afternoon was one of the latter.

'Good afternoon, children,' said Mrs Callaghan cheerfully.

'Good afternoon, Mrs Callaghan, good afternoon, everyone,' chorused the children.

'I would like to extend a very special welcome today to our two important visitors, Earl Marrick and Mr Gervase Phinn. Later this afternoon, children, Lord Marrick will be officially opening our new building and unveiling a plaque to celebrate the rebirth of Pope Pius X School. It is a very important day for us.'

What followed was as if Mrs Callaghan had chosen her words just for me.

'We always dreamt of a new school,' she said, looking around the bright new hall. 'We always dreamt of light, airy classrooms, long colourful corridors, a well-stocked library with a carpet and cushions and easy chairs. We always dreamt of a sports field and a playground, a modern kitchen, sparkling toilets and, most especially, a spacious school hall with high walls and a polished wooden floor. Some thought it would remain just a dream, just an idea that would never come true. We have had so many disappointments along the way, so many hurdles and detours and standstills, and there have been many times when we have felt like giving up. But we didn't. We believed in our dream and today our dream has come true. In an hour's time, our new school will be officially opened.' The headteacher paused for a moment to compose herself. She was clearly finding this quite an emotional occasion. 'All of you will have your dreams and you must never, never give up on them, for dreams *do* come true. In your own lives, children, there will be times when you have worked so hard for something and all your efforts seem to come to nothing. Times when you have walked a

291

thousand steps towards your goal only to find yourself back in the place from where you started. At times like these, you will feel disappointed, let down, bewildered. You will feel like giving up and asking yourself if there is any point in carrying on. Well, you must carry on. You must continue to believe in yourself and you must, we all must, follow our dreams.'

Mrs Callaghan then went on to talk about various events which would take place over the next week, and this gave me time to think about what she had said. I realised just how selfish and ungrateful it was of me to be so pessimistic and downhearted. What had I got to be so miserable about? I had a beautiful new wife, a lovely cottage and a good job and here I was feeling sorry for myself. I had to admit that I was still smarting at not being even interviewed for the Senior Inspector's job but they had all been right— Christine, Harold, Dr Gore and now Lord Marrick. It was far too soon for me to go applying for such a senior position and my time would surely come.

*   *   *

After assembly, Lord Marrick and I were taken on a tour of the school by two of the older pupils, a small black boy of about ten and a pale-faced girl with raven-black hair and the bluest of eyes.

'Hello Mr Phinn, hello Mr Marrick,' said the boy. 'We're your guides.'

'Hello,' said Lord Marrick, chuckling. 'And what's your name?'

'Anthony, but you can call me Tony. Everybody else does,' replied the boy. 'And this is Bernadette.'

'How are you doing?' asked the girl, in the lightest of Irish lilts.

'We are doing just fine, are we not, Mr Phinn?'

'I recognise you,' I told the girl. 'When we came into this school a couple of years ago you were writing a lovely poem about a horse.'

'Good gracious!' cried Lord Marrick. 'That's right, I remember. I've still got the copy you gave me.'

'Oh yes, I remember,' said the girl with a tilt of her head and a disarming smile. 'And I remember showing you the toilets, too, where the damp on the wall was in the shape of a big green monster. Would you be wanting to see the girls' toilets now? They're new and shiny and there's no leaks anywhere.'

'I don't think that is a place we are intending to visit today, my dear,' explained Lord Marrick.

'It is all tiled and painted now. It's a pleasure going to the toilet, so it is.'

The 9th Earl Marrick, Viscount Manston, Baron Brafferton, who lived at Manston Hall, one of the county's most magnificent houses, smiled benignly. 'I'll take your word for it, my dear,' he replied.

'Would you like to follow us,' said the boy, who had been getting increasingly impatient with a conversation from which he must have felt excluded, 'and we'll take you on a tour of the school.'

'And if there's anything you want to ask,' added the girl, 'just go ahead. As my mother would say, "If you don't ask, you'll never get to know."'

'We will,' said Lord Marrick as we followed the two small figures who headed off down the corridor at a cracking pace. We went from classroom to

293

classroom, looked in at the small library, examined the kitchens and, to please Bernadette, even put our heads into the new cloakrooms.

On our way back to the staff room for a cup of tea, Lord Marrick beamed with pleasure at the children. 'Well, that was splendid. You have both been excellent guides.'

'My brother's called Earl, you know,' announced Tony.

'Is he really?' replied Lord Marrick.

'Yeah. You're the only other Earl I've ever met apart from my brother.'

'Well, it's a pretty good name, I think.'

'Are you famous?' asked the boy.

'No, I'm not famous,' replied the peer.

'Mrs Callaghan said you were famous.'

'Have you heard of me?'

'No.'

'Well then, I can't be famous, can I?'

'No, I don't suppose you can.' Tony turned his attention to me. 'Are *you* anybody, then?' the boy asked.

'No, I'm not anybody, either,' I replied, amused by this interrogation.

The boy, obviously unimpressed, turned back to Lord Marrick. 'Mrs Callaghan said you were famous.'

'Well, I'm very sorry to have to disappoint you, young man,' Lord Marrick told him, 'but she is sadly mistaken. I'm not famous at all.'

'I brought my autograph book in specially,' said the boy, looking disappointed.

'I see,' said Lord Marrick, scratching his outcrop of hair. 'Well, would you like me to sign it?'

'No, because you're not famous. Well, it's been

nice meeting you. Now, I've got to get back to my class. Bye.' He gave a wave and was gone.

Lord Marrick laughed and turned to me. 'I reckon that if Pope Pius himself walked through that door, he'd find it pretty difficult to get into that young man's autograph book.'

'Could I ask you something, Mr Marrick?' came a small voice from behind us. We had forgotten all about Bernadette.

'Of course you can, my dear,' replied Lord Marrick. 'If you don't ask, you'll never get to know.'

'Is that moustache real, or have you put it on for today, it being a special occasion an' all?'

*   *   *

Lord Marrick and I now made our way to the staff room where the school governors were gathered with Mrs Callaghan and the teachers.

'Good afternoon, Mr Phinn,' said an elderly, quietly-spoken priest dressed in a cassock which had seen better days.

'Good afternoon, Father.'

'Delightful occasion, isn't it?' remarked the priest. 'We have so much to be thankful for. I do hope you will personally convey our gratitude to Dr Gore and the Education Committee for making this possible. Such a beautiful new building, don't you think?'

'Yes, it's very different from the old one. I don't think it had ever crossed the original architect's mind that it was a school he was designing and not a temporary army barracks.'

'Ah well,' said the priest, 'one shouldn't be too

295

hard on him. I imagine he was constrained by financial considerations. I am sure that if money had been no object we would have had an attractive, spacious building. You see, the school was constructed, like so many post-war Catholic schools, largely as a result of the efforts of the Catholic community hereabouts who raised the money. I'm afraid it didn't go far. It's so good to see the Education Department taking such an active interest in the school and providing us with this wonderful building. I'm Father Leonard, by the way. I don't think we've met.'

'Ah, *the* Father Leonard!' I cried. 'You must be Monsignor Leonard's brother.'

The priest's wrinkled face broke into a great grin. 'Oh no, Mr Phinn, he's mine!'

Some time later, after having done my duty and talked to the governors, I joined Lord Marrick who was holding sway over a group of teachers. The subject under discussion appeared to be an interview which, a short time ago, would have depressed me immensely but now the black cloud had lifted and I was in a much better frame of mind. In fact, I was feeling positively buoyant.

'I was just telling the present company, Mr Phinn,' said Lord Marrick, moving his bulk to allow me to stand beside him, 'that we were talking on the way over here this afternoon about the appointment of the new Senior Inspector and all those letters he has after his name. Father Leonard here was recalling that the headteacher before Mrs Callaghan had a similar string of qualifications.'

'But you appointed me, Father,' said Mrs Callaghan, 'with just a teaching certificate and not a degree to my name.'

'We did,' said the priest, 'and we certainly made the right decision. It's not the qualifications that matter in the long run. It's the calibre of the person. Indeed, the greatest teacher of all had no letters to his name.'

'Yes, indeed,' said Lord Marrick, 'yes, indeed. I don't mind saying, Mrs Callaghan, and you have heard me saying this on a number of occasions, that you run a cracking good school.'

'And that was a cracking good assembly earlier on,' I added. It had certainly given me food for thought.

At the end of the school day, Lord Marrick cut a long length of bright blue ribbon fixed across the entrance to the hall, pulled a silk cord to uncover a plaque set in the wall, and made a short but elegant speech. Then, as the children sweetly sang some country songs, I sat blissfully listening to their clear, innocent voices whilst staring beyond them through the large picture window at the sweeping green dale beyond.

*　　　*　　　*

One bright early June Saturday morning, Christine and I moved into Peewit Cottage, saying a thankful farewell to the flat over the Rumbling Tum Café and the cooking smells that wafted malodorously up the stairs. The woodworm and damp treatment on the cottage, the re-pointing, re-plastering and re-decorating had just about cleaned out our bank account but we couldn't have been happier. The sun was shining, the birds were singing and we were so excited at the prospect of starting our married life in our very own home. I had hired a van on the previous Saturday and, with David's help, had moved the bits of furniture which Christine had inherited from her great-aunt. There was a chest-of-drawers, rather worse for wear, two threadbare easy chairs, a large drop-leaf dining table and six ladderback chairs. My sister had donated some pots and pans, carpets and curtains; my brother Michael had presented us with a sideboard and Sidney had arrived unannounced one evening at my flat with an assortment of cutlery, garden tools, shelves and rugs.

'I've been having a clear out in the garage, dear boy,' he had told me, 'and thought some of these might come in handy.'

The final article of furniture we needed to buy was a bed.

The Sunday before we moved into the cottage, Christine and I spent a morning browsing around Roper's Saleroom in Collington. Roper's, auctioneers of fine quality furniture, paintings and effects, was housed in an impressive red-brick building set back from the road. The main room, where the auctions took place, was crammed with the most wonderful antique furniture: Regency mahogany sideboards, delicate inlaid rosewood tables, chiffoniers, satinwood desks, Edwardian wing armchairs, bow-fronted cupboards, Victorian balloon-backed chairs, Art Nouveau display cabinets, ornately-carved marble fire mantels and tall, highly-polished grandfather clocks. All of it was way out of our price range.

And then we saw the bed. It took up an inordinate amount of space at the side of the saleroom and, surrounded by such exquisite furniture, looked amazingly plain and ugly with its

298

dark oak headboard, thick buttoned mattress and heavy square legs.

'What do you think?' I asked.

'It's a bit large,' Christine replied, 'and it's not the most elegant of pieces, is it?'

'Looks aren't everything,' I pointed out.

'I'm not sure. Perhaps we ought to get a new one.'

'It's very comfortable,' I told her, sitting on the thick mattress and bouncing up and down. 'A modern bed wouldn't fit in. A cottage the age of ours needs to have older furniture and this is really well-made. I can tell. It will last for ever, this bed.'

'I have no doubt about that,' Christine remarked, giving a wry smile.

'Well, shall we stay for the auction and see what it goes for? I mean, it will probably be well out of our price range anyway.' When had we said that before? We should have learned by now.

So we stayed for the auction and sat through item after item, most of which fetched an exorbitant price.

'Ours is the next lot after this one,' I whispered to Christine.

'I really don't know whether we should bid, Gervase,' she said. 'Are you really sure about this?'

'Lot 367,' the auctioneer intoned. 'A unique nineteenth-century Louis XIV-style burr walnut and ebony banded cabinet with decorative stringing and ormolu mounts. This is a very special piece, ladies and gentlemen. I would ask you to note, in particular, the enchanting oval jasperwear plaques inset in the doors, the beautifully-turned pierced gallery back rails and the delightful gilt metal statuettes on the small plinths. The rope-twist

299

beading and the mirrored back undershelf are, as you can see, in immaculate condition. Shall we start the bidding at say, £500?' Bidding was brisk and the cabinet was soon sold.

'Lot 368. A turn-of-the-century solidly constructed, iron-framed and impressively large bed in oak. Shall we start the bidding at £100?'

'I am not sure about that bed,' Christine said, later that evening. 'I still think we should have gone for something more modern.'

'Well, it's too late now,' I told her. 'We've bought it and Roper's are delivering it next Saturday. It may not be a Louis XIV masterpiece but I think we got a real bargain.'

'By the time we've bought a new mattress, it won't be so much of a bargain,' said Christine, who had insisted we threw away the old mattress. 'But, I agree, it's a great bed.'

The bed arrived the day we moved in. I was exchanging pleasantries with my neighbour, Harry Cotton, over the drystone wall when a huge dark-green removal van bearing the words 'Roper's Auctioneers of Distinction' printed in gold lettering on the side drew up outside the cottage.

'More furniture, then,' observed Harry, scratching his shock of white hair. 'At this rate, you won't have room to swing a dormouse.'

'Just a bed,' I replied.

'Aahh, well,' he chuckled, tapping his beak of a nose and winking theatrically. 'Tha'll be needing a bed an' no mistake. I reckon you and yer new missus'll be putting that to good use, if tha follows my drift.'

I did not wish to follow his drift and went to greet the three men in green overalls, with the

Roper's logo embroidered in yellow, who had just jumped out of the van.

'Mr Phinn?' asked a young man with closely-cropped, dyed blond hair and a large gold stud in his ear.

'That's right,' I replied.

'We're here with the bed. Where do you want it?'

'Where do you think he wants it?' bayed Harry Cotton, shouting over the wall. 'In my experience, beds go in t'bedrooms, sithee.'

'OK, granddad,' said the young man. 'Keep your hair on. I was just asking.' Then he asked Harry mischievously, 'Are you going to give us a lift with it, then?'

'Am I 'ell as like,' he said. 'I've had a double hernia, me. Not a single one, mind, but a double, and t'eaviest thing I lift these days is a pint o' bitter.'

The three men, with my help, struggled and strained to get the bed out of the removal van and we dumped it at the door of the cottage. It looked gigantic.

'It's a fair old size,' panted one of the men, sitting on the bed's iron frame.

'And a fair old weight, as well,' added another, joining him.

'Do you think you'll get it through the door?' I asked apprehensively. 'It looks a lot bigger here than it did in the saleroom.'

'We'll get it in through the door, no trouble,' said the young man with the short hair and the stud. 'We can up-end it. Getting it up the stairs is a different matter altogether.'

'Well, they got it down,' said Harry as he

observed proceedings from the wall. 'So they must 'ave got it up.'

'How do you mean?' I asked.

Harry rubbed his chin and cocked his head in the direction of the cottage. 'That theer bed what you 'ave just bought, belonged to old Mrs Olleranshaw. It used to be in her front bedroom.'

'Mrs Olleranshaw!' I exclaimed. 'The old lady who owned the cottage before us?'

'The very same.'

'But I thought you told me she had died two years ago.'

'She did. It were her nephew, young Nigel, 'im what came into her money. He only got around to selling her stuff at t'beginning of this year. Some of it went to Roper's, I believe. Aye, that theer bed used to be in her front bedroom.'

'And how would you know that then, granddad?' asked the young man, smirking.

'Well . . . I . . . er . . . er . . . I saw it being brought out when young Mr Olleranshaw sent it to t'saleroom.'

'I believe you, granddad,' said the young man, giving a theatrical wink. 'Thousands wouldn't. Come on then, lads, let's give it a try.' The two men rose from the bed. He turned to me. 'We'll need a bit of help up the stairs, if you don't mind, so I hope you haven't had a double hernia like old Casanova over there. By the way, you haven't decorated yet, have you? It's just that there might be a bit of manoeuvring to get it in the bedroom. These old cottages often have very narrow stairs.'

'They do,' agreed Harry who, having regained his composure, had moved from the wall and now stood by the cottage door, the better to observe

302

proceedings. 'And Peewit Cottage has some of t'narrowest, if my memory serves me right.'

'Yes, I have just decorated,' I told him, my heart sinking into my shoes. 'Just last week.'

'Well, I can't promise we won't chip your paintwork,' he said.

Mr Cotton was now perched on the bed, running his hand over the oak headboard.

'Yes, this were Mrs Olleranshaw's bed, all right. Nice piece of furniture, this.' He chuckled, a long low chuckle. 'It's a rum do, i'n't it? All that heffort gerrin' it down and then it 'as to go up ageean.'

'Are you sure this is the same bed, Harry?' I asked.

'Oh yes, it's t'same bed, sure as eggs is eggs. She was ill for a long time was Mrs Olleranshaw. Spent a deal of time in that there bed a-moanin' and a-groanin'.' He scratched his chin and nodded sagely. 'Breathed her last in it an' all.'

At this point, Christine emerged from the cottage, looking radiant in the spring sunshine and smiling widely.

'Ah, the bed,' she said. 'It's arrived.'

'I was just saying to your 'usband, Mrs Phinn,' said Harry. 'This is the bed that old Mrs Olleranshaw died in.'

CHAPTER SIXTEEN

On a bright early June morning, I made my way to Barton Moor Parochial School, feeling on top of the world. Married life was seriously suiting me, I mused, and I whistled a little tune to confirm that I felt on top of the world. In fact, I thought, glancing at my watch, I had a little time to spare so I pulled into a gateway and climbed out of the car—I had borrowed Christine's small Morris Minor since my car was in for service.

I leaned on the gate and looked at the scene below me. The field, which fell away into Bartondale below, was full of contented grazing sheep, the warm morning sun falling on their newly-shorn backs. The sky was alive with darting swallows and the air with birdsong. I would have liked to have spent all day there, but I had a school to visit, so reluctantly I returned to the car and made my way to the small hamlet of Barton Moor.

I swung into the small parking area and as I got out of the car I saw two boys aged about ten or eleven sitting on the school wall, watching me with some interest.

'Hey up,' said one as I approached.

'Good morning,' I replied, waving.

'Grand day,' said the other, screwing up his eyes and surveying the sky.

'It is, a beautiful day.'

The bigger of the two boys pointed a finger at the car and said, 'I see tha got rid o' t'hearse then.' And I immediately remembered meeting the boys on my first visit to the school more than two years earlier.

Snow had been falling heavily ever since I had left Fettlesham, and I had thanked my lucky stars that I had been driving the large estate car that I had bought from my brother before moving north. Old and black—a 'wardrobe on wheels', as Sidney liked to call it—the vehicle was not the most attractive looking, but it was solid and heavy and

304

ideal for driving in such hazardous conditions.

I had felt a certain smugness as I had chugged slowly but surely up the ribbon of road, leaving behind me other vehicles unable to cope with the conditions. That morning, as I had clambered from the car, I had noticed two young lads watching me with great interest from their viewpoint on top of the school wall. They had been muffled up so thickly in woolly hats, thick coats and scarves that I had only seen two pairs of sharp dark eyes peering out at me. The two figures had looked like bundles of clothes one might see in the corner of a jumble sale.

'Come for t'body, 'as tha?' one of the boys had asked me, pointing a gloved finger at the car.

'Pardon?' I had replied, shivering in the cold air.

'For t'body. To tek away in t'hearse.'

'No, no,' I had said, laughing. 'I've not come for the body and my car isn't a hearse.'

'Looks like an 'earse,' the larger of the two had commented. 'I bet tha could get a body in t'back wi'out any trouble at all.'

'Tha could get a pair of 'em in theer,' his small companion had added.

'I suppose I could,' I had replied, 'but I'm not here for a body.'

'Are thy 'ere to fix t'frozzen pipes in t'lads' lavs, then?'

'No, I'm afraid not.'

'Pity. We've been crossin' us legs all week, 'aven't we, Roge?'

'Good sort of car to drive in this sort o' weather, I reckon,' observed the other boy. 'It's like a tank. Cooarse, tha needs a bit o'weight under thee, to get up Barton Hill.'

'You certainly do.'

'Keeps thee on t'rooad, then?'

'Yes, it does. Well, I must be getting on. See you in school.'

The headteacher of Barton Moor Parochial was a large, rosy-cheeked, good-natured woman by the name of Miss Sally Precious. When I had first inspected the school, it had received a good report but there had been one or two criticisms and suggestions. I had had a meeting with Miss Precious the year before but it had been in the Staff Devlopment Centre when she had been there for a course; the purpose of this visit was to see how much progress had been made in the school.

'Bit different from your last visit, eh, Mr Phinn?' she said, bustling towards me and then shaking my hand vigorously. 'My goodness, the snow was thick and then the fog descended. It's a wonder you got back home in one piece.'

'Yes, indeed, Miss Precious,' I replied. 'I won't forget that journey in a long time.'

She chatted on amiably as I followed her in the direction of her small office.

'I've put you with Mrs Durdon and the infants first and then you're with me after morning playtime. Is that all right?'

'Fine,' I replied.

'Then at lunchtime we can have a little chat about how things have improved since you were last here. Well,' and she gave a little laugh, 'I certainly think that things have improved.'

'I'm so glad to hear it,' I said, trying to keep up.

'Do you remember when you last came we had that interesting conversation about Joseph, the gifted pupil?'

'Yes, I was going to ask you about him,' I said, hoping to hear more about the intriguing boy I had met on the previous visit.

'Well, I'll tell you all about him later,' she told me, striding ahead. 'I'm sure you want to make a start.'

Joseph had been the very first pupil to whom I had spoken when I had last called at Barton Moor. He could have been a schoolboy of the 1950s. He had a short-back-and-sides haircut and was dressed in long grey trousers and a hand-knitted grey jersey, while his shoes were eminently sensible. He wore extremely thick-lensed spectacles. Joseph was probably the brightest pupil I had ever met, with a sharp enquiring mind, a remarkable general knowledge and an outstanding command of English, but he seemed such a sad, serious, lonely child. I had often thought about how he would fare moving from the small and friendly rural primary school to the large comprehensive in West Challerton. It occurred to me that he would be the perfect target for the school bullies.

Yes, I was looking forward to hearing from Miss Precious just how Joseph was getting along at his new school where he had been for nearly a year now.

*   *   *

There were just the two classrooms in Barton Moor School, one for the infants and one for the juniors. Both were long rooms with high, beamed ceilings and both were clean and orderly. A large picture window had been put in the junior classroom (how Miss Precious managed to get

307

planning permission, I will never know) and this gave the children an uninterrupted and quite magnificent view across the moor and down into the valley. The infant classroom, with its small, high windows, was darker and less cheerful and it was the headteacher's principal aim in life to have a similar 'window on the world' created there, too.

When I came into the infants' classroom, Mrs Durdon, who was a small, intense-looking woman, seemed extremely nervous and blinked rapidly. 'I'm afraid you've come at the wrong time,' she told me rather crossly. She sounded like an irritated housewife, confronted with a fervent member of some religious sect intent on converting her.

'The wrong time?' I repeated.

'We're doing mathematics this morning, not English. English takes place this afternoon. Can you come back?'

'No, not really,' I replied. 'I'm only here for the morning.'

The teacher blinked madly. 'After your last visit, Mr Phinn, you suggested that we planned our days more thoroughly and devoted greater time to the basic subjects, so we now have maths in the morning and English in the afternoon. I did tell Miss Precious.'

'Don't worry,' I said calmly, 'I'll just stay for ten minutes.'

'But we are doing maths this morning,' she repeated, 'not English.'

'Yes, you said. I'll just stay for a moment, if I may.'

The children had been set the exercise of identifying different geometrical shapes—squares, rectangles, circles, triangles, hexagons and so on—

which had been drawn on a worksheet. I approached a small girl busily writing away with a large pencil. She had completed the first two questions correctly: 'Is this a triangle or a circle?' and 'Is this a square or a rectangle?' but in answer to the third question she had written what looked like 'Melanie'.

'What is this word?' I asked, intrigued.

'Melanie,' replied the child.

'Melanie,' I repeated. 'Why have you written "Melanie"?'

'Well, it says, "Name this shape",' she replied sweetly, 'so I thought I'd call it Melanie.'

My laughter brought the teacher bustling to my side. I explained the reason for my amusement, before leaning over the child. 'You know,' I told her seriously, 'I think it's more of a Samantha.'

'Actually, it's an octagon,' said Mrs Durdon, without any trace of a smile.

The next child, a mousy-haired girl, as small as a sparrow, with tiny bright eyes and a little beak of a nose, had completed her worksheet and was reading quietly.

'All finished?' I observed.

'Yes, it was pretty straightforward,' she told me, looking up from her book. 'I'm pretty good at shapes.'

'And what is your name?' I asked.

'Anna Martram,' she replied.

'Can you spell that for me?'

'Of course I can,' she said pertly before doing so, slowly and deliberately as if she were in the presence of a slow learner. Then she added, 'Both my names are palindromes, you know.'

'Palindromes?'

309

'Spelt the same backwards.' She returned to her book.

Here is another Joseph, I thought to myself.

'The last time I came to your school,' I told her, 'it was very cold and wintry and on my way back I got lost, it was that dark and foggy.'

'Yes,' she replied without looking up, 'visibility isn't too good up here, is it? And now, if you will excuse me, I do so want to finish this chapter.'

At morning break I joined the headteacher in her small office and heard about Joseph's progress.

'Our Joseph is doing really well,' Miss Precious informed me proudly. 'He's taken to secondary education like a duck to water. I think it is living in an isolated house on the moor top with his grandparents, well meaning though they undoubtedly are, which makes him seem so serious and so old for his age. He has no other children to play with up there, and his grandparents are rather strict and sober people. They don't approve of television, cinema, fashionable clothes and comics, nothing of that sort, but they have certainly taken his education seriously. I don't think they felt that I had really stretched him intellectually here, but he's really coming on at the comprehensive, socially as well as intellectually. He looked as if he had the weight of the world on his shoulders some days when he was with me. Do you know, he got this scholarship to a top public school, which I thought would be ideal for such a child, but he wouldn't go.'

'He wouldn't go?'

'No, he said he didn't believe in private education or in private healthcare and was going to the comprehensive in West Challerton like the rest of the children. Wouldn't budge.'

'Why did he sit the scholarship paper for the public school if he never intended going there?' I asked.

'He said he wanted to see how he would get on. He always liked a challenge, did Joseph, and loved doing tests. He got top marks, evidently, and they were very keen to have him, I can tell you. The headmaster was on the phone here, morning, noon and night, asking me to get him to change his mind but Joseph was as stubborn as a mule.'

'And he's doing all right at the comprehensive?'

'Fine, as far as I know. He's been there less than a year and already he's won two national writing competitions and was selected to play in the England Junior Chess Team. He's become a member of Junior MENSA as well and has joined the drama club. And, what's really good to hear is that he seems to have developed a sense of humour. Now then, what about that?'

'You always said he would go far.'

'I did, didn't I? Well he's certainly on the road to fame and fortune is our Joseph Barclay, and what is really nice is that he calls in and lets me know how he's getting on. Comes in regularly for a little chat. I do like it when my former pupils keep in touch. It makes the job that bit more worthwhile, don't you think?'

'And you can be justifiably proud of the part you played in his success,' I told her, and I meant it.

'Get away with you,' she said, colouring up. 'Now, there's a little girl in Mrs Durdon's class I want your advice about. Bright as a button she is.'

'Ah, yes,' I said smiling. 'Anna the palindrome.'

Just two weeks later, I happened to meet Joseph again. I had been asked by the recently-appointed headmaster of West Challerton High School, Mr Raymond Pennington-Smith, to attend the school's annual prize-giving ceremony and speech day when the most successful students in the various academic subjects and those who had achieved highly in sport, would be presented with their awards, certificates, shields and cups. Mr Pennington-Smith was a very different character from the previous headmaster—a large, bluff, outspoken Yorkshireman called appropriately Mr Blunt. Mr Blunt was not a one for sherry receptions and speech days.

West Challerton High School was one of the first schools I had visited as a school inspector and when I had delivered my report to Mr Blunt he had bristled when he read that there had been so much as a hint of a criticism of his school. My attempts to explain that the report was, in general, a very favourable one and that he seemed to be taking the relatively few criticisms personally, were dismissed curtly. He had told me that when a school is attacked it was the headteacher who bled and then he had shared with me his uncompromising views about my chosen profession.

'I have always been of the opinion, Mr Phinn,' he had told me, pushing out his face like a bulldog with toothache, 'that school inspectors are like cross-eyed javelin throwers. They hurl a lot of spears in the direction of the schools, missing the point most of the time but occasionally, and by sheer accident, they happen to hit the right target.'

I knew that while Mr Blunt remained as headmaster of West Challerton High School, an invitation to attend a sherry reception and the annual prize-giving would not be forthcoming. Yet, despite his brusque manner and poor opinion of school inspectors, I rather liked the man. He was, like many a Yorkshire person, plain-speaking, unassuming and not a one for anything fancy—unlike his successor.

I arrived at the school an hour before the proceedings and chuddered through the gates in my old estate car in the direction of the reserved parking spaces near the main entrance. I had just negotiated the narrow bend in the drive when two smartly-dressed pupils waved me to stop.

'I'm sorry, sir,' explained one of the boys, 'but the spaces at the front of the school are for the VIPs only. Would you mind parking your car in the main car park at the back?' It was obvious that the young man did not number me amongst the great and the good—not that I blamed him when I saw that the cars in the reserved spaces were rather newer models and a great deal more flashy than my old 'wardrobe on wheels'.

'All right,' I said.

'You are a little early, sir,' the boy told me. 'Speech Day doesn't start until seven-thirty.' I resisted telling the young man that I was one of the VIPs in question and that I had been invited for sherry with the headmaster and governors prior to the ceremony. 'Perhaps, rather than waiting in the car, you would like a tour of the school,' suggested the boy.

'That would be splendid,' I replied. 'I'd like that very much.'

'Well, you park your car, sir, and I'll meet you back here.'

When Mr Pennington-Smith had taken over as headmaster at the beginning of the year, one of his first innovations was to commission a very impressive-looking school brochure; it was full of coloured photographs, grandiose 'mission statements', descriptions of the various courses offered and a list of the staff with their various academic qualifications appended. I recalled Harold telling me when I started in the job that a school is only as good as the teachers and the pupils. The best advertisements for a school, he had said, are not the glossy prospectuses, promotional leaflets, flattering newspaper articles, lists of examination results and publicity materials but the students themselves. They are the ambassadors and the school is best judged by the standard of their behaviour, their enthusiasm for learning and their achievements. The young man who took me on a guided tour of the school left me with the most favourable of impressions. He was confident, courteous and good-humoured, and kept up a running commentary as we toured classrooms and workshops.

'Have you travelled far, sir?' he asked, as we set off at a quick pace down a long corridor.

'I've just come from Castlesnelling, so not too far.'

'And what are your interests?'

'Pardon?'

'Do you follow the cricket? Terrible result from Headingley, wasn't it?'

'Yes, I follow cricket when I have the time, although there seems little point in getting excited about Test cricket at the moment.'

'Do you play rugger?'

'No, not any more.'

'Or are you more of a soccer fan?'

'I like soccer, yes.'

On my travels around schools, I am the one who generally asks the questions so this was a very pleasant change. I glanced at my watch. 'Well, I think I had better be on my way. Thank you very much for the tour of the school. It was most interesting.'

'Oh, you've plenty of time, yet,' the boy told me. 'You have another half hour. Is your son or daughter receiving a prize tonight?'

'Actually,' I said, 'I don't have a son or daughter. I'm not a parent. I'm a school inspector and one of the invited guests.'

'Oh crikey!' exclaimed the boy, his hand to his mouth. 'You are one of the VIPs. I'm really sorry. I thought you were just one of the . . . just an ordinary . . . I didn't know . . . oh help!'

'Don't worry yourself,' I said, smiling. 'I've very much enjoyed looking around the school. What's your name?'

'Andrew Winner, sir. Oh, sir, you won't tell Mr Pennington-Smith, will you, sir, about me getting you to park at the back?' he pleaded.

I smiled mischievously. 'No, we'll keep that to ourselves, shall we?'

It was certainly my intention to tell Mr Pennington-Smith how very impressed I had been with my young guide and to ask him to congratulate him on his initiative, good manners and excellent inter-personal skills. At a very brisk pace, I followed the scurrying figure and was very

315

soon delivered outside the headmaster's room.

'Goodbye, sir,' said the boy and hurried away.

My heart sank when I saw who was in animated conversation with the headmaster. Although he had his back to me, the huge neck with folds which overlapped the top of his collar, the mop of black hair and the bombastic voice were unmistakable. It was Councillor George Peterson, an insufferably garrulous and self-opinionated man who, on the several times we had met, always succeeded in irritating me beyond measure.

'Ah,' said the headmaster, catching sight of me entering the room, 'I think I can see Mr Phinn.'

The councillor swivelled round and I was confronted with the vast florid face. 'Oh, he's arrived, 'as he?' he stated loudly to anyone who happened to be listening. 'I thowt tha'd forgotten or 'ad summat better on.'

'No, councillor,' I replied, smiling sweetly. 'I've been having a tour of the school.'

'You know Councillor Peterson, then, do you, Mr Phinn?' enquired the headmaster, with an ingratiating smile playing on his lips.

'Aye, we've met,' the councillor replied before I could respond. 'At interviews, school plays, parents' evenings, Education Committee and such like. We never seem to be away from each other. I thowt we might 'ave seen you up for t' Senior Inspector's job, Mester Phinn, but they never called you for interviews, did they?' He had all the tact of a sledge hammer.

'No, they didn't, councillor,' I replied.

'I thowt to myself when I heard abaat it, you were a bit on t'premature side applying for such a top job. I mean you've only been in t'county five

316

minutes.'

Why don't you say it a little louder so all the room could hear, I thought to myself.

'You are probably right, councillor,' I said.

'Anyrooad, we appointed a very bright chap. Everybody on t'panel were very impressed with 'im. As Lord Marrick said at t'time, he's got more degrees than a thermometer.'

I steered the conversation onto another subject. 'And how is your wife, councillor?'

'Oh, she's champion.' He turned to the headmaster and took his arm. 'He inspected mi wife, you know.'

'I beg your pardon, councillor?' said Mr Pennington-Smith, rather taken aback.

'Mester Phinn. He inspected mi wife. Gave her a thorough goin' ovver.'

'He inspected your wife?' the headmaster repeated, now with a quizzical expression on his face.

'She's an 'eadteacher, my wife. Highcopse Primary School,' explained the councillor. 'Mester Phinn here went through her school like a dose of salts. Tha wants to watch out, headmaster, or he'll be standing on *your* doorstep with his ruddy clipboard one of these days.'

'Councillor Peterson is our Chairman of Governors,' said Mr Pennington-Smith, looking rather embarrassed. 'Now, perhaps I might go over the proceedings. The evening will commence with the school orchestra and some poetry recited by the students, followed by Councillor Peterson who will say a few words to welcome the parents. Then I shall give my annual report and this will be followed by the presentation of the prizes. I

317

wonder, Mr Phinn, would you do the honours?'

'Present the prizes?'

'If you would be so good,' said the headmaster.

'Well, yes, of course, I should be delighted.'

'And don't go droppin' any o' t'cups,' said the councillor, laughing at his own supposedly amusing comment. 'Or walkin' off wi' 'em.' Before I could reply, he consulted his watch and barked across the room. 'Well, I think we're about ready for the off by my reckonin'. Sup up, everybody, and we'll make a start and get the show on t'rooad.'

The party processed behind Mr Pennington-Smith, resplendent in his black academic gown with fur-lined hood.

'I asked t'headmaster,' chortled Councillor Peterson, indicating the hood with the white fur, 'when he was at t'University of Alaska but I don't think he saw t'funny side.'

We made our way into the school hall and up onto the stage to the accompaniment of the school orchestra. The first ten or so rows were full of smartly-dressed students and in the seats behind were the proud parents. After the school orchestra had played a selection of rousing melodies and three students had recited a Shakespeare sonnet, a dreary Robert Burns poem spoken in a very poor attempt at a Scottish accent, and an excellent rendition of John Betjeman's poem 'Original Sin on the Sussex Coast', the Chairman of Governors made his ponderous way to the lectern. Councillor Peterson's 'short' address, in which he lambasted wishy-washy, airy-fairy, modern teaching methods, and lamented the demise of gabardine raincoats and schools caps, and the disappearance of corporal punishment (which, he said, had never

318

done him any harm), lasted a good fifteen minutes but concluded on an unintentionally amusing note.

'Now, this school 'as 'ad its share of problems, there's no denying that. We've 'ad cracks in t'walls, asbestos roofs what 'ave been condemned, gas leaks, bomb scares and floods and the last inspectors' report—that was before the present headmaster was in post, of coourse—mentioned some shortcomings. So we 'ave 'ad a difficult year. Make no mistake about that. We are at t'edge of a precipice, not to put too fine a point on it, but, with the recent appointment of Mr Pennington-Smith, we are now moving forward with confidence.'

Mr Pennington-Smith decided upon a nautical metaphor for his address. 'Mr Chairman of Governors, governors, members of staff, parents, honoured guests and, last but not least, students of West Challerton High School,' he began, 'welcome, welcome, to the first, but certainly not the last of my Annual School Prize-giving and Speech Days. It is with great pride that I stand before you this evening as your new headmaster to report upon the school's outstanding academic and sporting successes. But, you know parents, I see myself not as a headmaster at all, but more as the captain of a ship, standing proudly on the bridge, scanning the horizon, with the salty spray of enthusiasm in my face and my sails full of an optimistic wind. And what is our destination? I hear you ask. Where are we going? Well, I will tell you. We are heading for the land of opportunity and the harbour of success. It will not be an easy journey. Sometimes we are buffeted by the stormy gusts of educational change. Sometimes we are carried off course by the cold currents of government policy. Sometimes we face the hurricanes and gales of school inspection.' He glanced briefly in my direction at this point and allowed himself a smug little smile. 'Sometimes we are inundated by a heavy downpour of yet more documents from the Ministry of Education. Sometimes we are becalmed by the shortage of the necessary resources. Yet we always keep a steady course, with a firm hand on the tiller, for the land of opportunity and the harbour of success. As captain of this ship of ours, I have the experience and skill to steer us onwards. I have all my correct navigational equipment intact and I have with me on the bridge, to help keep us heading in the right direction, my first officer—the deputy head—Mr Stipple, and my second officer—the senior mistress—Mrs Wellbeloved. My other officers—the teaching staff—are keen, capable and well qualified. They help me navigate this ship of ours to the land of opportunity and the harbour of success. They assist me to plot the course, steer the ship, make sail towards our desired destination. And you, the students here tonight, our precious cargo . . .' The headmaster paused to sweep his hand before him. 'You know well the name of this, our ship, a name that stands for history, for tradition and for the highest possible standards. What is the name of this our ship, I ask? What is the name of this vessel of ours riding the crest of the wave for the land of opportunity and the harbour of success?'

No one volunteered a name. The headmaster's eyes came to rest on a small boy in the front row. He was a strangely old-fashioned-looking boy, wearing grey trousers and eminently sensible shoes. He stared up from behind thick-lensed glasses like the bottom of milk bottles. It was Joseph. He was staring seriously at the headmaster. 'Yes, you, boy,' Mr Pennington-Smith commanded, 'Barclay, isn't it? Tell us the name of this ship of ours.'

'Is it the *Titanic*, sir?' enquired Joseph with a small smile.

CHAPTER SEVENTEEN

We could hear Sidney chortling to himself as he climbed the stairs to the office.

'Someone is in a remarkably good mood,' remarked David, looking up morosely and peering over the top of his spectacles. He pushed away from him the report he was attempting to complete and leaned back in his chair.

'It's Friday,' I reminded him, trying to sound cheerful, the prospect of a nice quiet weekend.'

'Huh!' snorted my companion, shaking his head wearily. 'Nice quiet weekend? Not if I haven't finished this wretched report which I have been working on for the best part of a week. Gerry did the right thing by going off early.'

A moment later, Sidney strode through the door, threw his briefcase onto his desk with a flourish and flopped heavily into the nearest chair. Then he threw back his head and laughed so loudly that Julie came bustling in to see what the noise was.

'Whatever is it?' she asked. 'Are you having some sort of a turn?'

'No, Julie,' replied Sidney, 'I am perfectly well, thank you. I am laughing. I am having a hearty laugh which, so the philosophers tell us, is a sign of a healthy soul.'

'Oh, for goodness' sake!' said David. 'I sincerely hope that you are not going to go all philosophic on us. I couldn't bear that after the week I have just had.'

'What an old grump you are, David,' said Sidney. '"A cheerful heart is good medicine but a crushed spirit drieth up the bones." Book of Proverbs.'

'Yes, well I feel as if I have a crushed spirit at the moment so I don't feel like laughing,' retorted David. 'Could we, therefore, dispense with your insufferable bonhomie and good humour?'

'"A merry heart doeth good like a medicine." Still Book of Proverbs,' continued Sidney, unabashed.

'"And a heavy fist doeth great damage to the features of the intolerably jovial." Book of David.'

'Well, this will warm those little Welsh cockles of yours,' smiled Sidney. 'I have the most wonderfully amusing story to tell you. It was so absurdly entertaining, I just cannot stop chuckling to myself.'

'Well, you can share it with us,' I told him. 'We're not feeling too happy with the world at the moment, are we, David?'

'That is putting it mildly,' remarked David gloomily, plucking the spectacles from his nose. 'Every blessed report I write, I keep thinking of the new Senior Inspector and what he said. I tell you, I've been put right off my stroke since *Mister* Carter criticised our reports. I'm certain he was referring to mine in particular. He was looking directly at me when he fired the broadside about flabby writing. I do tend to be a bit wordy, I have to admit, and am a little anecdotal, but I have always found that the schools appreciate—'

'You are sounding paranoid,' Sidney interrupted. 'He was referring to all of us. You are, if truth be told, rather loquacious, David, but at least you do not use that ceaseless flow of limp metaphors and memorised maxims beloved of management gurus like Simon Carter and our very own Brenda Savage. They use a sort of verbal wallpaper to cover the cracks in their thinking and the gaping holes in their arguments. Anyway, our new Senior Inspector was staring at me when he made that particular caustic comment. You are taking it far too personally. He thinks we are all as bad as each other.'

'I didn't like him,' observed Julie, leaning against the door jamb and examining a broken nail. 'He's got cold fishy eyes and warm clammy hands. He asked me if I was the clerical ancillary—I ask you!—and told me he would be reviewing my roles and responsibilities as soon as he's settled in. He also thinks that Frank is superfluous. If he starts interfering, I shall tell him to stick his job.'

'So don't keep this very funny story to yourself, Sidney,' I said, not wishing to prolong the depressing discussion of the new Senior Inspector. 'We could do with cheering up.'

'Well,' began Sidney, grinning like a hungry frog, 'have either of you been into West Challerton High recently?'

'Yes, I was there last week to attend Prize-giving and Speech Day,' I told him. It was now my turn to smile as I recalled the event on stage.

'And met the new headmaster?'

'Yes, of course, I did. He would hardly miss Prize-giving, would he?'

'You know, then, how inflated and self-promoting the man is and so full of his own importance, swanning around the place in his academic gown like Napoleon.'

'I was not aware that Napoleon wore an academic gown,' remarked David. 'He wore a sort of greatcoat, if my memory serves me right.'

'You know what I mean,' continued Sidney. 'The way he struts about the place with his hands behind his back.'

'Napoleon tucked his hand inside his coat, didn't he?' asked Julie.

'Am I allowed to finish this story,' demanded Sidney, 'without petty interruptions?'

'Go on, go on,' I urged.

'Well, you know the way he tells everyone how everything in his educational garden is so rosy,' continued Sidney, 'and how things have really flourished and blossomed since he took over? He likes horticultural metaphors, does Mr Pennington-Smith—'

'And nautical ones,' I interjected, thinking of his address at the Prize-giving again. 'I have a funny story about that as well.'

'The other chap, old Blunt, was a pain in the neck at times,' observed David, 'but you knew where you were with him. Blunt by name and blunt by nature, that was him. Always a man for speaking his mind. I recall that once—'

'David!' snapped Sidney. 'Who is telling this story, you or me?'

'Well, I don't know what story you're going to tell,' said David. 'I was going to tell you about the P.E. equipment.'

'Is it funny? It doesn't sound as though it could

324

be the least bit funny.'

'Well, it's not really.'

'Well mine is. It is very funny, extremely funny, so may I be allowed to continue?'

'Come on, Sidney,' I said, 'let's hear it. We'll be here all night at this rate.'

'Well, earlier this week, when I was on a two-day visit to the school inspecting the visual arts department, the headmaster had this final-year pupil in his room when I arrived. She was a tall, gangly, sullen-looking girl of about fifteen. Anyway, he asked me to wait in the outer room—that little glass adjunct which he euphemistically calls his personal assistant's office. As I sat there waiting to give him the oral report of my inspection visit, I could hear the conversation as clear as if he were sitting next to me. He says, "Well now, Delores, you are still sure you want to keep it?" "Oh yes, sir," the girl replies. "And you have given up any thoughts of adoption?" "Oh yes, sir," she says again. "You are very young to be bringing up a child. Have you talked it through very thoroughly with your parents and the social services?" "Oh yes, sir," replies the girl for the third time. "When is the baby due, Delores?" he asks. 'Not until October, sir," says the girl. "And are you getting on well with your studies at home with the private tutor?" "Oh yes, sir," she says. "When you come into school next week to take your final exams, we are putting you in the deputy headteacher's room rather than in the hall with the other students. We felt it would be a little less embarrassing for you with people staring and so forth." "Thank you, sir."

'At this point,' continued Sidney, 'I could hear the girl getting up and heading for the door. "Oh,
325

and Delores," the headmaster calls after her, "the Outward Bound week over the summer holidays is off." "Aw, no, sir," moans the girl. "I was looking forward to that." "Well, you can hardly go abseiling, canoeing, caving, orienteering, mountain-climbing and grass-skiing when you're five months pregnant, can you? Tell your mother that we will refund the deposit she paid for the trip." "Yes, sir. Thank you, sir." '

Sidney paused for effect.

'Is that it?' said David. 'It doesn't sound at all that amusing. In fact, I feel quite sorry for the poor girl, bringing a baby into the world as a teenage, unmarried mother. OK, so she shouldn't have got into that position in the first place—to coin a phrase—but it takes a lot of guts to do that.'

'My best friend is an unmarried mother,' chipped in Julie. 'And it's no laughing matter, I can tell you. She had a terrible time with all the gossip and people making comments.'

'It must be very hard bringing up a child on your own,' I said, thinking of Gerry.

'Look, all of you,' cried Sidney, exasperated, 'I haven't finished the story yet! This is not a general discussion about the trials and tribulations of teenage pregnancies.'

'Well, hurry up, will you?' said Julie, 'I've got a bus to catch at six and if I miss it, I'll have to wait another hour.'

'Please don't let me detain you, Julie,' replied Sidney curtly. 'I could make the story episodic if you would prefer and relate the dénouement tomorrow.'

'The what?'

'The conclusion to this very funny story which I am attempting to relate despite the frequent
326

interruptions. As I said, don't let me detain you.'

Sidney's sarcasm was wasted on Julie who was now attempting to cut her nail with a large pair of office scissors. 'No, I want to hear the end but can you hurry up and cut out all the conversation bits?'

'Those are the funny parts!' exclaimed Sidney. 'It's the conversation bits which make it interesting. It is the conversation bits which enhance the narrative and embroider the story.'

'And I thought I was wordy and anecdotal,' remarked David, closing the report and plucking his glasses from his nose. Then, with a cynical little laugh, he added. 'And you won't be doing any enhancing and embroidering in your school reports if Mr Simon Carter has his way.'

'Please don't bring him up again,' I pleaded.

'Right, well, if that is the way you want it,' Sidney told us. 'I will cut out the conversation bits and tell you, without gloss, what happened next. So the headmaster tells Delores—'

At this point the telephone rang.

'Leave it! Leave it!' ordered Sidney. 'I am determined to get to the end of this blessed story if it kills me!'

'No, I had better answer it,' I said, picking up the receiver.

'Well, go on,' said David, addressing Sidney. 'So the headmaster says to Delores . . .'

'Hello?' I said.

'It is quite impossible for me to continue,' Sidney told him, 'with Gervase prattling on in the background.'

'But I've got to get my bus,' wailed Julie.

'Gervase, it's me, Gerry,' came a distressed voice down the phone. 'I'm in a spot of bother.'

'What's happened?' I asked. I cupped my hand over the receiver. '*Will* you be quiet,' I told Sidney, who had decided after all to continue to regale Julie and David with the account at West Challerton High.

'My car's broken down,' said Gerry. 'It suddenly cut out and I'm stranded here in a lay-by on the wrong side of Fettlesham. I have to get home in a hurry.'

'Have you called the breakdown people?' I asked.

'I have, but they'll be quite a while and I have something urgent to do. I really *have* to get back. Could you possibly collect me and take me home? I wouldn't ask, Gervase, if it weren't really important.'

'Of course, no problem. Tell me exactly where you are.'

'Look,' I told my colleagues when I had put down the telephone and interrupting Sidney yet again, 'I've got to go and get Gerry. Her car's broken down.'

'I'm forever telling her about that old car of hers,' said David. 'It's not safe, an attractive young woman driving all over the county in an old jalopy like that.'

'It's not as if she can't afford a better car,' remarked Julie. 'Some of us, of course, have to make do with public transport. And on that subject, I'm off since I'll miss my bus if I don't get my skates on,' and, with a wave of her hand, she left the room.

'But what about my story?' shouted Sidney after her. 'I haven't finished my story.'

'Tell us another time—a shorter version,' called

328

back Julie.

'Well, I shall make a move,' said David, putting the report in his briefcase and rising. 'I've had this week in a big way.'

'I really don't know why I bother,' said Sidney, shaking his head and slumping back in his chair. 'I really don't know why I bother.'

*   *   *

Gerry was waiting at the side of the road, pacing up and down and looking uncharacteristically anxious and impatient. She was usually such a composed and easy-going sort of person and I had never seen her in such an agitated state.

'Oh, thank goodness,' she said breathlessly, as I opened the passenger door for her to jump in. 'It's really good of you to collect me, Gervase. I'm so grateful.'

'No problem at all. Now,' I said, as I eased out into the traffic, 'I take it we are heading for Hawthwaite?' I asked.

'Oh, yes please,' replied Gerry. 'I really am sorry to be such a nuisance. The car just suddenly cut out. For all my knowledge of science, I'm afraid the workings of the car engine are beyond me. I phoned the breakdown people but they said they'd be over an hour and I just didn't know what to do. Did I drag you away from anything important?'

'Just one of Sidney's long stories. I was glad to get away, to be honest. It was lucky you caught me because I was about to make tracks when your call came through.' Gerry did not reply but rubbed her hands together uneasily, then glanced at her watch. 'So, what's the emergency?' I asked.

329

'What?' she asked sharply.

'The emergency,' I repeated. 'You know, the something urgent you have to do.'

She was silent for a moment. 'Oh, it's . . . I really don't know what to say. I honestly don't know where to start.'

'You don't have to tell me if you don't want to,' I said, gently. 'I'll just drop you off home and ask no questions. But I can be very discreet, you know, and if you need any more help . . .'

'I do appreciate your coming out. I know you will want to get on home and Christine will be wondering where you've got to. And on Friday night as well.' She glanced at her watch again.

'Oh, she's used to my staying out late. Anyway, it's unlikely she's back from school yet. She stays late most evenings. I often get home before her and—'

Geraldine was clearly not listening. 'Actually, could you drop me off just the other side of Fangbeck Bridge? There's a row of red-brick cottages, just past the Three Feathers pub.'

'Oh yes, I know them. But I thought you said you lived at the other side of the village?'

'I do,' Gerry replied, 'but I have to collect someone.' She took a deep breath, and then said, 'And then actually if you could run us home. Fortunately it's Saturday tomorrow so I can sort the car out then.'

'Do you want me to collect you in the morning,' I asked her, 'and give you a tow to a garage?'

'No, no, you've been really kind as it is. I'll be able to deal with that myself.' She glanced at her watch again and then rubbed her hands together. 'Gervase, there is something I have to tell you,' she

330

began, 'and I really don't know where to start. The someone I have to collect . . . oh, this is very difficult . . .'

'I think I can save you the embarrassment, Gerry,' I said. 'I assume it is your little boy?'

There was sharp intake of breath. 'However did you know?' she whispered.

'I was speaking at the Totterdale and Clearwell golf club dinner and I sat next to Mrs Hills, the woman you rent the cottage from. She told me you had a child.'

'When was this?' Gerry asked, still in a shocked whisper.

'Oh, sometime before Christmas.'

'You've known for over six months?'

'Yes.'

Gerry released a huge sigh, then threw back her head and gave a little laugh. 'And here I was thinking that it was the world's best-kept secret. Why ever didn't you mention it?'

'I assumed you wanted to keep it a secret—although heaven knows why.'

'How many other people know?'

'None, so far as I know. I haven't said a word to anyone—and that includes Christine.'

'Thank you, Gervase, a hundred times. Heavens, that's another thing I have to thank you for.'

'And discretion being my middle name, I shall continue to remain as silent as the grave. But what I cannot understand, Gerry, is why you have decided to keep it such a secret? I mean, it is not as though we are living in the Dark Ages. Who nowadays is going to bother about someone who's a single parent? There's enough of them about.'

'It might not be the Dark Ages, Gervase, but this

331

is Yorkshire, not London. People can be very narrow-minded. And do you imagine for one moment that I would have had a hope in hell of getting this job if it were known that I had a three-year-old son to look after and no husband—an unmarried mother? Just think of some of those who sit on the interview panels—Councillor Peterson, for example, with his ghastly comments about young women not being able to handle the difficult lads and his prehistoric views on the woman's place being at home, cooking and cleaning, darning the socks and looking after the kiddies. It's difficult enough for a woman to get a senior position in such a man's world as it is, without being unmarried and with a young child. I just knew I could hold down this job and be a good mother as well.'

'Mmm, I see what you mean.' I immediately thought of some of the more 'traditional' governors, councillors and clerics I had come across who made Councillor Peterson appear positively liberal in his views. 'But, you know, Yorkshire people are generally very warm and generous and usually don't judge others too hastily. I think you would have been rather surprised at the reaction, had you taken the risk.'

'It will eventually have to come out,' continued Gerry. 'I realise that. Jamie starts nursery school after the summer holidays and you know what the jungle telegraph is like.'

'So no one, except myself, knows then?' I asked.

'Harold knows. I told him before they offered me the job. I thought it only fair to tell him, and he said it was nobody's business but my own and if it did not affect my work then there was no reason to say anything.'

'That sounds like Harold,' I said.

'He's been a tower of strength. In fact, he's been like a father to me, has Harold, and I will really miss him terribly. I'm not looking forward to the arrival of Simon Carter, I have to say. He doesn't strike me as the most understanding and tolerant of men. He has already told me he expects lots of late meetings and evening events. I've not stopped worrying since that dreadful encounter with him when he outlined all the changes he intends making. I cannot imagine Simon Carter being warm and generous and non-judgemental. I really am dreading his coming.'

'Join the club,' I remarked.

'Anyway, I'll have to face that when I have to. I always try to collect Jamie from the child-minder at six. She'll baby-sit for me as well so long as I give her good notice. It's worked out pretty well.' She glanced at her watch for the umpteenth time. 'Until today, that is. She's arranged to go out this evening.'

'Well, we are nearly there now,' I reassured her. 'And I wouldn't worry about Mr Carter. As Connie would say, "You can burn that bridge when you get to it."'

*   *   *

Early the following Monday morning Sidney, David, Gerry and I were at the Staff Development Centre for an inspectors' meeting.

'Thanks a million for Friday,' said Gerry quietly, placing a bottle of wine before me on the table. 'I was in a real state. I hope you and Christine will

333

enjoy this on one of the rare evenings you spend together.'

'Oh, you shouldn't have bothered,' I told her, 'but thanks. It's very thoughtful of you. Has the car been fixed?'

'No, not yet. I'm in a hire car this week but I should have it back next Monday.' She sounded her usual composed and confident self.

'As I said to Gervase the other night,' said David, peering over the top of his spectacles, 'you ought to get yourself a reliable vehicle, Geraldine. You could have broken down in some dark, deserted and dangerous place in the middle of nowhere with no sign of life for miles. Then what would you have done?'

'I shudder at the thought,' Gerry said.

'I mean, you read all the time about young women being attacked along lonely country roads, dragged into the bushes and assaulted, left for dead in a ditch, buried—'

'David,' I interrupted, 'must you be such a prophet of doom. You are getting more and more depressing lately.'

'It's a sad fact that there are all sorts of weird, violent, deranged and dangerous people at large,' he continued obliviously, 'who prey on young women. My sister's daughter, Prudwen, is a case in point. She was coming home from a pop concert in Colwyn Bay with a friend last year when one of these flashers jumped out of the bushes, baring all. Rather unfortunately for the flasher, Prudwen and her friend are big strapping girls and they were not the least bit frightened. More amused than anything. They had caught the drum sticks which the drummer in the band had thrown into the

334

audience at the end of the concert.' David nodded sagely. 'That little man will not be so keen on exposing himself again, I can tell you, not after Prudwen had finished with him. She's taken up playing those steel drums, so my sister was telling me last week, so some good came of it.'

Sidney entered the room, pursued by Connie who was wearing her usual bright pink nylon overall but, in place of the feather duster that morning, she held aloft a long and lethal-looking mop.

'I was merely pointing out, Connie,' Sidney was saying in a weary tone of voice, 'that there is little point in putting a notice which says "Wet Floor" right at the end of the corridor where no one can see it. The sign would be better, I would have thought, placed in the entrance to forewarn those who are foolhardy enough to venture through the door in the first place that the floor is like an ice rink. I very nearly fell full length.'

'Putting the notice in the entrance would cause an obstruction and be a health and safety hazard,' announced Connie. 'People could fall over it.'

'And people could, and I nearly did, slip on the wet floor,' said Sidney.

'I always do my floors on a Monday morning, Mr Clamp, you know that. Eight o'clock prompt before the teachers arrive at nine for their courses is when I do my floors. Then I do the brass fitments in the Gents and the washbasins in the Ladies. I always have done and I always will do. I never deleviate from my routine. Anyway, I did wait until the inspectors had arrived before starting on the floor, so it's your fault for being late.' Before Sidney could respond, Connie turned her attention to the

335

rest of us and smiled. 'Now, I called in to say I have had a phone message from Dr Yeats, who said he would be a bit late. He's tied up with that Mrs Savage at the moment.'

'I can't think of anything more unpleasant,' remarked David.

'So, since we have a little time on our hands,' said Sidney, glancing in the direction of Connie, before gently pulling out a chair and making sure it did not leave a mark on the highly polished floor, 'I shall conclude my story of Delores and the headmaster of West Challerton High School.' He looked in the direction of Connie as if to indicate that she could get on with her mopping but she remained where she was, standing sentinel at the door with her mop, like Britannia herself.

'If you must,' said David.

'Now, it is far too long for me to narrate the first part of the story,' Sidney told us, 'so I shall briefly summarise the story so far for your benefit, Geraldine. I was telling David and Gervase that I was doing a two-day inspection in West Challerton High School at the beginning of last week and on the first day eavesdropped on a conversation between that dreadfully pompous and self-opinionated headmaster and one of the older pupils. This girl was due to have a baby, one of these teenage pregnancies, and he was explaining to her that she could still come in for her examinations which she would sit in a small room rather than the hall. He was also informing her that the Outward Bound week over the summer holidays was off because she was not in a fit state, being five months pregnant, to go grass-skiing and abseiling. Well, on the following day old

336

Pennington-Smith stands up in assembly, before all the staff and pupils and announces, "There is a spare place now available on the Outward Bound week over the summer holidays because of a late withdrawal."' Sidney's face creased with laughter. 'I nearly died when I heard what he said. All the staff had to go out for laughing.' David gave a weak smile but I know I must have looked acutely embarrassed because I could not avoid immediately thinking of Gerry's circumstances.

'Well, I thought it was hilarious,' said Sidney, looking crestfallen. 'A spare place due to a late withdrawal!'

'Mr Clamp,' said Connie, who was still listening from the door and shaking her mop like a spear, 'Delores, for your information—and I assume you are talking about my Delores—happens to be my cousin's girl and I'll tell you this. Those who get into trouble like what she did are the innocent ones, those what men take advantage of. It is no laughing matter bringing up a child without a father. No laughing matter at all.' With that she stomped out.

Sidney hunched his shoulders, pulled the most excruciating expression and whispered across the table, 'Tell me where the hole is so I can crawl into it.'

'It was in rather bad taste,' remarked David. 'Even for you, Sidney.'

'Well how was I to know the girl was Connie's cousin's daughter?' moaned Sidney. 'She'll put toilet bleach in my tea after this.'

'Connie's right,' said Gerry. 'It's no laughing matter bringing up a child without a father. It's a real struggle. I should know.'

'And why should you know, my dear Geraldine?'
I opened my mouth to try to head Sidney off but I
was too late. 'Don't tell us that you have a love
child.'

'Well, yes, Sidney, actually I do.'

'Good God!' exclaimed Sidney and, for once,
was completely lost for words.

'It is perhaps not the most brilliant time to tell
you but I have a little boy called Jamie. He's three.
Jamie's father is married and has a family. I guess I
should have told you.'

There was what seemed like an interminable
silence. It was broken by Sidney. 'Well, Gerry, I . . .
er . . . congratulations! I mean about having a little
boy, not about . . . er . . . his father . . .'

'Stop digging while you can, Sidney,' advised
David. 'The hole is becoming a bottomless pit.'

'I really am sorry, Gerry,' said Sidney, giving her
a pathetic hangdog look. 'I didn't know . . . You are
quite right. It's . . . it's no laughing matter.'

'Actually, your Delores story was quite amusing,'
said Gerry, smiling, 'and you weren't to know.'

'But why didn't you say anything?' asked David.
'I mean, I know it's none of our business, but you
surely didn't think that we would think any less of
you? That we wouldn't be supportive.'

'No,' replied Gerry quietly, 'I never thought that.
I suppose I was just afraid of the gossip, what other
people would say. It was rather silly of me to keep
it a secret.'

'We all have skeletons in our cupboards,'
announced Sidney, now recovered somewhat from
his earlier embarrassment.

'Some more than others, I guess,' remarked
David, looking fixedly at Sidney. Then he turned

338

his attention on me. 'You are pretty quiet, Gervase. Aren't you surprised? Ah! Perhaps you already knew.'

'Yes,' I replied. 'I met Jamie on Friday night when I took Gerry home when her car broke down. A smashing kid.'

Gerry threw me a grateful glance. There was no point in letting on that I had known for months.

At that moment Harold breezed in. 'Sorry, sorry I'm late. I was tied up at County Hall with Mrs Savage and just could not get away.' He smiled indulgently at David and Sidney who were chortling like schoolboys. He placed himself at the head of the table, pulled out a wad of papers which he placed before him and rubbed his large hands vigorously. 'Well now, colleagues, I've got some rather interesting news.'

'This seems a morning for revelations,' remarked Sidney.

'I'm not sure to what you are referring, Sidney, and much as I would like to hear about it,' said Harold, 'there is really something of great importance that I must impart.'

'Don't tell us that you are running off with Mrs Savage,' said David.

'No, no, God forbid,' said Harold, clasping his large hands in front of him and leaning forward over the desk. 'Listen, let us be serious for a moment.' He took a deep breath, gave a great toothy smile and announced, 'I am staying on for another term, maybe two.'

'You are *what*!' we all exclaimed.

'Staying on,' repeated Harold, grinning his big toothy smile. 'Dr Gore has asked me to withdraw my resignation for the time being and hold the fort until my successor has been appointed.'

'But your successor has been appointed,' I said. 'Or have I missed something?'

'Mr Simon Carter, as you correctly point out, Gervase,' explained Harold, 'was indeed appointed but has unexpectedly resigned.'

'He's not coming, then?' announced Gerry.

'Exactly.' There was a distinctly gleeful tone in Harold's voice.

'He's really *resigned*?' cried Sidney.

'Yes, he has decided that the job is not really quite right for him,' continued Harold. 'He has been having certain reservations. If truth be told, I think he found the prospect a little too challenging. He has decided to return to management consultancy.'

'Well, he certainly knew all the buzz words,' said David. 'He seemed to have memorised all the catchphrases and clichés there are. I for one am delighted he is not taking over. It has lifted a great heavy burden from me.'

'This is great news indeed, Harold!' exclaimed Sidney. 'Carter promised a great deal which, to my mind, signified very little.'

'But is he allowed to break his contract?' asked Gerry. 'He accepted the position, didn't he?'

'You are perfectly right, Geraldine,' Harold told her. 'He would, under normal circumstances, be required to honour the contract he signed but Dr Gore has spoken to members of the Education Committee and sorted all that out. He certainly would not want a Senior Inspector whose heart was not in the job. I have to say, he was secretly very pleased, very pleased indeed, when Mr Carter asked for an interview and requested to be released from his contract. He had become increasingly unsure about the man. He found him very intense and tiring and had also received numerous complaints about his abrasive manner. And that is even before he has started. Evidently Mr Carter, on his several visits to the county, has trodden on a great many toes. He has already managed to upset the resource manager, the principal architect, the chief psychologist, the principal school librarian, various councillors and members of the Education Committee and then it came to a head with Mrs Savage.'

'He upset Mrs Savage?' demanded David in mock horror. 'Well, if he upset Mrs Savage then he just has to go.'

'It was quite a dramatic confrontation, I hear,' explained Harold, 'and the corridors of County Hall were echoing with their voices. Evidently Mr Carter got on pretty well with Mrs Savage at their first meeting but, having looked a little bit more thoroughly into her role and responsibilities and having studied all the various questionnaires, reports and circulars which she has produced for the inspectors, he found that there was room for improvement and for some "organisational realignment". Although it was hardly in his remit, he began to quiz her about her administrative duties, told her she spent far too much time on inessential tasks and then when he cast his covetous eye on that plush office of hers she evidently, in colloquial parlance, "lost it". She threatened him with Dr Gore and he threatened her with "downsizing".'

'Downsizing Mrs Savage!' I exclaimed. 'He certainly picked the wrong person to attempt to downsize.'

'Blowing up, yes,' added David, 'but downsizing, oh no. The thought is inconceivable!'

'Evidently he wanted to streamline everything,' chuckled Harold.

'I would have just loved to have been a fly on the wall,' said Sidney, leaning back in his chair. 'Simon Carter and Brenda Savage slugging it out in the long corridor at County Hall. What a sight that must have been. I am tempted to feel sorry for Mrs Savage but I will resist the temptation and just enjoy a small gloat.'

'So he's definitely not coming?' I asked.

'No, Gervase, for the umpteenth time, he's definitely not coming,' replied Harold. Then he added, 'And due to his late withdrawal, you are stuck with me for the time being.'

The whole room erupted into wild laughter.

'Is it something I said?' asked Harold, totally perplexed.

CHAPTER EIGHTEEN

I thought Harold had been exaggerating when, one day during my first year as a school inspector, he had told me about the day of the Fettlesham Show. 'From nine o'clock in the morning until seven o'clock that evening, I am at the mercy of a queue of difficult and demanding parents, teachers, governors and whatever pressure groups have decided to make my life a misery. I am bombarded with a battery of unanswerable questions about the state of schools and schooling, I am asked to sort out impossible problems, have instant advice on all manner of things educational at my fingertips and all with a smile on my face.'

I have to admit that I had taken what Harold had said with a pinch of salt until the day of the Fettlesham Show, when I saw the poor man facing alone a phalanx of disgruntled people.

My duties at the show that first year sounded as though they would be pretty straightforward: I had been deputed to judge the children's poetry competition. All I was supposedly required to do was judge the poems, say a few words, smile pleasantly and present the book tokens and rosettes to the five winners.

'It's a job of minimal duties, so you will be able to spend a very pleasant, uneventful day out,' Harold had informed me—and Harold had been wrong. The judging of the poetry competition had been a nightmare. My decision to award the first prize to a child who had written a delightful poem—albeit a non-rhyming one—about her grannie had seemingly been greeted with disbelief by everyone save for the winner's parents. The Dales poetess, Philomena Phillpots, a woman of apparently outstanding poetic talent and immense experience, felt that a piece of writing was not a poem unless it rhymed.

At the beginning of the summer term, Harold had called the inspectors together for another meeting to discuss the plans for this year's Fettlesham Show. We had sat there, glumly, waiting to be told what our duties would be.

I had hardly dared ask. 'Am I judging the poetry again?'

'No, no,' Harold had replied. 'Philomena

343

Phillpots has been persuaded to take that on, much, I guess, to your relief.'

'Phew! Yes, that is a great burden lifted.'

'However,' Harold had continued, pausing momentarily to give me a great, wide smile displaying his impressive set of tombstone teeth, 'you *have* been nominated to adjudicate the children's verse-speaking competition.'

'The what!' I had exclaimed.

'Now, don't get all flustered and difficult. It is the competition where youngsters recite their favourite poems. It's pretty straightforward and much easier, I should imagine, than judging the quality of a piece of poetry. Much more straightforward and less contentious and not subject to personal preference.'

'I imagined it would be pretty straightforward when I judged the poetry two years ago and it turned out to be an experience I would rather forget,' I had said.

'You'll be fine this time because you will have a couple of other judges to help you reach a decision so it won't all fall on your shoulders.'

'This sounds like another hot potato,' I had murmured.

'No, no, Gervase, not at all. It will be a piece of cake.'

'Who are the other judges?' I had asked warily.

'Well, there's Lord Marrick and Mrs Cleaver-Canning, both of whom I know you get on very well with. It will be like a day out. Like meeting old friends. Take Christine and enjoy yourself.'

One morning, a week after he had given us the welcome news that he would be continuing pro tem as Senior Inspector following the resignation of Simon Carter, Harold came into the main office. I was, in fact, the only inspector present so he sat himself down at David's desk opposite mine.

'Do you know, Gervase,' he said, 'the Fettlesham Show is imminent and for the first time since I have been involved, I'm rather looking forward to it.'

For the past few days, Harold had been a new man. I believe that he too had been worried by the appointment but since he had not been directly involved in it was unable to do anything more than try to ensure that he left his job as free from problems as possible.

'Oh, Harold,' I groaned, 'the Fettlesham Show. I can hardly bear to think about it. Do I really have to do that judging?'

'Yes, of course you do. To use the terminology of our late departed Senior Inspector designate, we all have to "run that extra mile, get on board, pull in the same direction, give it our best shot".'

'Don't you dare start on that gobbledegook!' I exclaimed.

'Well, you can't be the only one on the team to take his bat home.'

I aimed a ball of paper at him, which missed by a mile, and he laughed. 'Sorry, it just slipped out. But, to be serious, Gervase, Sidney will be judging the art competition as usual, David is organising the children's sports as he always does and Gerry has kindly agreed to arrange a children's modelling and craft competition and in addition mount a science display. She is really looking forward to it.'

'First-year fervour!' I snorted. 'She'll learn.'

'What about me,' Harold continued, 'stuck in that beastly hot Education Tent the whole day? At least this year Dr Gore has agreed to join me for part of the day and I shall have Mrs Savage by my

345

side the whole time.'

'Huh, well,' I grumbled, 'perhaps I've got off pretty lightly after all. The thought of a day behind a desk with Mrs Savage is an even more nightmarish scenario than the verse-speaking competition.'

'Splendid!' cried Harold. 'You know, I think you are all rather hard on Mrs Savage. She will be invaluable in deflecting the difficult customer and dealing with contentious issues. Evidently she has become quite popular, in fact, something of a cult figure, at County Hall since her clash with Simon Carter. She does have her faults, I will admit, but when the chips are down I would prefer to have Mrs Savage in my corner rather than the opponent's.'

*   *   *

And so it was that early on a bright and windless July Saturday, before the gates were opened to the general public, I made my way across the Fettlesham showground in search of the tent where the children's verse-speaking competition was to take place. Under normal circumstances I would have been extremely apprehensive and wishing that the whole thing were over, but that morning I was head over heels. I was walking on clouds. Nothing could possibly ruin the incredibly good mood I was in. The birds were chirping, the sun was shining, there was a spring in my step and all was right with the world—and it was not just because schools had gone on holiday the day before and we wouldn't have to see any more of the little darlings for weeks.

'Good morning!' I called to everyone I saw. 'Lovely morning, isn't it?'

The reason for this elation was that the night before I had heard the most wonderful news. Christine and I had been snuggled on the old sofa in the partially-decorated sitting-room at Peewit Cottage when she whispered in my ear, 'I think we will have to get the spare room decorated pretty quickly.'

'Why?' I had asked. 'I thought we'd agreed not to have anyone to stay quite yet, not while the place is such a mess. Are you telling me that we are expecting visitors?'

'Well, yes, we are,' she had said. 'Well, one anyway.'

'Who?'

She had run the flat of her hand over her stomach and smiled enigmatically at me.

'You don't mean . . .?' I had stuttered.

'Yes, I'm pregnant.'

Our nearest neighbour, Harry Cotton, must have fallen out of his bed with the noise that I had made. I had run around the cottage like a whirling dervish, whooping and screaming and jumping in the air. It was the best news I had had since—well, since Christine had said she would marry me.

My lovely wife was going to join me around one o'clock when we intended to treat ourselves to a bottle of champagne, a leisurely lunch and then spend the afternoon looking around the exhibitions and stalls. Christine was busy with someone else that morning. While Gerry was organising the modelling and craft competition, Christine had offered to look after Jamie since the regular child-minder was on holiday. 'We're having a baby!

347

We're having a baby!' I wanted to call out to anyone I met as I made my way across the showground. 'I'm going to be a father! Me! I'm going to be a daddy!' I wanted to run around the showground and yell the news at the top of my voice.

'Don't tell anyone just yet,' Christine had said quietly the evening before. 'Not until I know for sure that the baby is at home here.' She gently stroked her stomach again. So we agreed to wait a couple of weeks before announcing it.

On my way across the showground, I passed the Education Tent and decided to call in briefly to say hello to Harold. I would have loved to have told him our amazing news. To my surprise, I found Mrs Savage seated, as stiff and haughty as ever, behind a large desk in the very centre of the tent, the desk almost disappearing under a bank of potted plants and flowers. All around were display boards and exhibition tables giving details of the Education Department. Mrs Savage was dressed for the occasion in her 'ideal countrywoman's summer ensemble': bright yellow cotton jacket, wheat-coloured roll-top sweater, cream slacks, lime green silk scarf and expensive pale green boots. She was also bedecked in her usual assortment of heavy metal jewellery. As I would have expected, her make-up was faultless, her long nails were impeccably manicured and not a hair on her head was out of place.

'Ah, good morning, Mrs Savage,' I exclaimed, with the exaggerated good humour of a game show host. I was so happy I could have kissed even her. 'And how are you on this bright and sunny morning?'

'I'm very well, thank you, Mr Phinn,' she replied

formally. 'If you are looking for Dr Yeats, he has gone in search of a cup of tea. We have already been here a good half hour and no one has seen fit to bring any refreshments around.'

'It's such good news, isn't it, that Dr Yeats will be staying on for the time being?'

'Yes, indeed,' she replied in a non-committal tone of voice. She was clearly not wanting to prolong this topic of conversation. But I was.

'And so unfortunate that Mr Carter felt unable to join us.'

She looked me straight in the eyes and twitched slightly but merely replied, 'That is a moot point.'

My next comment seemed to wind her up like a clockwork toy. 'And he had such great plans for the department,' I remarked casually.

'Huh, he had great plans, all right,' she said malevolently and with a curl of the lip. 'The least said about Mr Carter the better, as far as I am concerned. I have never seen Dr Gore so angry in the whole of the time I have been his PA. He's such a calm, rational and even-tempered man but he was apoplectic when Mr Carter went back on his word. He had to take two aspirins and sit in a darkened room until he calmed down.' Mrs Savage was clearly unaware that Harold had already informed me of Dr Gore's delight when Mr Carter had reneged. Mrs Savage continued, 'All the time I spent sending out letters and application forms, all the time spent short-listing and convening the appointment panel, a full day interviewing on top of that and then, as large as life, he informs Dr Gore he wanted something more challenging. More challenging! And what a rude and insensitive man he turned out to be!' Her face was flushed with anger and she breathed out heavily. I had clearly touched an extremely raw nerve and I was enjoying the spectacle.

'I thought you rather took to him,' I commented, winding her up again.

'"Rather took to him?"' she repeated slowly. 'Rather took to him? He was an odious little man and, as you said, it is very good news indeed that Dr Yeats will be remaining with us.' Her voice suddenly softened. 'I have always found Dr Yeats a perfect gentleman and very easy to work with.' Then, a slight smile played on her lips and she looked again into my eyes. 'It will be a big man, or woman, who tries to fill his shoes, Mr Phinn.'

Touché, Mrs Savage, I thought to myself.

At that moment, the subject of our conversation padded heavily into the tent carrying two plastic cups of tea. Of all the characters in the showground that morning, Harold looked the least like a school inspector. With his huge frame, great broad shoulders and hands like spades and dressed as he was in a rather loud black and white striped suit he looked more like a Mafia enforcer.

'Hello, Gervase. Good to see you,' he said genially. 'Here we are, Brenda, one cup of tea.' He placed the plastic cup down before her. 'I'm sorry I couldn't get that herbal stuff you usually drink but this is warm and wet and better than nothing.'

'It will be most acceptable, Harold,' simpered Mrs Savage, giving him a charming smile. 'And thank you for taking the trouble to fetch me one.' She then reached into a pale canvas bag beside her chair and produced a china mug into which she poured the contents of the plastic cup. 'I cannot bear to drink out of plastic,' she told us. 'And, of

350

course, you never know what germs you can pick up using a receptacle someone else has used.' She took a sip and nodded. 'Most acceptable.'

It occurred to me that there would be little danger of contracting anything dreadful from a disposable plastic cup but I didn't say anything. Anyway, I was intrigued by their use of first names. I had never heard either of them address each other like that before.

'I can nip back and get you a cup if you would like one, Gervase,' said Harold pleasantly.

'No, thanks. The verse-speaking competition is scheduled for eleven-thirty, nice and early, thank goodness, so I can get it over and done with and then relax for the rest of the day. I'm on my way to check things are organised, and just called in to say hello.'

'Mrs Savage was telling me earlier, Gervase, that the CEO was well pleased with the "Literacy and Learning" initiative. I'm sure he will have a word with you when he arrives. I'm expecting him to join us later this morning.'

'Really?' I said, smiling as I realised that the pair of them reverted to formal names when it came to business. Well, why not? They had worked with each other for a good number of years.

'Yes, he was very pleased,' said Mrs Savage, looking at me over the rim of her mug as she took another sip of the tea. 'Dr Gore will be sending you a memorandum thanking you and your colleagues for your hard work with the initiative. He received some very complimentary letters from the headteachers of the schools involved who said they found the visit most valuable and informative.'

'Well, that's good to hear, Mrs Savage,' I said,

351

smiling smugly, and then rather wickedly decided to twist the knife another few turns. 'I think everything went like clockwork. It's good to know that Dr Gore is back to his calm, rational and even-tempered self after all the trouble with Mr Carter.'

'Mr Phinn,' said Mrs Savage, placing the mug down firmly on the desk, 'I am here to help Dr Yeats deal with enquiries from the general public about education and not to discuss Mr Carter whom you have an unpleasant habit of bringing up.' She was looking quite hot and flustered again. 'I admit I found Mr Carter a rude and detestable little man and we are well rid of him. And that, Mr Phinn, is my last word on the matter.'

'Yes, of course,' I said meekly, and then returning to the exaggerated good humour of the quiz show host, I bid them both farewell. 'Have a nice day!' I called as I made for the exit.

I had only gone a few more yards in the direction of the bright red and yellow marquee where the verse-speaking competition was to take place when a husky voice boomed behind me, a voice with which I was very familiar, 'Now then, Gervase!' I turned to find Lord Marrick in a bright striped blazer which had seen better days, a ridiculously large coloured bow-tie and sporting a rather battered, wide-brimmed straw hat. He carried a walking stick with a fox-head handle. 'Good to see you,' he said, holding out a hand. 'How are things?'

'Couldn't be better, Lord Marrick,' I replied. 'And what about you?'

'Bloody excellent! Rum do this about Dr Yeats's successor, eh?'

'Yes, I've just been talking about that.'

'Fellow upped and went like a fox with the

hounds at his heels, I hear.' He fingered the top of his walking stick. 'Didn't take to him myself. Clever man, no doubt about that, but far too much to say. Anyhow, how's married life treating you?'

'Marvellous! Best thing I ever did,' I said, meaning every word of it.

'Well, let's have a drink in the beer tent later to celebrate the good things of life—but we've got to get this judging over and done with. Shouldn't be a long job, should it?' He didn't wait for a reply. 'Any sign of the patter of tiny feet yet, eh?' He was nothing if not blunt.

I would have loved to have told him. 'Not yet,' I lied.

'Well, you haven't had much time yet. Now, come along then, let's get this verse-reading show on the road, shall we?'

On our way to the tent I was treated to a running commentary. 'Margot Cleaver-Canning is joining us. I know you've met Margot and her long-suffering husband. He's a martyr is old Winco. Mind you, Margot is a splendid woman—feisty, I should say. Salt of the earth. Calls a spade a shovel.' He stopped at the entrance to the tent and took my arm. 'My goodness, you should have seen her out hunting. She could hold her own with the best when she was out with the Totterdale. Never seen a more fearless jumper than Margot Cleaver-Canning—although, of course, that was before she carried the extra baggage, if you see what I mean. She'd gallop up to this drystone wall and if her mount refused, she'd sort of put her horse in reverse and the beast would kick down the bloody wall to let her through. Trained him to do it, she did. Nothing would stop her. All end of trouble her father had getting her out of such scrapes. And if you see her on the golf course, she's a veritable virago. Women like that are the backbone of Britain. Great-grand-daughter of General Cleaver-Bolling of the 12th Royal Lancers, you know. All in the bloodline.'

Mrs Cleaver-Canning was waiting for us in the tent. She was dressed in a shapeless multicoloured cotton tent of a dress, a huge red hat and wore pristine white gloves.

'Now then, Margot, my dear,' boomed Lord Marrick, 'how are you?'

'I'm very well thank you, Bunny,' she replied, 'and I see you're looking well.'

Bunny? I said to myself. Bunny! I looked at the rotund, red-cheeked character with his great walrus moustache and his hair shooting up from a square head. It would be difficult to find anyone who looked less like a rabbit than he.

'I'm as fit as a butcher's dog,' growled the peer. 'And look who I've found outside.'

'Good morning, Mr Phinn,' said Mrs Cleaver-Canning, extending a gloved hand regally.

'Good morning,' I replied. 'It's very nice to see you again. Is . . . er . . . Winco here too?'

'Good gracious, no! I've sent him off. Winco knows as much about poetry as I do about the Messerschmitts he used to shoot down. He'll be in the beer tent if I know Winco, regaling anyone who will listen to him about his war exploits. Now, Mr Phinn, Lord Marrick and I are relying on you to help us though this judging how-de-do. I was approached to do this as President of my local branch of the W.I. and, although I am very happy to oblige and I do have some limited experience in

354

this field, I have never judged children before.'

'And I don't know a bloody thing about poetry,' added Lord Marrick. 'Pardon my French. However, I am sure Gervase here will tell us what to do, Margot, so I wouldn't worry. It seems pretty straightforward, as far as I can see. We listen to a few kiddies performing their poems and pick the winners.'

'Let's hope so,' I said. 'But very often it is the parents who cause the problems, not the children.' I had a niggling feeling that this was going to be a re-run of the disastrous poetry competition and as the morning progressed that feeling grew.

Five small square staging blocks had been pushed together to form a makeshift stage at the end of the marquee, facing the judges' table. Behind us was row upon row of wooden chairs for the audience to sit on. The area would have looked a little more cheerful and welcoming had someone had the foresight to paint or drape the blocks in bright colours and put a few colourful plants here and there. As it was, it looked a rather drab environment for the children to present their poems.

The organiser of the event was an amiable but completely disorganised man with a soft voice and an absent-minded expression. He had the irritating habit of biting his bottom lip and punctuating all his replies to my questions with, 'Well, what do you think, Mr Phinn?' I checked that there was the requisite number of book tokens and rosettes to award, agreed to introduce the event and that Lord Marrick would present the prizes.

I went in search of the showground announcer to ask him to inform the public over his loudspeaker

355

that the verse-speaking competition would be taking place in thirty minutes. This had never occurred to the organiser. I could visualise the children presenting their poems to an empty marquee.

On the way back, I diverted to the Education Tent, which was already exceedingly busy, but I managed to attract Mrs Savage's attention.

'Might I borrow a few of your plants? I will bring them back very soon,' I said and without giving the woman a chance to object, I scooped up four big pots from in front of her table, gave her a cheesy grin and left quickly, ignoring her little bleats of 'Mr Phinn, Mr Phinn.'

When I arrived back in the marquee, I found to my surprise that the place was filling up fast. Things seemed to be looking up, I thought, as I placed the pots of flowers in front of the little stage. All the entrants had arrived, been told the order of their appearance and the judges had a full list of poems for recitation with names of all the children. At 11.30 on the dot, I welcomed the audience, told them what a treat was in store and introduced myself and my fellow judges. I then asked for the first child to deliver his piece.

Onto the rostrum clambered a nervous-looking boy with a startled expression. He entertained us with a laboured rendering of 'The Highwayman', prompted frequently by a parent who followed his progress in a large book from the side of the stage. After him came a large girl who gave a most original performance of 'Daffodils' by William Wordsworth. Dressed in a bright yellow dress, she took to floating around the stage like a cloud, waving her arms in the air, miming the fluttering

356

and the dancing of the flowers in the breeze and all the while reciting the verse in a loud sing-song voice. When she got to the lines: 'For oft, when on my couch I lie, In vacant or in pensive mood', she clapped her hand to her forehead dramatically as though suffering from a particularly painful migraine and put on a face which was neither vacant nor pensive. The remarkably thin youth who followed her mounted the stage with amiable lankiness and managed to deliver a piece of Shakespeare as if he were recalling a shopping list. Next was an older girl, dressed in a Victorian-style dress with lace-up boots, who accompanied her rendering of 'The Green Eye of the Little Yellow God' with the most elaborate movements and facial expressions. She pointed towards the audience, grimaced as if the boots she was wearing were too tight and belted out the lines with gusto.

And so the performances went on and on until the penultimate entrant strode to the stage like a giraffe. My heart sank. It was Pollyanna Phillpots. When I had judged the ill-fated poetry competition two years before, one of the entrants was the daughter of the Dales poetess, Philomena Phillpots. Pollyanna, at the time, had been a miniature replica of her mother: thin, gaunt-looking with waist-length sandy hair and dressed identically in a long, flowered-print dress. The child had produced a trite little verse about gambolling lambs and fluffy white sheep and she and her mother had not been best pleased when it failed to win a prize. Now here she was again, a great deal taller, and I had an unnerving feeling that in the audience somewhere was the Dales poetess herself, watching me like a hawk. I had heard that the poetry competition, which Philomena Phillpots would be judging, would be taking place at three o'clock and had made a mental note to give that event a wide birth.

'The poem I am going to recite,' started the girl in the bland tones of an undertaker giving his condolences, 'has been written by my mother, the famous Dales poetess, Philomena Phillpots.' There was a favourable murmur from the audience. 'It is called, "In the Country".

> If you are in the country
> Well, don't just walk on by,
> But stay awhile, squat on a stile
> And sit beneath the sky.
> In this very busy world
> A world that's full of care
> We never give ourselves
> The time to really stop and stare,
> To listen to the country sounds
> That fill the morning air.
> Hear the little beck a-gurgling
> See the great dark river burbling
> Feel the whispering wind a-teasing
> See the winter puddles freezing
> Hear the peewit's plaintive calling
> See the gentle snow a-falling . . .

I found myself switching off; the mention of the peewit made me think of our cottage, of Christine, and the news that I was keeping close to my heart.

I came to with a start when, the poem evidently having finally ended, there was a ripple of applause and some exceptionally loud clapping from the back. I didn't need to turn round. I could see in my mind's eye a thin, gaunt-looking woman with waist-length sandy hair and dressed in a long, flowered-print dress. Pollyanna gave a little bow and loped off the stage.

The final entrant, a sharp-faced boy of about ten with a scattering of freckles and wavy red hair, clambered on the rostrum.

'Well, well, well,' I murmured to myself. It was little Terry Mossup of Willingforth School. Miss Pilkington must have worked wonders to have persuaded him to perform.

'This piece of Yorkshire dialect verse was written in 1909 by Ben Turner,' said the boy in a clear, loud and confident voice. Then, looking directly at our judging table and the audience behind us, he began his poem:

> Whativer task you tackle, lads,
> Whativer job you do,
> I' all your ways,
> I' all your days,
> Be honest through and through:
> > Play cricket.
>
> If claads oppress you wi' their gloom,
> An' t'sun seems lost to view,
> Don't fret an' whine,
> Ask t'sun to shine,
> An' don't o' livin' rue:
> > Play cricket.
>
> If you're i' debt, don't growl and grunt,
> An' wish at others had
> T'same want o' luck;
> But show more pluck,

An' ne'er mak others sad:
> Play cricket.

If in your days there's chonce to do
Good deeds, then reight an' fair,
Don't hesitate,
An' wait too late,
An' say you'n done your share:
> Play cricket.

We've all a row to hoe, that's true,
Let's do it best we can;
It's nobbut once
We have the chonce
To play on earth the man:
> Play cricket.

The judges retired to the tea tent to deliberate.

'Well, I reckon this is going to be a long business,' said Lord Marrick, stroking his moustache. 'I mean there was a lot of talent there, a lot of talent.'

'And some very interesting, not to say unusual renderings,' added Mrs Cleaver-Canning. 'I thought the girl doing the mime to the "Daffodils" was going to fall off the stage at one point. If I didn't know better I should say she'd been on the cider. She did very well to keep her balance and continue to say the words. And another thing, if I were the mother of the young man reciting that Shakespeare, I would be extremely worried about his health. He looked unnaturally thin to me. Anorexic I should say.'

'Yes, well it's the poems we're here about, Margot, not the state of the entrants' health.'

'My father, God rest his soul,' continued Mrs

360

Cleaver-Canning, 'used to give a very impressive rendering of "The Green Eye of the Little Yellow God" with all the actions. It brought back many a pleasant Christmas at Cleaver Hall, that poem.'

'Well, I'm going to put my cards on the table,' announced Lord Marrick. 'I thought one stood out head and shoulders above the rest.'

'Yes, there was one I liked very much more than the others,' agreed Mrs Cleaver-Canning.

'So,' said Lord Marrick, 'how are we going to play this, then, Gervase? Shall we go through them one by one and compare our marks?'

'I, too, have my favourite,' I said, but didn't reckon that my two colleagues would agree. 'Of course, we are not judging the content of the poems, it's the performance, the presentation, use of the voice, timing, expression, how the words are interpreted, that sort of thing. Perhaps we should start by saying who each of us thinks is the best.'

'Very well,' said Lord Marrick. 'I'll go first. Never been one to be backwards in coming forwards, as my gamekeeper tells me often enough. The cheeky-faced little lad at the end. I thought he was the best. Not a line fluffed, good strong voice, bags of confidence and he got the dialect off to a turn. That's my opinion, for what it is worth.'

'Well, that's two of us,' said Mrs Cleaver-Canning. 'I loved the poem. My father was a stalwart of the Yorkshire Dialect Society for many years and was a great one for encouraging the production of Yorkshire dialect literature. I did think the little boy gave of his best. He was a delight.'

'This is not going to be protracted at all,' I said with a great sense of relief and satisfaction. 'I too

361

think the last entrant was the best.'

'Great Scot!' exclaimed Lord Marrick. 'We are unanimous.'

Little Terry Mossup jumped up onto the stage to receive his first prize. He beamed as he took the book token and rosette from Lord Marrick before thanking him. 'Cheers mate,' he said, giving the peer a wink and a thumbs up. He then faced the audience and, with a triumphant look, clenched a fist, punched the air and shouted, 'Yeah!' like a footballer who had just scored the winning goal.

*   *   *

Later that afternoon, I sat with Christine at a table in the sunshine outside the tea tent. I was so happy. We had had a delicious lunch, and then spent our money rather haphazardly. Christine had bought a stack of saucepans, and a patchwork throw for the bed, and I had fallen for a beautifully-made bird table which I thought would look great in the garden of Peewit Cottage. With our purchases piled on the ground beside us, we were now indulging ourselves with a cream tea.

'Got to eat for two, now,' said Christine, her eyes sparkling. 'But that doesn't mean you have to as well,' and she took the last bit of scone off my plate and popped it into her mouth with a grin.

At that moment, a small boy with ice cream smeared round his mouth and a cone nearly the size of his head walked past.

'Hey, Terry,' I called. 'Well done winning the competition. You did really well.'

The boy came across to where we were sitting. 'Aye,' he agreed. 'I didn't do too bad, did I?'

'This is the winner of the verse-speaking competition,' I told Christine.

'Congratulations,' she said. 'You must have been very good.'

'I was all right,' replied the boy, taking a great lick of his ice cream.

'And are you liking school a bit better now?' I asked.

'Naw, not really,' he replied. 'I wunt go if it was left to me.'

'And are you behaving yourself?' I asked.

'Allus do,' he replied, with a twinkle in the eye.

'And how's the football?'

'Not bad.'

'Did you get into the Junior Side, then?'

'Naw, they din't want me, but it's not end o' t'world, is it?'

'No,' I agreed. 'And you can always try again next year.'

''Appen I can,' he replied, taking another immense lick of the ice cream. 'Is this your girl friend, then?' he asked, nodding in the direction of Christine.

'No, this is my wife.'

'Have you got any kids?'

'No, we haven't any children,' I replied, smiling.

'Mi mum—mi real mum—says they're more trouble than they're worth, are kids.' He sniffed and took another lick. ''Appen she's reight.' He thought for a moment. 'It's not been a bad day this, 'as it?'

'No, it's not been a bad day,' I agreed. 'And what have you been learning at school then, Terry?'

'Not much,' he answered. Then after a thoughtful pause, he announced, 'I do know how to mek babies, though.'

Christine choked on the tea she was just at that moment drinking, and coughed and spluttered it all over me, herself and the table. Here we go again, I thought to myself: the inquisitive child who asks a tricky question or regales you with an embarrassingly blunt observation. I prepared myself to smile widely, nod sagely and be as evasive as possible. I tried not to look in the least shocked and replied in a very casual voice, 'Really?'

'Aye I do. I've just learnt how to mek babies.' He gave his ice cream cone another elaborate lick. 'Do you know how to mek babies then?' he asked.

'I do, yes,' I replied and looked over to Christine who was holding a handkerchief to her mouth in an attempt to smother her laughter.

There was another long pause. 'How do you mek babies, then?' the boy asked, looking me straight in the eye.

'You go first,' I told him.

'Well,' he said, looking up at the cloudless blue sky, 'I knock the "y" off and add "i-e-s". Is that how you make babies, then?'

'Exactly,' I replied and, putting my arms around the mother-to-be, I gave Christine a great hug and a kiss.

For Connie

’Tis on a certain Sunday,
A special time of year,
Old soldiers from all Britain
Stand to attention here.
The noise is hushed in London
On this very special day,
Poppies on the Cenotaph,
Red amidst the grey.
Two minutes’ special silence
As we think of those who fell,
Who died for King and Country
In that other place called Hell.
And those legions of old soldiers
Like shadows, march on by,
And they hold their bodies proudly,
And stare towards the sky.

Chivers Large Print Direct

If you have enjoyed this Large Print book and would like to build up your own collection of Large Print books and have them delivered direct to your door, please contact **Chivers Large Print Direct**.

Chivers Large Print Direct offers you a full service:

☆ **Created to support your local library**

☆ **Delivery direct to your door**

☆ **Easy-to-read type and attractively bound**

☆ **The very best authors**

☆ **Special low prices**

For further details either call Customer Services on 01225 443400 or write to us at

**Chivers Large Print Direct
FREEPOST (BA 1686/1)
Bath
BA1 3QZ**